YACHT DESIGNING AND PLANNING

Revised and Enlarged Edition

YACHT

Designing and Planning

FOR YACHTSMEN, STUDENTS & AMATEURS
REVISED AND ENLARGED EDITION

by

HOWARD I. CHAPELLE

New York

W·W·NORTON & COMPANY·INC·

Publishers

Contents

Preface to First Edition

YACHTSMEN who are content in merely sailing a boat are few in number compared to those who find pleasure in designing, building, altering or "improving" their craft. To this class of yachtsmen the credit for much of the progress in yacht design is due. Yet, in spite of the large number of books relating to naval architecture and yacht building that have been published, these yachtsmen suffer from the disadvantage of not having precise directions as to the proper methods of drawing plans, fairing lines, calculating and writing specifications. Information in regard to these problems is not easily available, as yachtsmen well know.

This book is designed to meet the needs of these yachtsmen. It attempts to lay down a comprehensive procedure of design suitable to the requirements of the beginner in the art of yacht design. In general, the methods described are those employed by professional designers, as actually carried out in the drafting room, rather than those of textbook theorists. In short, this book attempts to aid the amateur to plot a course for a fascinating cruise in the sea of yacht design.

HOWARD I. CHAPELLE

Scituate, Massachusetts

Preface

to Revised Edition

THE INTEREST in the design of small craft has grown steadily since the publication of *Yacht Design and Planning* in 1936. The fundamental problems of small-craft design remain unchanged, of course, but modern trends have added many new problems in practical design. Therefore revision and addition seem necessary.

In making all revisions and additions, the original treatment of information is retained here, in order to make it useful on the drawing board without much resort to theoretical processes. It is evident that more discussion of hull-form detail and of the results of selection is required. It is also necessary to discuss engine selection and installation problems. In addition, new construction methods that have come into favor require attention. Modern trends, especially in sail and rigging, produce practical design problems that need discussion.

Revision and correction of formulae and tables, as well as additions that make the book a better drawing-board reference, are required. Many matters in small-craft design change so rapidly that detailed suggestions as to their treatment are not possible, but these are usually of minor importance and their treatment becomes one of common sense and up-to-date information readily obtained from boating and yachting magazines. It should be emphasized, perhaps, that *Yacht Design and Planning* was intended for beginners and students in the practical steps in design on the drawing board. This remains its primary function.

HOWARD I. CHAPELLE

Washington, D.C.

Acknowledgments

THE author wishes to express his obligations to the following: the late Frederick A. Fenger, Walter McInnis, the late John Alden, the late Frank Paine, the late Ralph Winslow, the late George Buckhout, the late Wirth Munroe, the late Ralph M. Munroe, the late W. P. Stephens, W. D. McLean, Henry Rusk, Jan Olof Traung, the late Dwight Simpson, Professor Ata Nutku, Merriman Bros. Inc., Wellington Sears Co., L. Francis Herreshoff, John Gardner, Kenneth Smith and the many others who have generously given assistance in collecting data and for suggestions and criticisms. Articles in *Yachting, Rudder, Forest and Stream, Yachting Monthly* and *Yachting World* have been of great assistance, as have the books of Dixon Kemp, Kunhardt, Marett, Davis, Skene, Fox and Herreshoff in working out design procedures.

I. Tools and Materials

THE usual directions to the student of yacht design begin by describing the calculations. This is often very discouraging since the beginner has no conception of the practical application of such information; as a result he becomes lost and frightened in a maze of mathematical formulae. Though highly involved mathematical calculations are commonly considered to represent "scientific naval architecture," nevertheless mathematical formulae are of slight assistance in the first steps in designing a yacht. Calculations, in naval architecture, are primarily indexes of comparison and are effective only after some plans are drawn. With but few exceptions, calculations in yacht design are only approximate in accuracy and, though very useful, do not constitute the most important part in design.

Aim of Design

The end in view, in yacht design, is to turn out a boat suitable in every possible respect for the intended purpose, not to obtain a "coefficient" or any other mathematical expression nor to make "pretty" drawings. That sense of proportion and form, best described as "boat sense," which is obtained by critical observation and comparison of lines and details of successful craft is of far more importance than either the ability to make difficult calculations or to draw well. There can be no doubt that mathematics is an aid to yacht design; calculations are a "measuring stick" assisting the designer's boat sense. Overemphasis of calculation, at the expense of other methods of comparison and conclusion, should be avoided, however. In the same manner, good drafts-manship is an aid to design for it is the means of expression; nevertheless a handsome set of plans does not insure a good design.

The first step, therefore, is to get the designer's ideas into a visible and measurable form, a scale drawing. By this means fewer assumptions (guesses, to put it plainly) will have to be made when calculating or making comparisons. In order to make plans drafting instruments and materials are necessary; therefore these should be the first consideration.

Instruments Required for Study

The number of instruments required depends upon the drafting skill of the student and the amount of designing to be done; to say nothing of the state of the student's pocket-book. It is best to obtain the finest instruments possible, but for study purposes fewer and cheaper instruments may be purchased than when a great deal of designing is intended. The minimum equipment that will serve for study is as follows: a drawing-board, say about 24" x 36"; a 36" straightedge; two battens, 36" long, of hard rubber or celluloid; a 12" triangular scale, architect's division; a few "Copenhagen" or irregular curves; one medium size triangle, of celluloid, wood or hard rubber; box of thumbtacks; one H and one 3H drawing pencil; penknife; pencil eraser; drawing paper and a box of large desk pins, or common pins.

The pins are to hold the battens in the desired curves when drawing; this is done by sticking them into the drawing and board along each side of the batten, as it is being bent to the desired curve. This is not a very satisfactory method, it must be admitted, but it will serve when batten weights are not at hand.

This equipment will be sufficient for pencil drawings required to learn elementary yacht design. The backs of old charts make excellent drawing paper, for chart paper withstands erasing very well. Tracing paper, obtainable in drafting supply stores, will enable pencil tracings to be made that will blueprint. Soft lead pencils should not be used as they smudge and do not make sharp, clear lines. T-squares are not very satisfactory as the heads

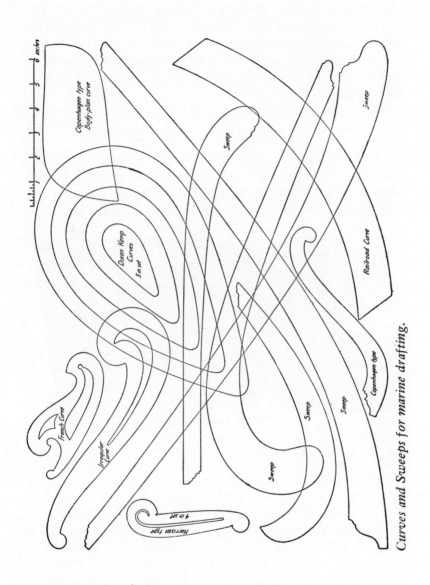

Curves and Sweeps for marine drafting.

get out of true; steel or wood straightedges are superior for marine drafting. In place of dividers strips of paper, made by cutting off the margins of magazine pages, can be used. These "tick-strips" are used to transfer lengths and widths from one portion of the drawing to another. Many professional draftsmen use these in place of dividers as there is less danger of punching the drawing full of holes.

Instruments for Amateur and Professional

For the man who intends to make yacht design a hobby or a profession, the following list of equipment will cover all requirements. Every instrument listed is not strictly essential, but possession of the complete equipment will lighten many tasks.

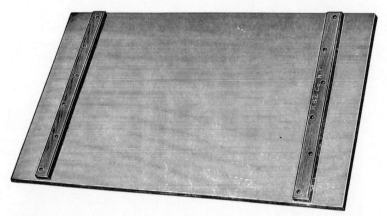

Typical drawing-board, showing the reinforcements on the underside.

1. A large drawing-board or table is necessary; the size may be fixed by the dimensions of the boats to be designed. The most popular size is 30″ x 60″. If space will not permit the use of so large a board, 24″ x 48″ will do. Too small a board is a nuisance.

2. Spline or batten weights, known to marine draftsmen as "ducks," are required; at least ten are necessary, fourteen are sufficient. Their weight should be between two and five pounds each. These ducks are usually made of lead or cast iron and may

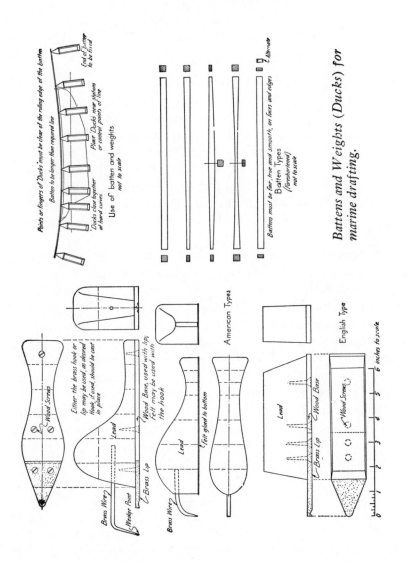

Batterns and Weights (Ducks) for marine drafting.

Spline or Batten weights.

be made from the sketches or purchased from manufacturers of drafting supplies. Most ducks have a wire hook or finger which is placed on top of the batten; the old or English type have lips or notches which are placed on or against the batten. A piece of felt on the bottom of the duck protects the drawing from being marked by the metal. Lead ducks are preferred by most draftsmen as they are smaller than cast iron ducks of the same weight. When ducks are being placed on a batten they should never be dropped as they will nick the batten; such damage is beyond repair.

3. Splines or battens are difficult to obtain in this country, except the parallel-sided type. English-made battens are often preferred. Battens from 18″ to 72″ in length may be purchased. As a guide for length, a batten should be about 12″ longer than the hull being drawn, regardless of scale. The best materials for battens are lemonwood, pearwood, lancewood, red pine, spruce, applewood, celluloid and hard rubber; each material has a different degree of flexibility. A good set would number about 20 battens of various lengths, shapes and materials, as follows: five tapered at one end, five tapered at both ends, five tapered from both ends toward the middle and five parallel-sided. By having battens of varying flexibility every need will be met. The parallel-sided battens sold in this country are usually made of hard rubber or celluloid and are rectangular in section with grooves cut in the two narrow faces to take the fingers of the ducks. With this batten, to draw a slight curve (as a sheer line) it is laid flat; to draw a strong curve (as a waterline) it is laid on edge. To draw a curve having reverse in both ends as waterlines often do, it is necessary to draw each end separately, setting the batten twice and making a joint amidships. Hence the advantage of the variously tapered battens; they may be made by a good wood-

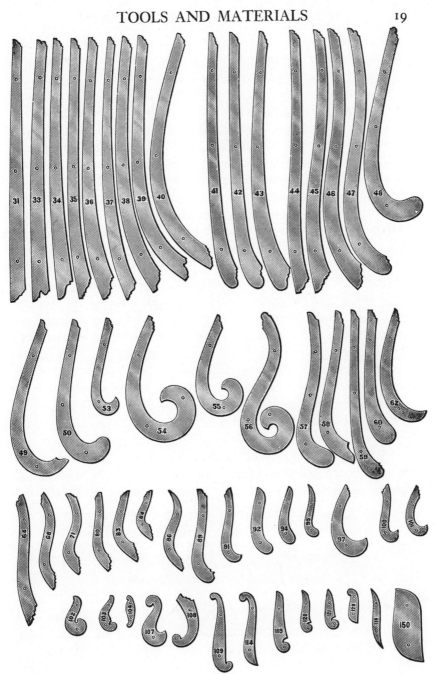

Ship curves.

worker, but imperfect ones are useless. The celluloid strips used to edge some T-squares and straightedges may be converted to battens if the latter are not procurable otherwise.

4. Curves and sweeps are usually obtainable in sets and are made of wood, hard rubber or celluloid; the last is best, and most expensive. The English curves, such as Stanley's "Dixon Kemp" pear-shaped curves, are excellent. The "Copenhagen" curves are much used, though more curves are required to make a set than with the "Dixon Kemp" model. The long curves in the "Copenhagen" set are called "sweeps" and replace battens to some extent but are expensive and require much practice to use properly. However, they are very handy when tracing as they save much time since ducks do not have to be set. There is great difficulty in obtaining fair sweeps and usually the draftsman must refair them with a file. A set of "Copenhagen" curves usually numbers between 40 and 50 pieces, including sweeps; it is best to purchase each one separately as the sets contain many curves and sweeps that are very rarely of use. "Dixon Kemp" curves number 5 to a set, in two sizes. Some English firms sell special sets of "Copenhagen" curves, of wood, specially selected for yacht design; the cost is usually low. "French" curves, such as are used in mechanical drafting, are useless for marine drafting, with but one or two exceptions. The sketches show some useful curves and sweeps selected for yacht design.

5. Straightedges may be of steel; wood edged with celluloid, hard rubber, ebony or other hardwood; or may be made of a single piece of hardwood. One edge may be beveled, but the

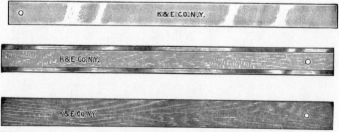

Three types of straightedges, steel, xylonite edged, and hardwood.

other should be square, against which a ruling-pen may be used. One straightedge about the length of the drawing-board and another 24″ or 30″ long will be found useful. Steel straightedges should be about one-sixteenth of an inch thick for it will be found that a ruling pen cannot be used with a thinner one.

6. Triangles can be purchased, made of either steel, celluloid, hard rubber or wood. Some English firms make a wooden "gal-

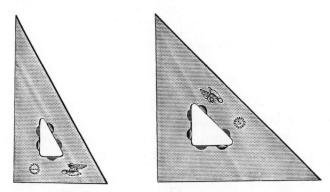

30 x 60 degrees and 45 degree triangles.

lows square" to replace the common triangle in squaring lines, an excellent tool for the use intended. One 45° triangle, about 5″ long, and one 30°–60° triangle, 9″ or 10″ long, are usually sufficient. The smaller triangle may be one of the various "letter-

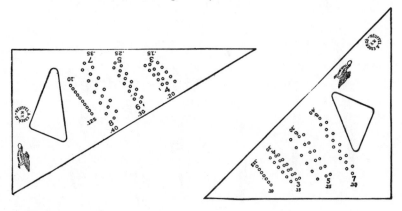

Lettering triangles.

ing triangles," thus serving two purposes. These "lettering tri-angles" are similar to the common type except that they have variously spaced holes or slots in them. By placing the pencil point in these holes or slots and sliding the pencil and triangle along a straightedge each time, spaced guide-lines for lettering are drawn without the extra effort of measuring to obtain a standard size of letters.

Dividers.

7. One pair of dividers, 4″ to 6″ long, is required for trans-ferring measurements on plans.

8. A spring-bow pencil, pen and dividers can be purchased separately or in sets; 1½″ or 2″ are good sizes.

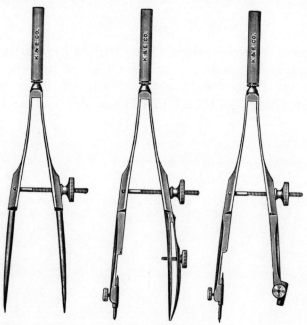

Spring-Bow dividers, pen and pencil.

9. A compass, 4″ to 6″ long, fitted with pen, pencil and lengthening-bar attachments, is needed.

A compass with extension bar and pen attachment.

10. Ruling pens, also called "right-line pens," should be the best procurable. The nibs should be long, narrow and sharply pointed. The "wedge" type, with the adjusting screw at the top of the handle, is recommended. Ruling pens may be obtained in

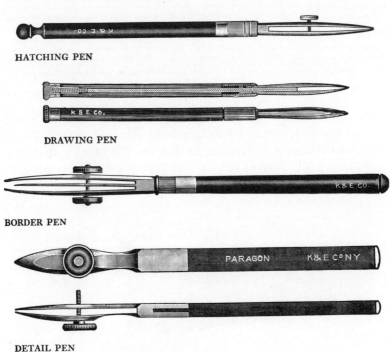

HATCHING PEN

DRAWING PEN

BORDER PEN

DETAIL PEN

Ruling pens, or "right-line" pens.

many shapes and sizes, to suit the taste of the purchaser. "Swedish detail pens" or "Border pens" are useful for drawing heavy lines but are not absolutely necessary.

11. A pricker can be made by inserting the eye of a common sewing needle in the eraser of a pencil, or a commercial tool can

Pricker.

be purchased. This instrument is useful in laying off accurate measurements with a scale and for copying plans when tracing cannot be done. The pricker should be held perpendicular to the surface of the drawing when in use.

12. One 12″ triangular architect's scale, or set of flat scales of the same division, must be at hand. The divisions used most

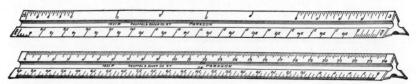

Triangular scales—upper, Architect's; lower, Engineer's.

commonly are ⅛″–¼″–⅜″–½″–¾″–1″–1½″–3″; each representing one foot and divided so that feet and inches may be measured. White-faced, open divided, are the best. A triangular engineer's scale, divided 10—20—30—40—50—60 parts to the inch, will be found useful in calculation.

13. A planimeter, though rather expensive, is worth the cost

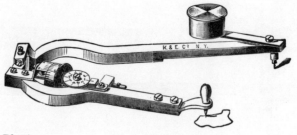

Planimeter.

if much designing is done. This instrument measures areas and makes displacement calculations less tedious. The cheapest planimeters are large enough for yacht design; a good one can be purchased for about thirty dollars.

14. An erasing shield of steel or brass should be purchased. The shield will protect the drawing when an erasure is neces-

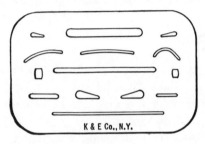

An erasing shield.

sary in the midst of a plan and will save much unnecessary redrawing.

15. Erasers for pencil and ink are required; for use on tracing cloth the "Emerald" or "Ruby" erasers are best. They can be used on other materials as well. The hard gritty eraser should be avoided for this type will destroy the surface of most papers and tracing cloth. It is better to use too soft an eraser than one too hard. It is unwise to try to erase very rapidly for friction of even a soft eraser will damage the surface of some material.

16. Lettering pens are important; these are also to be used for freehand drawing. Crow-quill pens are suitable for fine lines and

A quill pen.

small lettering; the Gillot 170 or 303 are preferred by some draftsmen and will serve for coarser work. Special penholders are required for crow-quill pens, common penholders will do for the others.

17. A good quality of "waterproof drawing ink" should be

obtained. Higgins' inks are preferred by many; there are other popular brands, however. Black is the only color that is required, though other colors, such as red, blue, green and yellow, are often used in complicated or superimposed drawings. A cloth ink-wiper should be on hand, to be used to keep all pens clean.

18. An ink-bottle-holder should be purchased; nothing is more annoying than to have the ink capsize on a finished plan. A very fine holder is made by Theo. Altenedar & Sons, which combines holder and filling quill and allows the pen to be filled with one hand.

19. Spline pens, while not absolutely necessary, are very handy instruments. They must be made to order, unfortunately, but are not expensive. The spline pen is somewhat like a bow-pen, but has a flat blade instead of a compass point and a longer handle. The flat blade is held against the batten or straightedge, then parallel lines can be drawn, by adjusting the set screw that separates blade and pen to the desired distance. A bow-spring compass can be made to serve the same purpose by backing out the compass needle and its holding screw. An old "railroad pen" can be converted for this use by replacing one of the two pens with a flat blade; a job any jeweler can do.

20. Drawing paper should be of good quality, having a hard, smooth surface that will withstand much erasing. Whatman's "Hot Pressed" drawing paper is excellent but expensive. Good roll papers in white, buff, and green are obtainable at less cost, but soft paper should be rejected. Tracing paper should be of good quality, hard and smooth, white is best. Colored tracing paper and vellums discolor with age and soil easily. Bond paper withstands the effects of age very well but is not very transparent. Some papers become brittle with age, particularly the more transparent, nearly all tear easily. Very fine sharp lines can be drawn on tracing paper and good blueprints can be obtained. The low cost of tracing paper, as compared to tracing cloth, is another advantage.

21. Tracing cloth is preferred by professional draftsmen because of its strength and ability to withstand hard handling. Tracing cloth is not affected by age to any great extent but is

damaged by moisture. A good tracing paper will serve the student or amateur as well. "Imperial Tracing Cloth" is standard; the dull side is generally the one drawn on because it takes ink and pencil while the glossy side will only take ink. Another grade of tracing cloth is known as "pencil tracing cloth"; it is rather too opaque for tracing but will serve for detail drawings in pencil that must be blueprinted. It is more expensive than paper and soils very easily, but blueprints very well and is durable.

22. Tracing cloth pounce is a chalk dust that is sprinkled on tracing cloth or paper, rubbed lightly with a soft cloth or blotter and then dusted off, before drawing with ink. Pounce removes an oily film which will cause broken and ragged lines if allowed to remain. All tracing cloth and most tracing papers require this treatment. Talcum powder will serve in place of pounce if the latter is not available.

23. Thumb tacks are needed to hold the paper or cloth to the

Thumb tacks stamped out of metal disk.

drawing-board. Tacks that are stamped out of a flat disk are best as their flat heads do not interfere with triangles and straight-edges; also they are easy to pull out.

24. Pencils should be of a good grade of drawing pencil; not writing or copying pencils. The degree of hardness should be decided by experiment, to fit the material drawn upon. For sketches and preliminary drawing, HB or H are good; for pencil tracing cloth H, 2H and 3H are used; for most tracing papers H will serve, though on vellums and other rough-surfaced papers 3H or 4H may be required; for hard drawing paper, such as Whatman's, 4H, 5H or 6H may work well. Much depends upon the draftsman's preference, some men use a 7H or 8H where others use 5H or 6H. The general rule is that hard, rough-surfaced papers require hard pencils, while soft- or glossy-

surfaced papers require soft pencils. Pencils with adjustable leads of required hardness, used in conjunction with a sandpaper pencil sharpener, are time-savers.

25. Lettering guides are necessary when good lettering is desired; the various "lettering triangles" on the market will serve. One of the popular instruments for drawing guide-lines for lettering is the adjustable "Ames Lettering Instrument" which has a large range of letter sizes. None of these tools help in shaping letters; this is done freehand. There are stencils for the purpose but they are expensive; it is better to learn freehand lettering than to depend upon stencils.

26. An erasing knife, a sharp penknife will do, can be used for correcting over-run corners and in making small erasures. A knife should not be used for extensive erasing and must be used

Sand paper block for pointing pencils.

with care as it quickly damages the drawing surface of paper or cloth. Some professional drafting offices do not permit the use of a knife on tracings for this reason.

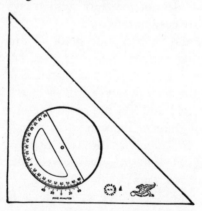

An adjustable protractor triangle.

27. Desk scissors and other miscellaneous tools are required, table brush, adjustable desk lamp, slide rule, sandpaper block, Arkansas oil stone for sharpening pens and knife, protractor, thumb tack lifter, sponge rubber or "Art Gum" for cleaning finished drawings, soft cloth and a stick of soapstone complete the list. Soapstone is used to prevent ink spreading when drawing over an erasure, on tracing cloth. The soapstone is crumbled slightly and rubbed over the erasure with the crayon or stick, then dusted off, before drawing.*

Directions for Use of Instruments

A few directions for the use of instruments can be given; it is recommended that they be supplemented by reference to textbooks on engineering or mechanical drafting. A list of these will be found at the end of this chapter.

Dividers should be opened and closed by one hand, as should compasses. Open by pinching the chamfer on the inner side of the legs with thumb and second finger. Hold dividers with thumb and forefinger on the outside of the legs and the second and third fingers inside. In this way the thumb and forefinger close, while the second and third fingers open, the dividers. When spacing, hold the dividers by the handle at the head, or by the pivot. Compasses are held the same way, by the head, and are revolved by rolling the handle slowly between thumb and forefinger. Bow-spring ·instruments are similar in operation, except that the sweep is adjusted by set screws. Needle-points of compasses should be slightly longer than the pen or pencil point when properly adjusted. The pen, on compasses, should be vertical to the surface of the drawing when in use, as should the needle-point; there are joints in the legs for this reason. A length-

* The names and addresses of dealers in drafting instruments and materials mentioned here are: Keuffel & Esser Co., 127 Fulton St., New York City; Eugene Dietzgen Co., 136 Camp St., New Orleans, La.; Theo. Altenedar & Sons, Philadelphia, Pa.; B. K. Elliot Co., 126 Sixth St., Pittsburgh, Pa.; Kolesch & Co., 138 Fulton St., New York City; A. C. Thornton, Ltd., King Street, West, Manchester, England. The American firms have agents or dealers in most large cities; catalogues may be obtained that will assist in choosing instruments and supplies.

ening bar is used to increase the sweep of the compasses.

Ruling pens should never be used freehand. They should be held with the handle nearly vertical, slightly inclined to the right if used right-handed. The nibs should be kept parallel to the ruling edge and not too close. Both nibs must touch the paper. These pens should never be dipped in ink but should be filled by touching the quill (attached to the cork of the ink bottle) between the nibs. The pen should not be filled too full; ⅛" to ¼" is enough in most pens. Be sure to clean the pen before laying it down even if only for a moment. Draw with a smooth, even motion, taking care not to tip or turn the pen. Most lines can be drawn with the arm resting on the drawing-board; long lines and those drawn with battens can be drawn by supporting the hand by the last three fingers.

It is helpful to the beginner to practice by drawing curves with the aid of "Copenhagen" or other curves; attempting to join one to another fairly, without visible joints. By "fair" is meant a smooth, even curve, without breaks, humps or angular bends. Practice drawing variously shaped and joined curves until blots, runs and unfair or visible joints no longer appear. The knack of being able to join curves and straight lines, or a series of curved lines, fairly and smoothly, without breaks or overlaps, can be soon acquired with practice and observation. In joining one line to another, start at the exact point at which the first line ended; do not over-run. It is a good rule to draw sharp curves first, then long curves; or curves first and then the straight lines if they are to join. Do not bear heavily on the pen for if you do it will cut into the paper and clog. The weight of the pen, loosely held in the hand, should be sufficient if the pen is sharp. It is easier to draw with fine lines than with heavy as joints are easier to make; but if heavy lines are required do not run a line until the ink is totally expended as a good continuation cannot then be made.

Use of "Tick Strips"

Instead of dividers, some draftsmen use "tick strips," mentioned earlier. The use of these is as follows; a strip of paper with at least one straightedge is laid along the line whose length is to be transferred, straight side to the line, and then the required length is ticked or marked on the edge of the paper strip with a sharp pencil. The measurement thus recorded may be transferred to another part of the drawing. Here the operation is reversed, the line is ticked from the strip. A number of measurements may be transferred in a single move, on one strip. Dividers are perhaps more accurate unless the tick strip is used with care.

Use of Battens

In laying out a curve with a batten, the ducks should be placed close to the points through which the line is to pass. It is very important that the ends of the batten be held by ducks, continuing the curve beyond the required length, else the line will show flat spots at the ends when drawn. Hence the requirement is that the batten be longer than the line to be drawn so that the curve of the batten can be carried beyond the extremities of the required line. After running the batten through the desired points it may be found that a hump or hollow appears (the line is unfair), which is corrected by lifting the duck, at which the unfairness appears; to allow the batten to spring into a fair curve. Before drawing the line, step to each end of the drawing-board and sight along the batten to make certain that it bends fair along its whole length; if not, correct it by resetting the ducks. However, do not allow the batten to design the line for it can be forced to any desired curve as long as it is a fair one. If the desired curve proves to be too sharp to bend a batten around, use sweeps or curves. A common error in the use of the batten is to employ too many ducks; only enough to hold the batten to the desired curve are required. If the batten moves at a rather hard part of the curve, place a couple of ducks on top of those that slip; the extra weight will usually correct the trouble. Choose a batten to fit the intended curve; do not attempt to use a very limber batten on a long gentle curve nor a stiff batten on a short quick curve. Use a batten whose taper is fitted to the shape of the curve; the thinnest portion of the batten should be placed where the sharpest bend is required or where there is to be reverse in the curve, while the thickest portion of the batten should be located where the curve to be drawn is slight.

The planimeter has directions for setting up, adjusting and using in its case. The outline of the figure to be measured is usually traced in a clockwise direction. The pivot-point should be firmly fixed for an error in the readings will result if the pivot-point slips while the instrument is in operation.

Use of Scale Rule

The use of the scale is easily understood. In drawing objects that cannot be represented full size because of the limitations of the drawing-board or other reasons, it is necessary to reduce the actual dimensions in some fixed proportion. By use of the architect's scale the proportion can be fixed at one-quarter the full size (3″ equal 1 foot) down to one-ninety-sixth the full size (⅛″ equals 1 foot). The draftsman does not think of the scale in this manner, however, but imagines each division (⅛″–¼″– ⅜″–¾″–½″–1″–1½″–3″) as a foot. Inspection of the scale will show that it is possible to measure feet and inches in each of these divisions. Look at a triangular scale, architect's division, and lay it on the drawing so that the end marked ½ is to the left and 1 is to the right. With the scale in this position it is possible to lay off dimensions in either ½″ or 1″ to the foot scale. The division nearest the end marked ½ is divided into inches and half inches at a scale of ½″ equals 1 foot, while the division nearest the end marked 1 is divided into inches, half and quarter inches on the scale of 1″ equals 1 foot. A little inspection will show how measurements are made to scale in feet, inches and fractions on these two scales and the others.

The use of the other instruments requires no explanation here; reference to text-books on drafting will give more detailed directions than can be given in these notes. The only remaining suggestion is that the drawing-board be covered with a sheet of drawing paper, over which the sheet to be drawn on is laid; by covering the board in this manner the old thumbtack holes and

Tools and Materials

It is important that a boat designer draw well. This requires much practice in order to obtain skill with the tools and to produce precise, neat plans. Poor drawings, so far as accuracy is concerned, result in uncertainty in design, and the builder will then have to interpret the plans instead of follow them. Interpreted plans may produce quite a different boat than the designer intended.

Small craft design is based on a long history of development during which thousands of intelligent and skilled builders and designers strove to produce good boats to suit given requirements. In the last hundred years they also experimented with engines of various kinds and with propulsion methods as well as with fittings, marine hardware and rigging details. While only a small proportion of their work has been recorded there is a great reservoir of technical information and basic ideas. It is folly to neglect this and to work with only an ill-informed imagination and the inadequate engineering knowledge of the present. Hence a very important tool of the designer is a collection of plans of old small craft and a library of reference books and magazines.

Drafting Suggestions

In fairing purchased sweeps and curves, or in making these, a flexible nail file about six inches long will be found very useful.

To lay off stations, a 24-inch triangular architect's scale is very handy. Stations and other spaced measurements are best made by measuring from a given point, say a perpendicular or base, to each station in turn, by adding up the accumulated spacings in feet, inches and fractions.

Pencil lines may be removed from tracing cloth by numerous cleaners on the market or with dry-cleaning fluid or white gasoline applied with a soft clean cloth.

The use of "drafting tape" or "masking tape" in lieu of thumb tacks is now popular with draftsmen. The drawing is secured with short pieces of the tape, which may be purchased in rolls.

Good drawing and tracing paper should be used, as much erasing will be necessary and only very good paper will withstand such treatment. Tracing paper that does not discolor or become brittle with age may be obtained; the medium or heavy weight is recommended. A smooth, transparent tracing paper of this class will take ink well and make very good blueprints. However, if a tracing is to be handled a good deal it is better made with tracing cloth. Such a tracing must always be protected from dampness, however.

It is convenient to have some information available in a notebook; looseleaf scrapbooks and notebooks are therefore desirable as part of a reference library.

II. Preliminary Design

Choice of Type

THE yachtsman who desires to design or to build a yacht has developed definite ideas as to the proper type of boat for his particular choice. It is therefore hardly necessary to discuss the questions relating to choice of type in detail. It is noticeable that most yachtsmen have some particular yacht in mind which, with changes in dimensions, profile, arrangement, rig or hull form, satisfies their desires. Some yachtsmen prefer standard types of yachts that are popular and fashionable at the moment, some would like to revive an old local type, while others are interested in experimental craft. These preferences are often modified by other considerations, of course; such as local requirements, prejudice, economic considerations and the intended use. Personal opinion governs the choice of type to a far greater extent than any quantity of argument, logical or otherwise. This statement is borne out by the countless and unending discussions and arguments in the pages of the yachting papers and in every gathering of yachtsmen. It is safe to assume that the reader has a definite type of yacht in mind, which he wishes to design, to have designed, or wants to build.

Compromising

It is often stated that the design of a yacht is a matter of compromising conflicting elements; speed, accommodation, seaworthiness, dryness, weatherliness, ease of handling and other qualities. This cannot be denied; yet it can be observed that the fewer the compromises the better the design will be. The owner must decide what particular qualities he desires most, or requires to the greatest extent, to meet his particular needs; to these elements he should sacrifice the less important. Too many yachts are designed by attempting to obtain all the qualities of the perfect yacht without regard to the limitations of the chosen type and intended use. It is very tempting to try to obtain all the good features seen in designs, yet if attempted the results prove very disappointing. To obtain a good design it is necessary to decide definitely the intended use; weigh the requirements of this carefully to fix the really important features that are necessary; then choose a type that has these elements of design to the fullest degree. When the type is chosen it should be held to religiously throughout the process of design.

In order to trace the process of making a design, it is necessary to have an example. Next, it is necessary to limit explanation to standard hulls and rigs for otherwise the discussion would be without end. Before the student can be successful in the design of experimental craft he must be well grounded on the basic principles of design which are well illustrated in standard types of hull and rig. The process of design is the same, regardless of type or size. The design of a motorboat is a similar procedure to that of a sailing yacht and the method used for drawing the plans of a 30 footer apply to a 70 footer. The interest of most yachtsmen is in sailing craft and auxiliaries, and since the design of these craft requires the most explanation, it will be proper to choose such a boat as the example for discussion. The easiest way to observe the preliminary steps in the design of a yacht will be to show the professional designer's methods.

Proposal for the Design

We are in the office of a designer, where we find a prospective client outlining his desires to the architect. The client speaks: "I have a winter home on the coast of Florida and I plan to build a yacht for use in neighboring waters. My house is on a rather shoal bay; this limits the draft of my boat to four feet or less, since I wish to keep her off my private dock. I want a boat that is capable of cruising in open water, say across the Gulf Stream to the Bahamas, and she must be reasonably fast. I expect to handle her with the aid of my wife and, on long runs, with a paid-hand. I shall also want to use her for taking out a few friends for an afternoon sail so I want a roomy cockpit. Personally, I like the schooner rig, gaff-rigged, with four lowers and perhaps a main gaff-topsail or perhaps a fisherman staysail. I shall have to have auxiliary power, enough to move her in calms and around crowded anchorages. While I shall not live aboard the yacht for long periods, nevertheless I want comfortable accommodations: stove, icebox, sink, toilet and roomy, comfortable berths. The stove should be able to burn wood, charcoal or anthracite. The sink must be a useful size, not a toy. The toilet must be a practical one. I should like to have berths for four in the cabin and a pipe-berth forward for the hand. The galley must be aft, close to the cockpit, as we shall eat out-of-doors in good weather. I want 6' headroom in the cabin as far as is possible without having excessive crown to the roof of the cabin trunk or too much freeboard. As I shall be short-handed, the rig must be simple and the finish plain, no bright-work as I must take care of her myself. I don't want her cut up inside with bulkheads for she must be easily ventilated. If it is possible, I would like extension berths in the cabin, but if not, upper and lower berths will do. I'd like a nice clipper bow and counter stern; here is a picture I found in a magazine that shows the profile I want. I must have a centerboard yacht, I know, but I would like a little outside ballast too as it will give me greater confidence in the boat. I do not feel that I can afford a boat much longer than 42 feet on deck, for I must consider cost. I want to have the boat built by some experienced builder, preferably some Maine builder as I expect to be Down East while the boat is building. Is it possible to get all this and have a good seaboat and a good sailer?"

Here is a typical problem; the owner has specified the type of hull, rig, accommodations, dimensions to some extent and the appearance of the boat he wants designed. To a great extent, the dimensions are subservient to the accommodations. He has stated the use to which the boat is to be put and has expressed, in general terms, the waters in which he expects to use her. Some of his requirements are the result of experience, others are based on opinion or merely "because I like it."

Roughing Out

The first step is to see if the requirements can be met in the specified length. By sketching the arrangement freehand, on a scrap of paper, and then estimating the dimensions of each item, it is possible to discover whether the arrangement is feasible within the given limitations. The sketch must show the general location of each portion of the arrangement and every important feature must be laid out. The study of published plans will aid the beginner a great deal in judging what is practical and what is not, as well as the allowance necessary for bow and stern.

The main considerations to be kept in mind when making these sketches and estimating accommodation are:—that full headroom cannot be had the full length of the hull (except in large craft) but can be had only under the cabin trunk in most small yachts; that full headroom cannot be had in yachts under 28 feet overall length unless the draft and displacement are abnormally large; that floor space is limited by the shape of the hull to a great extent, and by the deadrise of the sections; that cutting up a cabin with bulkheads is usually undesirable in yachts under 35 feet overall; that berths, lockers and other cabin fittings should be of practical size; and that the whole space enclosed by the outline of the deck of a given length and beam is not available for accommodations. There should be at least two hatches of reasonable size, one forward and one aft, opening into the cabin; and finally, some thought must be given to the effect of the arrangement on the appearance of the yacht, as well as upon the underbody and fore-and-aft trim. It is clearly impossible to give fixed rules; judgment, commonsense and experience must govern.

Estimating Dimensions

As a guide in estimating required dimensions, however, it is possible to make useful suggestions. Berths should not be less than 6'-2" long, nor less than 21" average width. Pipe berths are usually 6'-2" x 2'-6" if not shaped to the side of the hull. The minimum width for comfort is 21" except in cold climates, where greater width is highly desirable. The space between upper and lower berth must not be less than 21", nor should there ever be less headroom than this over any berth. All seats and transoms should be at least 16" wide and, if possible, 12" above the floor; but the width may be increased as the height is decreased. 20" depth of seat and 10" to the top of cushion make a good proportion. The lower the seat the wider it must be. There must be 3'-6" headroom òver all seats and transoms. A person sitting requires about 24" frontage.

The minimum floor space in front of a seat or transom should not be less than 24" for comfort; if transoms face one another there ought to be about 30" footroom, though this is rarely achieved in a small cruiser. The higher the transoms, the less will be the required floor space or footroom. As most yachtsmen sit in their cabins far oftener than they stand or recline, it is wise to give sitting comfort much consideration.

In estimating length, allow an inch or two for each bulkhead or locker-side. The stove, if coal burning, will require a space not less than 18" x 24"; this depends upon model, of course. The space under the stove is generally utilized for fuel. If an oil or alcohol burning stove is to be used, it is possible to obtain stoves as small as 15" x 15" (single-burner) or 15" x 24" (two-burner). Allowance must be made for fuel tanks, according to the maker's requirements. The same remarks apply to gas stoves and space must be allowed according to the catalogue dimensions. The top of the stove ought to be 30" above the floor if there is full headroom, a height of 36" is preferred by some. There must be at least 15" in the clear above the stove top in any case. It is a good idea to place a zinc pan under the stove. A ventilator over the stove is often desirable. In locating a coal or wood burning stove the chimney must be considered.

Clothes lockers, if used to hang clothing in, ought to be 16" in either width or depth and have 40" headroom. If doors are used, allowance must be made for their swing.

Iceboxes should be as large as possible; the space for ice should be equivalent to 15" x 15" x 18" at least. Boxes with two compartments on the same level, one for ice and one for food, and fitted with lift tops are known as "club iceboxes," and are superior to the household type fitted with doors, since the cold air does not flow out, nor does the food capsize into your lap every time you reach for the beer. The household icebox requires battens across the doors for this reason; battens are anything but convenient. In very small cruisers the icebox can be in the form of a large, well insulated drawer.

The sink, if built-in, should never be less than 10" x 10" x 6"; a larger one is preferable. It ought to be about 36" above the floor if there is standing headroom; there must be 15" in the clear above it. Allowance must be made for pump and drain. In single-handers and other small cruisers the old-fashioned dishpan and wash basin are superior to miniature sinks.

Tables may be folding or fixed; the size must depend upon cabin accommodations, of course; allow 24" x 18" of table space for each individual. The standard height above the floor is 30" with full headroom; in any case the top of the table must be 12" above the top of the seats or transoms.

Work tables, or "dressers," in the galley are very useful; they should be not less than 20" x 18" on the top, and ought to stand 36" to 40" off the floor when there is standing headroom. It may be remarked that there has been a tendency to make sinks, stove tops and work tables too low in yachts; a height of 38" is a good average when the owner is of medium height.

Water closets should be chosen with regard to the size of the boat. While dimensions vary with make and model, the minimum floor space required is about 16" x 18", to take care of the bowl and pump. Marine water closets require careful locating, for the plumbing and necessary valves must be taken into consideration. Practically all marine water closets require pumping to flush; this must be considered in locating the fitting. The well-known practice of singing the "Volga Boat Song" with variations while flushing the water closet with the pump, as well as the complication and cost of the fitting, has led many yachtsmen to prefer the "sanitary bucket," particularly in small craft. This is usually placed in a hinged box or locker; both locker and bucket are easily cleaned. The "sanitary bucket" requires less room than a water closet and enables the difficult plumbing of the latter to be omitted. There should be 40″ or 42″ headroom above the seat of a water closet. When a water closet or bucket is being located, it is very important that it be placed in such a position that the fitting and the floor about it can be easily cleaned. If the fitting is to be placed under a seat or in a hinged box, the seat or box should unship so that it may be cleaned. It is suggested that there be a zinc pan, as large as space permits, under a water closet or bucket. Toilet spaces should be well ventilated, even in small craft. Lately, metal piping outlets and inlets of waterclosets have been replaced with non-collapsing rubber hose, which has many advantages. Space must be allowed for valves or seacocks in *all* outboard hull connections.

Bureaus and buffets should be of convenient height, not less than 36″ when there is full headroom. The drawers should be of practical dimensions. As a guide, drawers should not exceed 9″ in depth, nor have greater dimensions than 30″ x 20″ x 9″. There must be exceptions, occasionally, but this is a good rule to follow. If the drawers must be very narrow, say under 8″, the depth may be increased to the maximum of 15″. If a drawer is to be used to hold heavy weights, as in the case where a drawer serves as an ice-box, it can be mounted on rollers.

Ladders should not be less than 16″ wide, but this will depend upon the amount of room available and upon the height. The maximum pitch for ladders is about 60°; long ladders should have less pitch than short ones. Stairs should rise 7″ to 9″ per step and the treads should not be less than 7″ or more than 10″, as a rule. However, space must govern in these matters. It is important that headroom at the lower steps of ladders and stairs be considered.

Generally speaking, it is bad practice to have ladders and stairs rise athwartships; they should always rise fore-and-aft. Berths placed athwartships are occasionally seen; the arrangement is a lubberly one.

Companionways should not be less than 18" x 24" in the clear; 18" x 28" is perhaps a safer minimum. Ventilating hatches may be 18" x 18", but ought to be larger so that they will serve for escape hatches. Cockpit floor space will be governed wholly by the owner's requirements; there has been a fad for unnecessarily small cockpits. Flush decks are not particularly desirable on small yachts where reasonably high bulwarks are not practical. Alleyways, or deck space between cabin trunk and rail, should not be less than 12" in width; if this minimum cannot be met it is better to carry the sides of the trunk out to the sides of the hull.

Engine and Tanks

The engine and tanks must receive attention in the working out of the arrangement. In small craft it is common to place the engine under the cockpit floor or under a bridge deck between the cockpit and cabin trunk. In large yachts the engine is sometimes located in the same manner, though installations forward or amidships are equally popular. By use of gearing, it has become possible to put the engine into a hull in almost any desired position. The use of gears increase cost, however. Dimensions of the engine, gears and other auxiliary machinery must be obtained from the engine-builder's catalogues. In fast vessels, having a fine run, there is rarely room for the engine aft, so forward positions are usually chosen. In locating the engine, some thought should be given to accessibility for repairs and adjustments. Arrangement for manual starting as well as mechanical starting should not be forgotten. In small yachts, the use of the outboard-engine may solve many problems. In placing the engine, the probable location of batteries and exhaust should also be considered. Placing the propeller shaft off the centerline of the hull may aid in finding a suitable location for the engine. Many designers prefer having the propeller on one side of the deadwood to employing an aperture for the wheel as the former is considered very efficient in sailing craft. Tank tests indicate that the centerline installation is the most efficient in sailing craft, theoretically. In actual practice there are so many things that may affect the efficiency other than installation position, that the subject is of relatively little importance compared to practical considerations of arrangement requirements.

Tanks are the most difficult fittings to locate, and are the most neglected in design. Too often tanks are an afterthought and are located haphazardly, without regard to convenience or safety. It is probably best to place fuel tanks aft, on each side of the cockpit or engine below deck. It is by no means uncommon to find these tanks under the cabin floor in modern yachts—perhaps the most dangerous location imaginable. It is hardly necessary to stress the danger of improper fuel tank installation, for it is obvious to all. Fire and explosions due to gas in the bilges or leakage have been all too common. Water tanks likewise require consideration. They, like fuel tanks, ought to be placed so that they are removable without disturbing joinerwork or structure. All tanks ought to be as low in the boat as possible and as near the centerline as they can be placed. They should be accessible for they will need cleaning occasionally and may need repairs. Water tanks have been located under the berths, but the noise of the water when the boat rolls is disturbing. Practically, the small water tank is best located in a deck locker, but this is often impossible. Such an arrangement, however, enables the use of gravity feed and permits inspection and cleaning. Waste or sewage tanks are sometimes required by the use of bath tubs or other plumbing, particularly on large yachts; these tanks can be placed under the cabin floor. In locating tanks, it is well to remember that they represent great weight which has an effect on trim, particularly fore-and-aft, and wing tanks affect stability. Tanks are usually of iron or copper, tinned inside, for fuel or water.

It is quite impossible to lay down absolute rules and dimensions

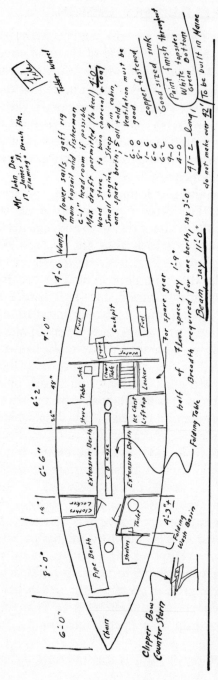

The sketch contains the following handwritten notations:

Mr. John Doe.
17 James St. "Beach Fla.

Tiller Wheel

4 lower sails gaff rig
main topsail and fisherman
6'-1" head-room if possible
Max draft permitted (to keel) 4'-0"
Wood Stove, to burn charcoal & coal
Small engine, Sleep in cabin,
one spare berth; Sail told
Ventilation must be
good

copper fastened
Good sized sink
Paint finish throughout
White topsides
Green bottom
To be built in Maine

6-00
6-6
6-2
4-0

41-2 long,
do not make over 42' To be built in Maine

Clipper Bow
Counter Stern

Chain

Pipe Berth

Shelves

Toilet

Folding Wash Basin

Clothes Locker

Extension Berth

CB case

Extension Berth

Stove Table

Sink

Chart Table

Ice Chest

Lift top Locker

Folding Table

Stove

Water

Cockpit

Fuel

Fuel

For spare gear

Breadth required for one berth, say 3'-0"

half of floor space, say 1'-9"

Beam say 11'-0"

6'-0"
8'-0"
18"
6'-6"
26"
6'-2"
48"
4'-0"
4'-0" Wants
4'-3"±

FIGURE 1. Sketch made by designer while discussing the design with the owner; showing method of estimating dimensions and roughing out arrangement prior to making a scale sketch. Note record of details discussed, for use in plans and specifications.

for all fittings that are required in the arrangement sketch. Lighting plants, stowage, method of carrying the dinghy, spare sail lockers, radio and similar items are matters of individual design; to be located as conditions warrant.

The application of many of the foregoing remarks to the proposed schooner is seen in the reproduction of the designer's rough sketch in Figure 1. It will be seen that the length requirement can be met, apparently, and that the beam required by the proposed arrangement can be fixed to some extent. The proportion of beam to length is, obviously, a matter of type. If it appears that the arrangement cannot be obtained in the desired length, or within the limitations on beam imposed by the choice of type, then further study is necessary. It must be observed that many yachtsmen expect altogether too much accommodation in a given length. It does not necessarily follow that the arrangement cannot be obtained, in such cases, but the result is generally a slow, deep and heavy-working boat.

When the make, model and power of the engine is decided, and the owner and designer have come to agreement as to arrangement details and other features, a scale preliminary drawing can be made. This will incorporate the arrangement plan as worked out in the rough estimating sketch, and show the profile of the hull and the rig as well. Sometimes a deck plan is shown also, particularly in large craft. Very often a midsection is likewise drawn, to check the transverse accommodation in a general way.

Scale of Preliminary Sketch

The scale of the sketch or plan will be governed by the size of the vessel and the limitations of the draftsman's board. It is best to use a small scale; the following is a good guide;

boats under 30' overall, ½" equals 1'-0"
" " 40' and over 30' overall, ⅜" equals 1'-0"
" " 70' " " 40' " , ¼" equals 1'-0"

Yachts over 70' overall may be drawn on a scale of ⅛" equals 1'-0". The purpose of making the drawing rather small is to enable the plan to be seen as a whole rather than in part. In this way an accurate impression is received. It is customary to hang the preliminary drawing on the wall, in professional design, and inspect it from a distance to discover whether the appearance of the yacht will be pleasing. An artist's "reducing glass" can also be used.

Preliminary Arrangement Plan

The first step in making the drawing is to lay out the arrangement plan. It is easiest to make the drawing on tracing paper; the procedure is as follows. Take a scrap of drawing paper and lay off a line equal to the length of the proposed hull, to the desired scale. Locate, along this line, where the greatest beam is to be (52% to 55% of the L.W.L. length from the bow is the most common proportion; usually this is about half the length overall) and erect a perpendicular. The bow end of the drawing may be taken to the right or left; the bow is usually to the right. On the perpendicular just erected, measure off to scale one-half the greatest beam and sketch in, freehand, the upper half of the desired deck plan. The shape of the deck outline, from the centerline out, is thus obtained. Alter until the eye is satisfied with the shape and then draw in with the aid of a batten and ducks, using a clean black line. The freehand line, lightly drawn, will serve as a guide; and aid in preventing the batten from designing the line. If the curve is too sharp for a batten, use sweeps and curves. Take care to avoid too sharp a bow on deck. Now half the deck plan is before you.

Take a piece of tracing paper (or cloth) large enough for the finished drawing, which will show the arrangement plan and profile (with sail plan) one over the other, and perhaps a deck plan in addition. Allowing sufficient room for the lower half of the deck outline, trace the drawing just made. Turn the sheet over and trace the other half, making certain that the centerline coincides and that the bow and stern agree. In this manner, both sides will be alike without the trouble of having to space lines in with the dividers. As the tracing paper (or cloth) is transparent the lines are visible from either side. If desired, both sides of the deck-line may be inked in on the working side of the tracing so that they will not be accidentally rubbed out in making erasures.

Deck Outline

A few remarks can be made about the shape of the deck outline, but it is supposed that the student has a definite hull form in mind and so has fixed upon the deck plan or outline by study of similar designs. Generally speaking, pinched-in bows and very curved sides are to be avoided. Except in catboats and other wide, shoal centerboarders, the width at transom is a good deal less than three-quarters the greatest beam. The shorter the stern overhang the wider the transom, as a rule, though exceptions are by no means rare. The deck plan or outline is fair, of course, unless there is to be a break in the sheer, when tumble-home or flare may cause a break in the outline of the deck when viewed from above. The use of "deadflat" (sides of the deck parallel amidships for a short distance) such as is seen in cargo steamers is rarely employed in yachts, though it can be used to advantage in some types of hull.

When the shape of the deck plan or outline is decided and drawn, the arrangement as worked out in the rough freehand sketch is drawn, carefully, and to scale, within the deck outline. This must be done with judgment; allowances for the thickness of the sides, the frames and ceiling, the limitations of floor space, headroom, hull shape and similar considerations, all must be kept in mind. It may prove necessary to make further changes, or even a totally new arrangement if it is found that one has made incorrect estimates of available space. It is important that the stove, sink, engine and other fittings are drawn to accurate scale; catalogue dimensions should be used. At the same time, the make and catalogue number of each fitting should be listed for ready reference. In working up the details of the cabin layout, due allowance for thickness of bulkheads, swing of doors, clearance of drawers and similar things must not be forgotten. Over the arrangement, when it is finally completed, the outlines of the cabin trunk, the cockpit, hatches, skylights and stove-pipe are drawn in dot-and-dash lines; to locate them in reference to the arrangement. If desired, a separate deck plan may also be drawn in the same manner as the arrangement, on which may be shown the plan-view of deck structures and fittings as the work progresses. These plan-views of deck and arrangement cannot be completed until the outboard profile is worked out, so should not be inked in now. It may be necessary to make extensive changes when the final position of the mast or masts is decided or the centerboard located. It will be found most satisfactory to work all three views together after they are once outlined, as by this method the effect of each item and specification can be studied.

Deck Plan and Outboard Profile

The deck plan, if there is to be one, should be directly above the arrangement plan, with the centerline of both views parallel and the ends on the same perpendiculars. Projecting the end perpendiculars further upward, and drawing another line parallel to the centerlines just mentioned (at some location that will give room for the underbody profile below it and the sail plan and above-water profile above it), the load-waterline of the outboard profile is obtained. The perpendiculars erected at the bow and stern of the arrangement plan will fix the length of the hull, of course, in the profile drawing. It may be well to take notice, here, that "plan" will hereafter designate a view taken from above the hull unless otherwise stated, and "profile" will indicate a side view or elevation. The outboard profile that is now to be drawn will show a side view of the completed boat, above and below the waterline; the appearance of the bow, stern, sheer, cabin trunk, hatches, skylights and other fittings that show above the rail; the complete sail plan showing at least the standing rigging; all are to be drawn. As the position of the cabin trunk, hatches and other details are projected up from the positions fixed in the arrangement or deck plans, their effect on the appearance of the finished boat will become apparent and changes may be required as the design develops. Before drawing the outboard profile it is necessary to have a mental picture of the desired appearance of the yacht. Since individual ideas of beauty and taste, as well as the requirements of hull-type, will govern the appearance of a boat, it is clear that explicit directions cannot be given here.

Nevertheless, there can be a general discussion of each feature to be designed which will aid the reader in working up the profile.

Freeboard

Beginning with the sheer line, the first step is to locate and fix the least freeboard. The measurement of the least freeboard (lowest portion of the top of the hull at the side, above the water-line) will be fixed by the limitations imposed by draft, headroom, arrangement of the cabin, the appearance desired and the type of yacht. The student will decide this by reference to published plans of craft similar to the one he is designing, for there is no mathematical proportion that would fit all types or designs. Generally, the freeboard should be kept as low as conditions imposed on the design will permit. Many modern yachts have excessive height of side, many yachtsmen and some designers labor under the delusion that high freeboard is desirable in a seagoing yacht. However, the windage and weight of excessively high topsides are actually a grave handicap, producing a sluggish sailer and, usually, a wet boat. Great freeboard has the tendency to make the hull appear short and chunky and this is not conducive to grace and beauty in hull-design. When the proportion of free-board in relation to length that is employed on liners and other large steamers is considered, as well as the actual measured height of side in these vessels, the fallacy of the relation of great free-board to seagoing ability and dryness becomes evident, for every winter brings forth tales of decks being swept by heavy seas and similar accidents to such vessels. It will be found, also, that most seagoing fishermen and other commercial sailing craft have com-paratively low freeboard, yet these craft do not commonly meet disaster at sea. Experience shows that it is better to sacrifice some headroom in small craft rather than to have excessive freeboard; in fact it is a good rule to keep the least freeboard as low as pos-sible in any sailing yacht.

The fore-and-aft position of the point of least freeboard is fixed by the type of sheer used, as well as by the taste of the de-signer. If the conventional concave sheer is employed, the least freeboard is usually located two-thirds, or a little more, of the overall length abaft the bow. If the sheer is to be convex or "humpbacked," as is sometimes employed in power craft and a few experimental sailing yachts, the least freeboard is located at the transom or extreme stern. In double-enders, such as lifeboats, sailing canoes and bugeyes, the least freeboard is usually amidships or a little farther aft.

Sheer Types

The conventional concave sheer may be laid out to the following specification. Draw the sheer nearly straight for the forward third of its length, working into a gentle curve with the lowest point at the place of least freeboard, then sweeping up sharply to the transom or sternpost. The sheer line, it is understood, may be the top of the rail cap or deck in this drawing, as desired. The amount of curve required in the forward third of the sheer should be governed by the amount of flare in the topsides forward, the fullness of the deck forward (in plan-view), and the shape of stem as will be explained farther on. If there is much flare forward or if the deck-line is full, there ought to be more curvature in the sheer forward than when the deck-line is sharp and the forward topsides have little flare. If this rule is not followed, a marked "hump" or reverse curve will appear in the forward portion of the sheer in the finished hull.

The sheer of a yacht has much to do with her beauty, which in sailing craft, as well as in houses, is based largely upon tradition and custom. It is well to take notice that the type of sheer, and the amount of sheer as well, should be fixed by the choice of hull type. The sheer used in the well-known "Friendship Sloops" will serve to illustrate the point; should a different sheer than that commonly employed in the type be used, the innovation would create an unfavorable impression. The amount of sheer to be given a design must be left to the designer's judgment; there is no mathematical proportion or given rule that will apply to all cases. The conventions of the hull type being followed, which have been established by usage, are the best guides. To some extent, the amount of overhang, beam, and freeboard, the shape of the deck-line, stem, stern and cabin trunk or deck erections and the form of the hull sections will have some effect on the amount of sheer that ought to be used, as will be explained shortly.

Amount of Sheer

In drawing, it is better to fix the location and amount of least freeboard, then sketch in the sheer freehand to suit the eye, rather than to try to fix the freeboard of bow and stern beforehand. A perfectly straight sheer line should be avoided, as such a sheer will not appear straight in the completed hull unless the vessel is wall-sided and more or less parallel-sided as well. If the hull has any shape, such a sheer will have an appearance of being "wavy" due to optical illusion brought about by the varying curves in the hull elsewhere. If it is desired to have a sheer that appears to be straight, a very slight amount of sheer will accomplish the result. In such a case, the greatest curvature is usually in the forward third and the after fourth of the overall length of the sheer line. In fixing the amount of sheer there is one rule that will aid in achieving the desired appearance to a hull; that is, the measured amount of sheer should be twice the amount that is to *appear* in the finished yacht. The amount of sheer always appears to be about half of what it really measures because of perspective. When the hull is viewed broadside on, the bow and stern are farther from the eye than the middle length, the perspective effect of which is heightened by the fact that the sides of the hull curve away toward the ends. As a result the sheer is lessened and often distorted. This matter will receive more attention later on.

Relation of Deck-line and Profile

There is a slight similarity between the shape of the deck-line in plan view and in profile, as has been suggested. This is illustrated by the fact that it is generally best to give a wide double-ender a canoe-like sheer. The effect of beam on sheer may be expressed in general terms as follows: narrow, wall-sided yachts require only a small amount of sheer, while wide hulls, particularly those with well-rounded deck-lines, require great sheer. It may be mentioned, here, that it is customary to give schooners and ketches more sheer than cutters, sloops or yawls, though this is by no means an absolute rule. Cruising yachts are commonly given a fair amount of sheer as they are not affected by the limitations set up by rule measurements. The wise designer takes advantage of such freedom when he can.

Illusions

The "Friendship Sloop" will serve to illustrate another matter in regard to sheer. This type of hull has an oval transom with much tumble-home to the quarters; these features give the illusion of much less sheer aft than really exists because the sheer is thus brought nearer the centerline of the hull and so farther from the eye when viewed broadside on. Therefore, if the transom tumbles-home (falls inboard at deck) the sheer aft should rise sharply and to a greater degree than if the sides of the transom flare outward or are vertical. In any case the sheer aft should *never* parallel the load waterline, for if it does the stern overhang will appear to droop in the completed hull. It is usually well to have a marked curve in the after portion of the sheer, as it approaches the transom or sternpost. As has been pointed out, these matters are modified by the traditional sheer of the hull type being designed.

Concave Sheer

The advantages of the conventional concave sheer are; that by this means reserve buoyancy is properly distributed along the length of the hull, a graceful appearance is obtained, and a dry deck is made possible. The most marked disadvantage is that windage is increased, particularly forward where it is most effective in setting up resistance. Cruising yachts and all types of seagoing fishermen and commercial craft employ this type of sheer. Formerly American sailing vessels had very little sheer, as may be seen in plans of sailing men-of-war, clipper schooners

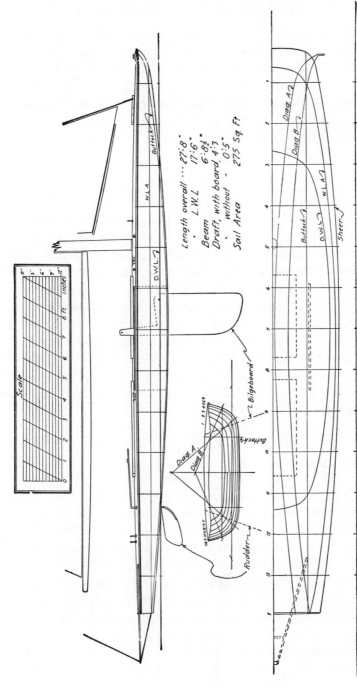

Scale

Length overall···27′·8″
 ″ L.W.L   17′·6″
Beam   6′·8¼″
Draft, with board. 4′·3″
 ″ without ″   0′·5″
Sail Area   275 Sq. Ft.

One-design racing scow, leg-of-mutton mainsail and jib; showing typical bow and deck half-breadth, reverse sheer, flaring topsides, bilgeboards and double rudders, typical deck layout, and method of fairing this type of hull.

and similar vessels. In recent times, many cruising yachts have appeared which had little sheer, for no other reason than it is fashionable in racers and therefore gives the impression of an ability to sail fast in the minds of the designer or owner. When in doubt it is better to use much sheer rather than a little. As a rule, the greater the freeboard the greater the sheer, though today this rule is often violated.

Reverse Sheer

The "humpbacked" or reverse sheer is now rather popular in cruising yachts, and often used in racing and power yachts. It has the advantage of increasing room amidships where it would be desirable for accommodation, and in a sailing yacht it places the greatest freeboard where it is needed, when the hull is heeled, to keep the deck free of water. The low ends, however, are disadvantageous in rough water, though undoubtedly aiding in the reduction of windage. To most yachtsmen this class of sheer is ugly as it is unconventional. Its use in sailing yachts has been limited almost entirely to shoal centerboarders of the "scow" models. In these, the highest freeboard is usually located just forward of amidships, to give the currently fashionable "streamline" effect.

Compound Sheer

The "compound" sheer has not been mentioned for it is now rarely seen. It may be described as being somewhat like the letter "S"; in other words it is the conventional concave sheer with a marked and intentional hump in the forward third of its length. This sheer was once popular in America, particularly in the 1870's, when it was used in a number of fishing and coasting schooners. Sometimes known as the "powder-horn" or "Noank" sheer, it may be laid out as follows: with the bow as the point of greatest freeboard, the sheer is carried aft for about one-fourth the overall length almost parallel the load-waterline, then it dips downward in a fair curve to the point of least freeboard, say at three-quarters the overall length abaft the bow, and finally sweeps sharply upward to the transom or sternpost. This sheer is graceful and is particularly suitable for small open boats, since it brings a high "shoulder" at a point where water is usually shipped by an open boat. The English "Coble" and "Yarmouth Yawl" are examples of the use of the "powder-horn" sheer in open boats. Its introduction was probably due to ease of construction in clench (lap-strake) built craft as it was used in early British cutters. On the whole, it has the same disadvantage as the conventional concave sheer and its use is merely a matter of individual preference, particularly in decked yachts.

Raised-deck Sheers

Broken, or "raised-deck," sheers may be divided into two classes: those with the raised-deck forward and those with the raised-deck aft. The latter is a very old feature, still seen in fishing and coasting schooners. The raised quarterdeck thus obtained gave increased room aft and a dry place for the helmsman. The modern raised quarterdeck is low, compared to that of earlier years; in this our ancestors had a distinct advantage for the high quarterdeck gave very fine accommodations aft. If the bulwarks on the maindeck are high enough, the sheer could be unbroken, or at least, the "break" in the sheer could be small. The minimum length of hull in which such design of sheer can be used to any advantage appears to be about 50'-0" overall. A low raised quarterdeck could be used on a shorter hull but there would be little practical advantage in such a design. When the raised quarterdeck is low, as in fishing schooners, the "break" in the sheer may be located amidships or thereabouts, but if the quarterdeck is much elevated above the maindeck and the resulting change in height of the sheer at the "break" is great, then the "break" should be farther aft; a high quarterdeck should not be longer than one-third of the overall length of the hull, preferably somewhat less. The "break" in the sheer is properly called the "drift" and may be of varying design, ranging from a simple angular or rounded one to ogees and carving, to set off the change in height of the rail-cap. The use of the low quarterdeck in hull-design was well illustrated in the New England fishing schooners and needs no special explanation. The problems in the use of the high quarterdeck are less simple and the designer should study plans of sailing craft of the late eighteenth century to obtain inspiration. The modern overhanging counter is out of place in such designs. The architectural possibilities of stern and quarter windows, as well as windows at the forward end of the quarterdeck (in the bulkhead at the break in the deck), are well worth study. In both classes of raised quarterdecks, the main sheer line should be carried from bow to stern by means of false rail-caps, if necessary.

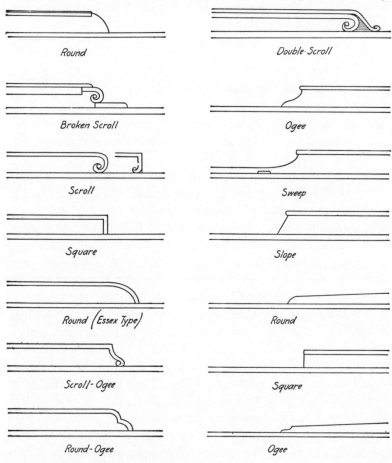

Types of Sheer Breaks or "Drifts."

It may be well to reassure those whose fancy turns toward designs having the ancient high quarterdeck; unless carried to extremes, the high quarterdeck will not harm sailing qualities of a boat. It is doubtful that the high quarterdeck was as harmful to sailing qualities as the high deck structures now so fashionable in sailing cruisers.

Designs having the raised deck forward have been popular, both in power craft and in small sailing cruisers. The advantages of this type of sheer are that accommodation is increased and a cleanswept deck may be obtained in a comparatively small hull. Structurally, the raised deck design is stronger and cheaper than the cabin trunk. The one serious objection to the use of the raised deck forward is the windage thus set up; as has been mentioned, windage forward is most objectionable. In this class of sheer, the drift should be forward or abaft of amidships if the appearance of "sagging" is to be avoided. Usually this sheer is employed in small craft where the difference in elevation of the main and raised sheer is necessarily great, therefore the profile requires careful study. The main sheer should be carried fore-and-aft by means of false mouldings or a cove-line (groove cut into the planking and gilded or painted with some contrasting color). Usually the main sheer is located below the real sheer aft as well as forward; in such designs the space between the two sheer lines should taper from amidships toward the ends; furthermore, it is well to stop the main or false sheer a little short of bow and stern to avoid possible illusions as to the profile of the ends of the hull. The shape of the drift needs much consideration as it is prominent in this class of sheer. Mouldings, made of tapered half-round battens, serving as guards, are more effective in setting off the false sheer than are cove-lines or painted stripes. The use of arrow-heads and large scrolls, in conjunction with a cove-line or stripe, has now gone out of fashion; if used such ornaments should be small. In small cruisers, a combination of raised deck and cabin trunk is sometimes employed.

There is a third type of broken sheer; that formed by extending the sides of the cabin trunk to the sides of the hull. The sides of the cabin usually tumble-home sharply in cross-section (above the main sheer) to reduce windage. This class of sheer is an excellent one for small cruisers as it combines the maximum of usable room in the cabin with excellent ventilation. It is less desirable in large craft, as in addition to the problem of stowing the dinghy there is the objection that the crew must climb over the cabin trunk when going forward. The two drifts required in this sheer should be located with care, as in other broken sheers, to avoid the illusion of the hull sagging. The most common drift seen in this sheer is formed by sweeping up the rail-cap in a short, hard curve to the top of the trunk. It is well to employ less sheer in the top of the cabin trunk sides than in the main sheer. The main sheer should be carried fore-and-aft by use of a half-round or other moulding. In most yachts having this sheer there are low bulwarks forward and abaft the cabin structure.

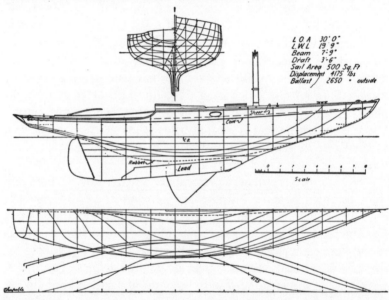

Knockabout centerboard sloop jib-headed mainsail, to show treatment of raised-deck forward, false sheer by cove-lines, long overhang bow, yacht counter, cut-away profile, and raking sternpost.

Cove-lines

When the freeboard is necessarily great, the use of cove-lines below the true sheer will aid in reducing the apparent height of freeboard. It is important to avoid parallel sheer lines; the rule is that the amount of sheer is decreased as the height above the waterline is increased, when there is more than one sheer. Thus, the sheer of the top of the cabin trunk should never parallel the main sheer, but rather, should be straighter. This matter will receive further attention when deck structures are discussed.

Heights of Bulwarks and Waist

When bulwarks are employed in the design it is well to taper their heights from the bow toward the stern; the top of the bulwarks being taken as the sheer line. It is not necessary to set off the deck-line, in this case, with a cove-line or stripe. If the bulwarks are high in proportion to the freeboard, the height may be the same throughout the length, however. In this case it will be found pleasing if the height of the bulwarks is made less apparent by use of a "waist" line, made by reducing the thickness of the planking of the bulwarks, at about one-third the height of the bulwarks below the rail-cap. The waist may be emphasized by placing a cove-line or stripe just below it. The cove-line or stripe should stop just short of the bow and stern; it is usual to sweep up the waist at the stern in a short, hard curve so that it meets the rail-cap a few inches forward of the transom. If the yacht is large enough to require hawse-holes these should come below the waist line at the bow, not above it. The waist line and its cove-line or stripe may parallel the rail-cap as the distance between waist line and rail-cap is small. If the bulwark height is less than 18″, the waist line may be omitted, as a rule.

The wide range of choice in design of sheer is no greater than the range of choice in bows and sterns. Here again, the designer should follow the conventions of the particular type which he is drawing. There are principles of design that govern the shape of each type of bow and stern, and also the combination of the two in a hull. Illusion plays a great part in the design of both the bow and the stern; in order to avoid accidental impressions this matter must be understood.

Straight Stem

For example, it will be found that a stem, whose profile is formed by a dead straight line, will appear to have a slight hollow unless the hull is quite wall-sided in section, forward. It will also be found that a stem that is nearly straight, with its upper portion perpendicular to the waterline, will appear to tumble-home slightly. Sometimes these illusions are desired, it is true, but ordinarily they are to be avoided.

To design a stem that will appear to be straight in the completed hull, its profile should be given a slight, gradual curve from the waterline up to about two-thirds the height of the stem,

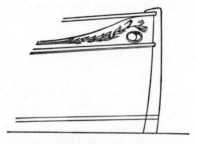

Straight stem power yacht.

above which it becomes straight. Sometimes the curvature increases as the waterline is approached. In order to avoid the illusion of tumbling-home the stem must flare outward at the top; the rake being at least one inch for each foot of freeboard. In drawing, the rake is first sketched in, then the curved portion is drawn. Rake of stem should be great in power boats that lift forward when at speed, as a perpendicular stem then shows excessive tumble-home and an unpleasant "chin" appears. If a scroll is used, it should be placed well abaft the stem, with its large end forward. It is possible to use a shield or even a small figurehead with the straight stem though this type of decoration is now out of style. It may be added that it is possible to use greater freeboard with the straight stem than with any other form of cutwater.

Catboat Bow

The tumble-home or ram bow, seen on catboats and some canoes, looks best if it has a slight curve for its whole height or if a distinct "chin" is employed. In catboats the tumble-home

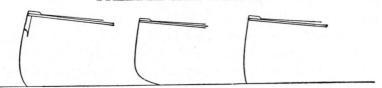

Typical Catboat Stems—Tumble-home Bows.

may be fixed at two-thirds the angle of the forestay (measured to a perpendicular through the extreme bow); if the forefoot is cut away below the waterline, the stem, after the tumble-home is fixed, should curve outward slightly from the fore end of the sheer line until it almost reaches the bow perpendicular (at one-third or one-quarter the freeboard at stem) from whence the curve may round sharply in a fair curve until it can be faired into the forefoot. The profile of the stem becomes tangent to the

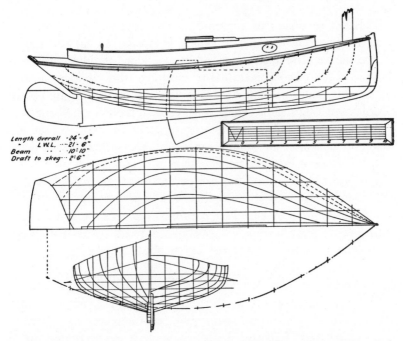

Length overall ·24·-4·
LWL. ···21·6·
Beam ·· ·10:10·
Draft to skeg·· 2:6·

Typical Catboat; showing strong sheer, the effect of forefoot and bow profile on shape of waterlines, and high cabin trunk of this type of hull. Note proportion of length of centerboard to L.W.L. and also design of V-stern.

bow perpendicular where the curve is sharpest, and since this is usually well above the waterline there is often a slight overhang as a result. If the forefoot is to be deep, the stem should curve gently outward from the stemhead to the waterline, without the rounding of the forefoot being visible above the waterline. Hollow ram bows, such as old battleships had, are wholly out of place in yachts or sailing craft.

Fin Keels

Under the influence of racing rule measurements a number of cruisers have appeared employing a more or less spindle-like hull fitted with a very short, deep, ballasted fin, with the rudder placed well abaft the after end of the fin. The rudder is often of the "spade" or balanced type. Sometimes the rudder is hung on the afterside of a small skeg which is independent of the fin.

This is a reversion to a type of yacht experimented with and used rather extensively in the 1890's. However the fin keel model of the above description too often produced wild steering; as this was difficult to cure in many instances, this type of fin keel did not long survive. But now is it back in favor and one recent example has established what seems to be a record—she broached 33 times in 3 hours! Poor steering qualities in some degree are now too common in sailing craft and are sometimes difficult to avoid in new designs, particularly in very short-keel models. There is evidently some misinterpretation of the model testing data that has revived the old short-fin of about one-fourth the waterline length or less. The combination of a very short fin with a short-base high-aspect sail plan appears to have inherent tendencies toward longitudinal unbalance.

Overhanging and Round Stems

Overhanging and round stems are, in various forms, the most fashionable type of bow employed in sailing yachts. Extravagant claims have been made on behalf of the overhanging bow; that its use insures speed, seaworthiness and a dry deck. It does give additional deck space, if yachts are judged arbitrarily by waterline length, and it does give some reserve buoyancy, but these advantages are also obtainable with the clipper bow. It is only when the bow overhang is of such form and length that it is waterborne when the hull is heeled that there can be any gain in waterline length, and so any gain in speed on the basis of waterline measurement. The short, overhanging, curved stem now popular in sailing cruisers has little to recommend it over the straight or clipper bow, practically; its use should be based on the taste of the designer, not on technical grounds. It is sometimes argued that the use of the bow overhang shortens the distance that the bowsprit must reach outboard, but a little consideration will show this is purely a matter of rig, not of hull design.

In drawing round or overhanging stems, never use the arc of the circle for this lacks character and is very ugly. The short, overhanging, curved stem may be somewhat the same as the straight stem, in design, except that there should be more curvature in its lower portion. Very often such stems show a hard, quick curve just above the waterline; this is formed by coming up from below the waterline in a nearly straight line until it emerges, then going into a short, hard curve and then continuing upward and slightly outward to the stemhead in a very gentle curve. This design may appear somewhat hard and exaggerated on the plan but will be pleasing in the finished hull; it is best represented in the stems of some Gloucester fishing schooners, such as the famous *Elsie*. The amount of hardness or "chin" in this type of stem may vary a great deal but the "chin" should never be too high above the waterline. A stem in which the "chin" is too near the sheer does not look well. The other type of short, overhanging bow may be described as the straight stem set at great rake or tumble-out. The method of drawing the straight stem that has been already described should be applied to this type; the rake being decided by the designer's sense of proportion.

When the bow overhang is long, the profile of the stem should be drawn nearly straight, from the waterline, well outward and upward, until about half or two-thirds the freeboard at the bow is reached, where a very hard curve is worked in, then nearly straight and sharply raking outward to the stemhead. The well-known Star Class boats will serve as an example of this type of bow. The curve worked into this stem should not be swept in an arc to the stemhead, nor should the portion of the profile between the waterline and the "chin" be given much curvature if a heavy appearance is to be avoided. While the profile of stem described here may appear somewhat angular on the plan, illusion will soften its hardness in the completed yacht. The designer must always keep in mind that a drawing gives only the *actual* lines of the profile of a hull, not the *apparent* lines that represent the effects of perspective and illusion in the finished hull.

Length of Overhang

Length of overhang must be governed by the relation of over-all to waterline length; it must be assumed that the designer has fixed this relationship by his choice of type or by some such limitation as a racing rule. Except in the latter case, perhaps, the overall length is the important measurement and the waterline length can be fixed to suit the designer's taste in overhangs or the requirements of type or fashion. It may be said, however, that long, thin overhangs are useless and unnecessary weights that serve no useful purpose and that cruising yachts should not have extremely long forward or after overhangs. All that need be given is enough to carry out the fair lines of the bow with a reasonable amount of flare or flam to the topsides forward and to give, perhaps, a pleasing appearance. The straight, almost plumb, stems used in power craft and such sailing types as the old pilot schooners of New York and Boston will serve to illustrate that bow overhang is not an absolute necessity in a seagoing yacht. The shape of the hull abaft the stem and the distribution of weight in the hull decide whether the yacht will be dry or wet, not the profile of the bow, in spite of many theories to the contrary.

Power Boat Stems and "Soft Nose" Bows

In recent years, the stem profiles of power boats, and to some extent of sailing yachts, have come under the influence of "streamlining." This has produced what is called the "soft nose" bow. The profile is usually straight and strongly raking in power boats, but many designs call for a clipper-like stem profile. In sailing yachts, the stem profile is usually of the "chin" form, straight and raking from rail downward and then curving aft at the load waterline, the bow overhang being rather short. In plan the rail or deck edge is brought in full and round, often to an exaggerated degree in power boats, and the flare in the forward sections becomes very marked. In sailing hulls, the flare is usually less great and the "snubbing" of the rail or deck line is moderate, except in sailing scows. The soft nose bow has been very fashionable in liners and naval vessels and particularly so in yachts. It is claimed that such bows produce drier hulls in a seaway. It is probable, however, that the chief attraction of the soft nose bow is its modernity and fashion, rather than any practical structural advantages. Stem-form is always expensive to build compared with conventional stems—particularly in wood construction. Most designers appear to think the soft nose bow is most attractive when its profile is nearly straight and moderately raking and when the "snubbing" at rail or deck is also moderate. Exaggerated rake or a marked overhanging "clipper" bow profile is commonly ugly—particularly so when the freeboard is relatively high. Practically, the snubbed deck and soft nose profile is of proven advantage only in the shoal racing sailing scow and even then it is not irreplaceable by some other form of stem of less costly build.

Scow Bows

Another form of stem, suitable for protected waters though also used in certain types of seagoing vessels, is the transom, scow or "swim" bow. This type varies greatly; the most common is shaped very much like the ordinary stern transom and counter, though that formed like the tip of a teaspoon is more popular in racing scows. Usually these forms of stems are employed in shoal draft centerboard craft, generally combined with hull forms having angular bilges or "chines," such as the common scow or punt. The scow sloops once so common in Maine and Chesapeake Bay waters, and the scow schooners of San Francisco, the Great Lakes, the Gulf of Mexico and the protected waters of the Atlantic Coast, all had the ordinary scow

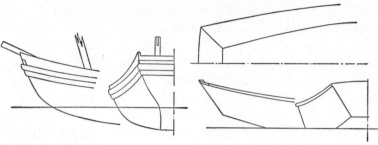

Chinese Junk Bow.   *Punt or Scow Bow.*

bow, built with a small transom generally set at a sharp rake
forward and with the bottom curving up from below to meet it.
Various forms of the scow bow were once to be seen in English
waters and are still employed in some Dutch and Chinese craft.
The Inland Lake scow sloops are now about the only type of
yacht, outside of some very small experimental classes, that employ the scow bow. The advantage of such a form of stem is that
it commonly permits a marked gain in sailing length when the
hull is heeled. It is usually quite cheap to build and gives the
maximum amount of deck space forward. Its disadvantages are
that its use tends to develop hulls that pound in rough water and
which are wet. Since the scow bow is used with success in many
types of Dutch and Chinese seagoing fishermen it is apparent
that the disadvantages may be overcome to a great extent by
proper design. The possibilities of obtaining increased accommodation by the use of some form of scow bow, as well as the
economic consideration, should encourage a study of this form
of stem when the design would permit its use. A sharply raking
transom bow combined with a strong V in the sections forward,
short overhang and shoal forefoot, in a chine or angular bilged
hull, might serve in a small coastal cruiser. It may be observed
that the Chinese junk's bow is usually formed so that the hull is
very narrow at the waterline, spreading out rapidly towards the
deck, the overhang being comparatively small. In this class of
vessel, the transom bow is often curved in profile, curving away
aft from the underside of the deck forward and fairing into a
rockered keel profile.

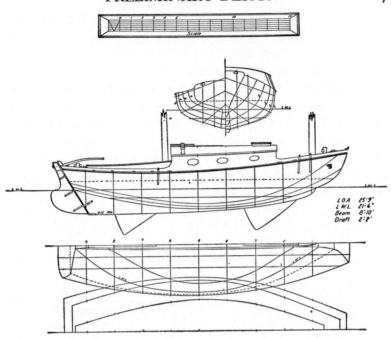

Single Hander; showing raised-deck amidships, Chinese Junk Bow, flat transom stern, double centerboard, tapered keel, outboard rudder, flaring topsides. (Rig:—cat-ketch, two leg-of-mutton or Chinese lug sails.)

Clipper Bows

The handsomest and most graceful of all forms of stem is the clipper bow. This type of stem is also the hardest to design for even a small error in proportion or line will spoil its appearance. Unfortunately, modern yachts built with this form of bow generally illustrate the fact. The clipper bow may be divided into two classifications, one in which the rabbet (line formed by the junction of the outboard face of the planking with the stem) follows the profile of the stem by flaring outward in a hollow curve and the other in which the rabbet is nearly straight, raking outward but little.

The latter is the older form, and the clipper bow is shaped outside the rabbet by use of a knee and, in large craft, other timbers.

The knee was supported on each side by trail-knees, usually two to a side, reaching from the billet or figurehead to abaft the hawse. Between these knees it was customary to place carved planks, the trail-boards. In addition, the knee of the stem was supported by straight or curved timbers reaching from the after side of the billet or figurehead to the sides of the hull, above the trail-boards. These timbers, called "rails of the head," were supported in turn by knees placed on each side of the stem knee, to act as struts to the rails of the head. In large craft there were usually two rails on each side and three or four knees to support them; in small vessels, such as schooners, one rail and three knees sufficed. The trail-knees and rails of the head were not employed as decorations, primarily, but to give the stem knee support laterally so that it would not be twisted off by the strain of the gammoning (fitting which holds the bowsprit to the stem) or

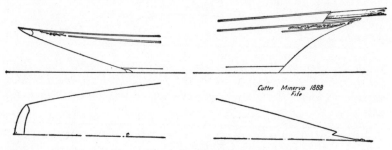

Bow and Stern profile and deck plan of Clipper Bow and counter stern.

knocked off by a sea that hit the stem broadside-on. When the heavy headrails and trail-knees were omitted the stem knee was much reduced in size, or was supported by a single trail-knee that was designed to extend the apparent line of the planksheer or a moulding forward to the billet. Later still, a single iron strut on each side of the stem knee served to give the head lateral support. Only on very small craft or where the stem knee itself is small can the lateral supports be omitted. If a figurehead was used its weight made the use of some kind of lateral support doubly necessary. Drawings of the old clipper bow will illustrate its

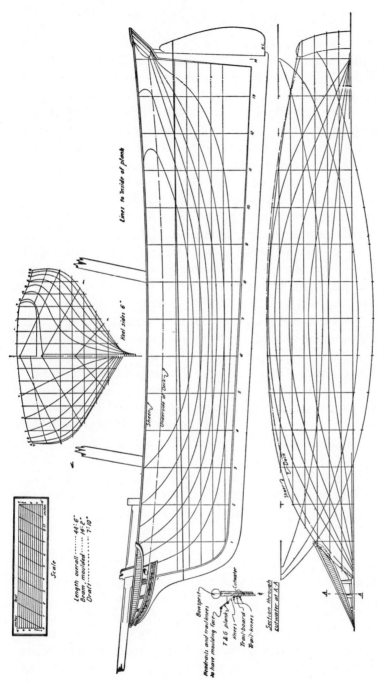

Boston schooner yacht built 1848 by Louis Winde; showing clipper bow with billet, trail-boards, headrails and supporting knees; short counter; strongly curved transom; drag to keel, and moderately high bulwarks. The straight rise of floor is about maximum, unless hollow garboards are employed. Ballast, iron, all inside. The position of the bowsprit and the prominent knightheads and hawse-timbers were common in small craft of this date.

Lines to inside of plank

Keel sides 6"

Scale

Length overall ...... 44'-6"
Beam, moulded ..... 14'-2"
Draft .... 7'-10"

Section through cutwater at A.A.

Headrails and trailknees to have moulding faces

Bowsprit

T & G planks

Knees

Trail-board

Trail-knees

Cutwater

features better than further description. The conventions of design that establish the correct appearance of the clipper bow were developed in early times and these conventions are as absolute as those of the Classical Orders in architecture.

The clipper bow in which the rabbet follows the outline of the stem more closely is the modern form, introduced in England about 1839 and in America a few years later. This form of clipper bow is that often employed in yachts, particularly when built of steel. Large sailing yachts, many steam yachts and a few large motor craft have been built with this type of bow, even in recent years. Most of these have been decorated with trail-boards and false trail-knees at the stem; in rare cases false rails of the head are seen. While it is impossible to describe every combination of design that is permissible in the clipper bow, there are certain rules that, if followed, will prevent errors. These rules express the conventions mentioned earlier and reference to the drawings of clipper stems shown here will make their meanings clear.

In the modern type of clipper bow the shape of the trail-boards, and the curve of the trail-knees (also called "cheek-knees") in profile, are of first importance. In drawing, the rough profile of the stem should be sketched in, then the shape and curvature of the trail-boards and knees worked up; these will be found, very often, to require some change in the profile of the stem. If there is no figurehead other than a billet or head of an eagle, the trail-board should be narrow at its outboard and gradually widening as it goes aft. If there are no trail-boards and a scroll of conventional foliage is used (with or without a single moulding), the scroll should taper similarly, the widest end aft. It is necessary to call attention to the fact that this rule has been broken far too often, not only in yachts, but in iron and steel sailing ships; this is the reason that their stems appear so heavy at the billet or figurehead. If the overhang of the clipper bow is small, the scroll should be small and may, if desired, run down the stem instead of aft over the rabbet, though this latter design is rarely pleasing. If a full-length figurehead of a man, beast or bird is used care should be taken that it is not too large; it must be proportioned to the freeboard and overhang and the rake of the figurehead

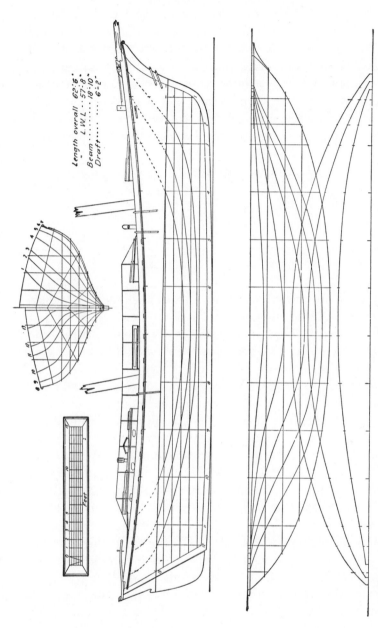

Length overall .... 62'-6"
" L.W.L. .. 57'-8"
Beam ...... 18'-10"
Draft ...... 6'-2"

Double-ended schooner, showing canoe sheer, life-boat stern, clipper bow supported by single trail-knee, hollow waterlines and flat buttocks applied to this type, deep forefoot, rise of sheer forward combined with full deck line, flare at bow, flam at stern and rockered keel. Designed to sail with slight heel, hence shoal draft, ballast all inside.

must be laid out with care. No rules or exact proportions can be given to meet all cases; the eye of the designer is the best guide if he has taken the trouble to study many examples of well-designed figureheads. With the use of a large figurehead, the taper of the trail-boards may be reduced; as the curvature of the trail-boards, in profile, is increased it is permissible to reduce their taper to a minimum, making them *almost* parallel-sided. In all types of clipper bow care must be taken that the trail-boards

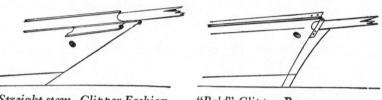

Straight stem—Clipper Fashion.   *"Bald" Clipper Bow.*

or scrolls are not carried too far aft. In the old clipper bow, where the rabbet does not follow the profile of the stem and when trail-boards are used in conjunction with one or more rails of the head, the curvature of the trail-boards in profile should be rather great so that the after ends are fairly low on the hull, say below the hawse-holes or deck-line. The hawse-holes may be placed in the trail-boards, or above or below; but the amateur's love of hawse-pipes on even small craft should not be permitted to lead him astray. Hawse-pipes, leading below the deck-line, are undesirable until the freeboard exceeds ten feet at the bow, and even then are not absolutely required. By having the trail-boards strongly curved in profile at the outer end, the inner end abaft the rabbet can be brought low; the advantage of this is to reduce the apparent freeboard.

It is possible to obtain a pleasing profile by employing a straight stem, drawn with a dead-straight line, set at a rather extreme rake and set off with trail-boards or false rails. The illusion in respect to the straight-line stem will make this appear to be a clipper bow, but this design should not be employed when the freeboard is high.

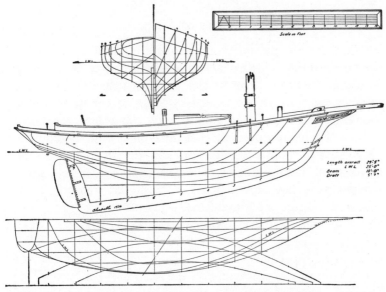

Design of a Friendship Sloop showing orthodox sheer, elliptical transom and treatment of "log" rail, rockered keel, clipper bow supported by trail-board and knees, drag of keel, heavy quarters, immersed counter, raking midsection, and combination of hollow garboards with hard bilges to obtain sail-carrying power, the ballast being all inside.

Overhang Bows on Racers

Some racing yachts having long bow overhangs show some reverse curve in the lower portion of their stem profiles due to the limitations set up by a racing rule, but this design should never be used in a cruising yacht where no such limitation exists. When the designer is drawing a yacht that does not follow any particular conventions, say an ocean racer-cruiser of modern type, he should take advantage of his freedom in design and allow neither fashion nor prejudice to govern his work, but rather follow the dictates of common sense and beauty in the choice of sheer, bow profile, or other detail, with due regard to practical considerations of economy, use and actual efficiency.

Choice of Stern

The first principle in the choice of stern is that it must balance the bow profile. This balance is less of a matter of having the same amount of overhang at bow and stern than of conforming with certain conventions. Generally speaking, the stern overhang should exceed that of the bow, though this rule is occasionally broken. The conventions are that the clipper bow should be employed with a counter or with a marked stern overhang, as should all forms of overhang bows. The very short round stem and the straight stem may be combined with the flat transom, set at a rake and with no other overhang, but usually it is best to avoid this combination if the freeboard is great. If the sharp, raking stern is employed, as in the Chesapeake "Bugeye," it is possible to use the clipper bow, but commonly such a stern is used with the straight or round stem unless the stern is of the "canoe" type in which there is a marked overhang. In the latter case an overhang bow looks very well. There is also the matter of rake of stern—usually the rake of transom or sternpost is at least half that of the stem; perpendicular transoms and sternposts are permissible, however. The rake of the sternpost, so far as the underbody is concerned, will be fixed by the designer's judgment since it may have some bearing on steering: hulls having long, straight keels and deep draft require the most rake, cutaway profiles and shoal draft hulls the least.

Flat Transom and V-stern

The flat raking aft transom, usually employed in hulls having short bow overhangs, has become somewhat popular in cruising yachts of all sizes. Unless the sternpost is well inboard, the rake of transom and sternpost is the same. Sometimes the transom is partially immersed while in other cases it is designed so that its bottom just clears the water; in sailing craft the immersed area should not be great. The transom stern is best illustrated in the Cape Cod Catboats and the ordinary dinghy. If not excessively wide it is an excellent type of stern for it is strong and cheap to

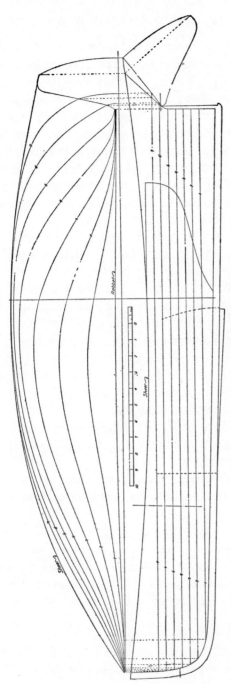

Lines of a centerboard sloop built in 1871; showing V-stern, hollow entrance, raking midsection, straight keel, and flaring topsides. Lines to inside of plank. Drawing shows lines as taken off half-model by taking lifts apart (see Appendix), before being faired.

construct. A seagoing yacht should have a rather narrow transom, well raked and with good deadrise. The transom often has some curvature, in plan-view, which is thought to improve its appearance, but this adds greatly to its cost and serves no useful purpose other than beauty. In large yachts, such as schooners, a form of transom stern is sometimes used that approaches the counter in profile, accomplished by setting it at a great rake. This stern, when faired into the hull, takes a V form and is therefore called a "V-stern." The V-stern was once popular in yachts, being copied from pilot-schooners; the famous schooner-yacht *America* illustrates this transom.

At one time there were two transoms, a lower one that was either set at a great rake or on a hollow curve when viewed in profile and an upper one set at a smaller rake. The lower one reached to the deck; the upper one was really a part of the bulwarks. This type of stern was the first step in the development of the conventional counter and was employed in the famous Baltimore Clipper schooners during the early nineteenth century. This form of stern is most attractive, also, when used with a high raised quarter deck; in fact it is apparently the only one that looks "right" with a prominent quarter deck having stern cabin and stern and quarter windows.

In small transom-sterned craft, where there is no overhang other than that caused by the rake, the sternpost is often brought up outside the transom to give support to the rudder; this gives a very strong construction. Usually the transom sterns having no overhang are combined with outboard rudders, as in the case of most catboats.

The flat transom is also the most popular form in motorboats. Usually the transom has some camber athwartships. In very fast boats it is nearly vertical in profile, as a rule, and the stern may be V-shaped in plan view in lieu of being curved athwartships. This might well be combined with a smart rake in seagoing motorboats.

Very large transoms must be designed with care as they may be ugly in a finished boat if too wide and deep. An outboard rudder reduces the apparent size of such transoms. Otherwise decorative name boards and mouldings can be used to advantage.

Tumble-home Transom

The tumble-home transom appeared in the 1870's, created in sailing craft by a racing rule measurement in which it was assumed that the greatest length would be on deck. This form of transom also appeared about 1905 in motor launches. These transoms had short periods of popularity, as they served no useful purpose other than rule evasion. But this form is now popular in sailing craft and is generally accepted as a mark of fast-sailing qualities.

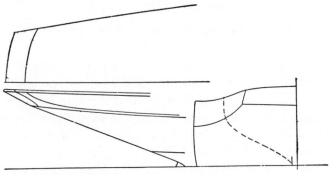

Yacht Counter Stern.

Counter

The counter stern is the conventional yacht finish, and was also used in most commercial schooners. In some yachts the counter is very long, ending in a small transom; in others the counter is short and the transom comparatively large. In most seagoing vessels the counter is either short or partially immersed, as in the more recent Gloucester fishing schooners. The advantages of the counter are the increased deck room that is obtained when compared to the sharp stern and the opportunity to obtain better buttock lines, particularly in a hull having a large midsection, when compared to both the sharp and flat transom sterns. In some classes of racing yachts, such as the Thirty-square Meter

Class, the counter is very long and light and ends in either a very tiny transom or in a form somewhat like that of the tip of a teaspoon. In most cases where the transom is employed with the counter, the transom is set at a sharp rake aft and is much curved athwartships.

The disadvantages of the counter stern are: the liability of pounding that this form of stern can develop, great cost when compared to other forms and, in long counters, structural weakness. Most of these disadvantages can be overcome in a great degree by proper design, though the factor of cost is inherent.

Elliptical Stern

Another form of counter that has had periods of popularity is that known as the "elliptical stern." This is a short counter in which the planking is brought up from below to a knuckle, usually at deck level, above which the bulwark is brought around at a rake. In plan view this form of stern is either round or elliptical, hence its name. The plan view of this class of stern ought never be an arc of a circle. The stern of the common towboat is an example of the elliptical stern, though in sailing craft the bulwark above the knuckle rakes sharply aft instead of being vertical or tumbling inboard as in the towboat. In the design of the elliptical stern the appearance of the counter viewed from astern must be studied as well as its profile. This form of stern is suited for narrow hulls having a fine run, but if applied to a full, beamy hull the result is too much like the appearance of a bathtub to be considered handsome. The advantages of the elliptical stern are those of the ordinary counter with the addition of not having any corners to catch the mainsheet or to be knocked off in working around wharves and piers. As to disadvantages, its most serious are the weight of construction necessary, due to the form timbering required, and cost. The elliptical counter is accounted seaworthy since it is invariably short and well rounded below the knuckle; it was once very popular in pilot schooners and is now very common in auxiliary fishing schooners built in Maine. The name "elliptical stern" has been erroneously applied to the

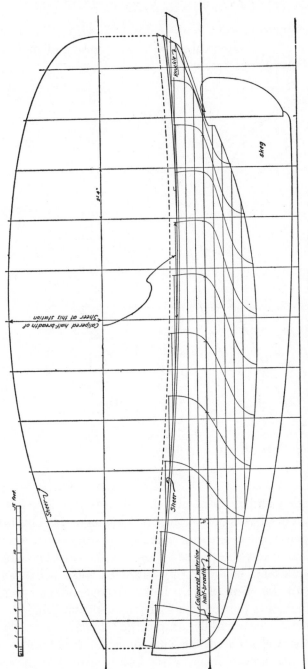

Lines of Sloop Yacht Enterprise designed by D. J. Lawlor, 1878; showing elliptical or "round" stern, with knuckle below deck-line, tumble-home bow, heavy quarters, hollow garboards, skeg or deadwood built up outside of rabbet, and rockered keel. Lines to inside of plank; drawing shows lines as taken off half-model by lead bar method (see Appendix) before being faired.

counter-and-transom stern of the Essex-built Gloucester fishing schooner, due to the elliptical shape of the transom of these vessels when viewed from astern.

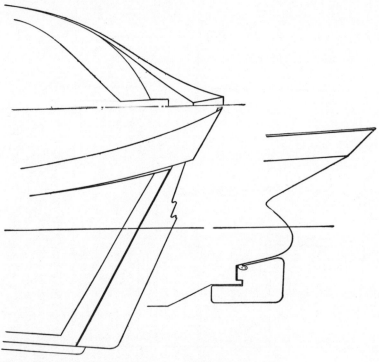

New England "Pink" Stern.   *"Bustle" Stern.*

Bustle Stern

The "bustle stern" is to be seen among large steamers, power and steam yachts, but is not employed in sailing craft. This type of stern is merely the conventional counter, transom or elliptical, with the addition of a "bustle" or "blister" at the waterline which prevents "squatting" or settling by the stern when under way. The profile of this form of stern looks like that of the counter stern with the upper portion of a rounded rudder showing above the waterline. There is usually a submerged knuckle, into which the run of the hull is faired; this knuckle or chine is sufficiently spread from the upper portion of the hull to give enough bearing to prevent the squatting that would otherwise result in a sharp run. This form of stern is most expensive to build and is difficult to fair on the drafting board. Except that its use enables the designer to obtain the conventional counter in a fast steam or power vessel, there is no practical excuse for the existence of this form of stern.

Lifeboat Stern and Variations

The lifeboat stern is merely a sharp stern, like a straight stem in construction, in which the deck comes to a point in plan view. The sternpost is sometimes vertical, particularly in shoal draft

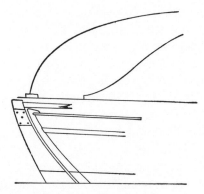

Lifeboat Stern—North Sea Type.

hulls, but usually there is much rake. In most cases the sternpost is straight; the sterns of some yachts of the Scandinavian model are exceptions. The lifeboat stern is represented in American types by the Chesapeake Bay "Bugeye," the old Block Island Boat and the New England Pinky. This type of stern, and the variations exhibited in the hull-forms just mentioned, have the advantages of being cheap and easy to construct; the seaworthiness of the sharp stern has been highly spoken of by experienced seamen and requires no discussion here. In spite of the apparent simplicity of the lifeboat stern it is very difficult to design so that a fast boat can be obtained. This is due to the fact that this form of sharp stern has a tendency to produce very round buttocks in the run, the result of which is invariably a comparatively slow boat. The failure of many modern sharp-sterned yachts can be traced to the designer's lack of judgment in the shaping of the run. In sailing craft the sharp stern commonly reduces the power to carry sail. This is particularly noticeable in light displacement hulls. Very full deck lines are often employed to overcome this objection, as well as to give more room, but full deck line increases cost as it adds to the planking difficulties.

In order to combine the lifeboat stern and a well-shaped run it is necessary to employ hollow waterlines aft, as well as to use sections having marked hollows in the garboards throughout the length of the run, so that the buttock lines will be fairly flat and straight below the waterline. Convex waterlines aft make such buttock forms impossible. Inspection of the runs of fast bugeyes and other sharp-sterned craft, whether keel or centerboard, power or sail, bear out this theory. The disadvantages of the sharp stern of the form under discussion are the lack of room on deck, and, due to the hollow in the run, a lack of accommodation below-deck aft. The first disadvantage can be overcome by the use of a platform over the stern, as in the case of the so-called "Patent Stern" used on most bugeyes or by use of the old "Pink Stern" that distinguished the New England Pinky. In the Scandinavian models, room on deck is obtained by having a very full deck-line, when viewed from above, and the use of very flaring sections aft. This stern is rather hard to build for the planking, particularly the sheer strake, often requires wide stock and steaming, and this adds to the expense.

Canoe Stern

The "Canoe Stern" is a variant of the older lifeboat stern and was developed in England. It is a true overhang, framed and planked in much the same manner as the conventional overhang bow. The deck-line is usually rather full and the sections in the overhang are generally U-shaped. This form of stern gives more space on deck and more room below-deck aft than the lifeboat stern; furthermore, it is easier to obtain flat buttocks with the canoe stern. This form of stern is somewhat expensive and requires good workmanship, particularly if the deadwood is

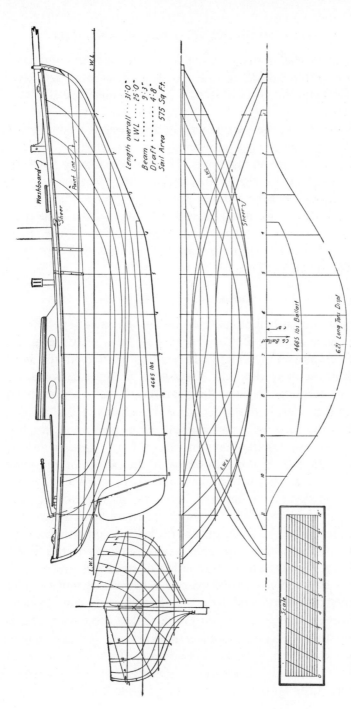

Length overall . . . . 31′0″
LWL . . . . . 25′0″
Beam . . . . 9′3″
Draft . . . . 4′8″
Sail Area   575 Sq. Ft.

Single-handed cruiser, cutter-rig; showing "chin" in profile of the short overhanging bow, canoe stern, cabin trunk, straight keel (tapered fore and aft in siding),
and flat buttocks worked into sharp stern.

planked up instead of being a mere skeg or fin. If not exaggerated, the canoe stern is suitable for a seagoing yacht of large size. Generally speaking, this form of stern is more popular abroad than in our waters.

In power boats the canoe stern is best designed quite full at deck, as this stern, and all sharp stern forms, are liable to squatting tendencies in fast boats. This is overcome by flattening the bottom of the overhang athwartships, but this adds to planking difficulties and may produce slamming or pounding in rough water. The canoe stern is also called "cruiser stern" when applied to power craft and is often finished off as a "soft nose" stem, rounded as the stern port approached the deck, but sharp at and below the loadline.

Elliptical Transom

The counter and elliptical transom has been mentioned; it has been popular in New England waters for over fifty years and has been employed in sailing craft ranging in size from the small Friendship Sloop to the large Essex-built fishing schooners. By use of the elliptical transom the quarters become very rounded and tumble in sharply to the deck-line. Usually the rail is brought around in the form of a flattened ellipse in plan view; there is neither rake nor tumble-home in the profile of this. In fishing schooners the top of the transom is at the height of the main sheer and the rail that is brought around over it is the "monkey rail"; the portion of the bulwark, above the main sheer, required by the raised quarterdeck. In small craft, such as Friendship Sloops, the top of the transom is at deck level and either a very low rail or a mere strip is brought around similarly to the fisherman's stern. The reason for this design of stern was probably to overcome the tendency of the mainsheet to become fouled under the corner of a sharply raking transom, such as these craft have. This form of stern is not easy to build unless the constructor is acquainted with it, and it is somewhat expensive. It is also difficult to design and record so that the builder may follow the designer's intentions accurately. However, it gives very graceful quarters and lightens the appearance of a heavy, wide, flat counter. The transom should have some curvature athwartships, in this form of stern, if the counter is at all wide.

Underbody Profile

The sheer, bow and stern have been discussed; the next detail is the profile below the waterline, the underbody profile in other words. This is a matter that will have to wait until the lines are described before being discussed in great detail. To a great extent, the underbody profile will be fixed by the type or model of hull the designer is using. As a preliminary consideration, however, it is well to employ as much straight, or nearly straight, keel as is possible. Very shoal centerboarders may be an exception, though cruising centerboarders ought to have a marked forefoot, as will be explained later. Though long, straight keels tend to produce a hull that is slow in stays, this can be largely overcome by the use of "drag"; that is, sloping the keel downward from the bow toward the stern. The advantages of the straight keel are: steadiness in steering, particularly in rough water; likelihood of the hull being self-steering under certain conditions; and lastly, ease and safety in hauling out.

For the last forty-five years yachts have been designed with very rockered keels, in some cases the underbody profile is almost triangular. Many yachts have had fins of varying lengths and shapes; the forefoot being cut away to an extraordinary extent in many examples. Undoubtedly the tendency to shorten the keel has been carried to undesirable extremes under the influence of the theory of wetted-surface resistance, better described as "skin friction." This is a matter for discussion when the lines are being studied; the practical objection to the underbody profiles just mentioned is this; hauling out for repairs or storage becomes very difficult, and dangerous so far as the life of the yacht is concerned. The deeper the draft the greater the difficulties. As the yacht is placed in the cradle, preparatory to hauling out, blocks must be set to keep her from falling over as she emerges from the water. Yachts with very rockered profiles have been damaged by slipping forward on the keel-blocks in the cradle until their bows struck the railway or ground, as they ceased to be waterborne. Furthermore, the keel blocks often require the attentions of a diver to be properly set. It is obvious that all yacht yards, particularly small ones in unfrequented ports, are not equipped to do such careful work and so hulls are often damaged or strained. This subject is not one that affects the racer, for she is usually hauled out in some of the yachting centers where yards are equipped to handle such craft. Cruisers, however, ought to be so designed that they can be hauled out and repaired without extraordinary care and equipment. Shoal draft hulls are less of a problem, if they have rockered keels, for obviously the rocker cannot be very great and the low bilges make the exact placing of blocking on the marine railway of little importance. This is one of the reasons why centerboard and shoal-draft cruisers are less expensive to maintain than deep-draft craft of equal length.

It has been argued that a short keel makes for quickness on the helm and quick staying. This is undoubtedly true, yet there are other factors that should be considered. A boat that is quick on her helm requires steering *all* the time, whereas most cruisers prefer a boat in which the helm can be left unattended for a few moments, particularly if the craft is a single-hander. The straight keel is much cheaper to build than any form of rockered keel or fin. Perhaps the best principle on which the length of the keel can be fixed is this: the shorter the base of the sail-plan, measured from boom-end to tack of foremost headsail, the shorter the keel or fin. No set proportions can be given, for this is a matter of individual design. The straight portion of the keel profile is usually just forward of the rudder or sternpost and its length should exceed one-fourth the waterline length of the hull; in cruisers over fifty-feet waterline the straight of the keel should approach one-third of the waterline length, as a minimum. Needless to say, the designer has complete freedom in fixing the amount of straight keel for he must decide how important the cost and ease of hauling-out factors are in his particular requirements. The size and shape of the rudder will be treated when the lines are discussed and the student can turn to that chapter for guidance in drawing its outline in the preliminary sketch.

Cabin Trunk and Deck Structures

The cabin trunk and deck structures can now be considered. The relative position of these on the hull must be decided by the cabin layout; this also governs their dimensions. However, the effect of these structures on the general appearance of a yacht is very great and deck structures that are improperly proportioned or poorly designed in relation to the hull may spoil the beauty of the whole yacht. The cabin trunk is the most common deck structure in yachts, particularly in sailing craft, and so may be discussed first. The centerline of the roof, where the crown is greatest, should nearly parallel the load-waterline, or slope down slightly toward the bow, in profile. This line may have some sheer or be a straight line; if the crown is great it may be hogged. The sides of the trunk should be lower in height forward than aft, in any case, and if the cabin trunk is long the top of the sides should have sheer, but less than that of the rail, of course. If it is necessary to have a high trunk the crown of the roof should be great in order to reduce the apparent height of the structure. But extreme crown is difficult to walk on and if the alleyways alongside the trunk are narrow, extreme crown should usually be avoided. The roof, at the sides and ends, is usually finished off with a moulding or cornice which accentuates the sheer of the top of the sides in profile. In general, the remarks in regard to cabin trunks apply to deck-houses. In recent years there has been a fashion for rounding off the corners formed by the juncture of roof and sides of deck structures, probably under the influence of the fad for "streamlining." This construction is a matter of individual taste; it is expensive and requires good workmanship to be satisfactory.

Long cabin trunks, in proportion to hull length, often spoil the appearance of an otherwise attractive hull. This is the case particularly when the trunk reaches well aft. The monotony of the long trunk is enhanced, of course, by the long line of round or rectangular ports of the same size. This can sometimes be overcome by raising a portion of the trunk at fore end, at middle, or at after end, a few inches or a foot above the rest of the trunk, say for a distance of ¼ or even ⅓ the total length of the trunk. This not only breaks the monotony of the long trunk, it allows larger ports in the raised portion, which helps appearance. This may be useful treatment to give really full headroom in some part of the cabin, galley or toilet, where otherwise headroom would be scant. If the "break" is low, as it should be, it should not be joined with a raking line but should appear as a vertical, short "break."

In laying out trunks and deck structures, and particularly in coordinating cabin arrangement with deck layout, give much thought to a working ship. This is not fashionable, it is true, for nowadays owners are inclined to sacrifice working qualities of a deck arrangement to obtain maximum cabin space, particularly in motorboats where a really big "greenhouse" steering shelter may be more prized than the ability to get forward from the steering wheel to the bow, to pick up a mooring or to fend off from a wharf. This is a great mistake now that the "paid hand" is nearly extinct. As much thought should be expended upon the deck arrangement as upon the cabin arrangement; indeed more, for the owner's life, and the lives of his guests, may depend upon getting forward quickly and safely in rough weather. It is also important in large cabin boats to be able to get out of the cabin and to bow or stern quickly—and by more than one way. Therefore, sufficiently wide and clear side decks are a *must*, and so are *well*-placed deck openings, grab rails on trunk tops, wire-and-stanchion rails, working space forward for handling ground tackle, deck storage chests, room to work the windlass and winches, low "breaks" in the deck and easy movement in getting from cockpit to deck. In your enthusiasm for cabin space, beware of creating the deck profile that requires a combination of mountain goat and acrobat to get forward in a hurry.

This business of being able to move fast about the deck, to handle ground tackle, to fend off and to get to running gear, is the practical objection to the "streamlined" sailing or power boat so often shown as the "design of the future" and also, regrettably, in some present boat advertising. Perhaps it should be emphasized that, while high speed on the water is an attractive and perhaps desirable feature, so is the ability to stay alive.

Rake

Plumb lines should be avoided; all vertical edges or lines, such as the forward corners of the cabin trunk, or masts, ventilators, stacks, corners of deck-houses and the doors, windows and panels therein, should rake aft. The rake for these details may be decided by finding the mean between a perpendicular to the waterline and a perpendicular to the sheer, taken at the place where the foremost vertical edge or line shows above the sheer; the foreside of the cabin trunk will serve as the location for deciding the proper rake in most small sailing craft. Once the rake is decided it is used for all deck structures that show above the sheer or rail-cap. If the sheer is very great, the rake of vertical lines in the profile should reduce as the stern is approached. In such cases the rake of the aftermost vertical line is about half of the foremost. Inspection of the deck-house of an ordinary harbor towboat will illustrate the practical application of this rule. The use of rake in deck erections is necessary to prevent the illusion of falling forward in these structures. The sides of all cabin trunks, deck-houses, high hatches, large skylights and other large deck erections should tumble-home in cross-section; otherwise they will appear wider at the roof or top than at the deck, a most unpleasant illusion. One-fourth of an inch of tumble-home to each foot of height above the deck is the usual proportion.

In sailing craft the mast or masts may rake more than other vertical lines, but the proportion of rake in the latter is usually fixed as just described. The higher the deck structure the more effective the rake of its vertical lines; for this reason the rake is most important in power craft having pilot-houses or similar deck erections, if a pleasing appearance is required. When stanchions are employed the rake should follow that of the nearest deck erection, and the spacing of the stanchions should be greater aft than forward. In fact the stanchions should be spaced on the profile and not on the deck plan since their appearance can only be decided in the sheer elevation.

Working Up

Returning to the sketch, these directions for the design of details in the profile may be put in practice. After the location and amount of the least freeboard is decided, the sheer, bow, stern underbody profile and deck erections can be sketched in; it is best to do this with light pencil lines, drawn freehand, as a great deal of erasing and altering will be necessary. The length of the cabin trunk and all deck erections, and their positions as well, is obtained by squaring up from the arrangement plan below the profile. The sheer, profile of the ends and the deck erections should be worked up together as they all relate to one another in appearance. The underbody profile will be fixed by the limit of draft that has been decided upon in the preliminary steps of design and, also, by the choice of hull type or model. To some extent, the profile will be affected by the form of bow and stern that is used, though this is basically a matter that comes under the heading of choice of hull type or model. The temptation to draw a "pretty" underbody profile by making the outline a series of graceful curves should be resisted for the practical reasons that have been given earlier in this discussion. A profile made of straight lines and angles is not indicative of a slow hull, by any means.

As the outboard profile develops under the pencil of the designer he will be able to decide whether or not his design would look better with the additions of false sheers, cove-lines and mouldings or scrolls; also whether or not the position of the cabin trunk, hatches, skylights and similar deck erections should be changed or whether their height or other dimensions ought to be altered. If the student has trouble in making freehand lines, say the lines are too rough and irregular or unfair, making them of dotted-lines (dots or dashes very close together) will be found helpful. A little practice in such freehand sketching will enable the beginner to accomplish satisfactory results.

The design has now taken shape to a degree that its appearance may be judged. Do not become down-hearted if the dream-ship appears to be an ugly crate, many a professional has made a similar discovery when a design has reached this stage of evolution. The thing to do is to alter the profile until the appearance is pleasing, and then to work back to the deck and arrangement plans to see how these changes are going to affect them. By working back and forth on the various views harmony will quickly result. Usually a great deal of erasing and redrawing takes place at this stage of development. Sometimes it will be found necessary to start a new and entirely different design if the first arrangement proves unsatisfactory when worked up to this point. Very often the overall length must be changed slightly, or the sheer, freeboard, cabin trunk, hatches, skylights, ports, bow and stern may need alteration; it is astonishing to see the difference the smallest change in these details will make in the appearance of a design. A great deal of study and drawing should be expended in this stage of design, for here the beauty of the yacht is made or lost. Small details are of great importance here; for example, too many or too large portlights in cabin trunk or hull may spoil the whole appearance of the hull. Another common fault is in location of ports; often they are too close together or otherwise wrongly placed. The use of deadlights in the deck or cabin roof, or skylights, will enable the designer to reduce the number of ports and still obtain good lighting below-deck. Care should be taken to space the portlights so that they are properly located inside the hull in regard to the accommodations and so that they show good spacing in the profile as well.

The preliminary design for a motor cruiser requires particular care at this stage. In the first place, the relatively shallow draught and the demand for headroom in the cabins of power cruisers under 45 to 50 feet create very high freeboard in proportion to length. In addition, the trend toward such conveniences as steering shelters or deck houses, flying bridges and trunk cabins, above the already high freeboard, readily produces a hideous profile—as may be seen in many modern cruisers—and even in liners and steamers. It is only by careful "massing" of high superstructure that the *least* ugliness can be had. Until the superstructure is probably massed or grouped, it is bootless to draw in mouldings, windows, raking windshields or mast, or to "streamline" by fancy profile-curves.

The whole problem of high freeboard plus superstructure goes farther than mere beauty, however, for a power cruiser having the two in extreme is both dangerous and unmanageable in heavy weather. The best advice is to *keep it down.* Yet superstructure to some degree is generally required and should be designed with due regard to appearance.

It is difficult to give precise instruction on massing of superstructure, but one rule is to raise the superstructure in steps, not abruptly, to the maximum height. Another is to group all superstructure at one center, usually pilot house or steering shelter, with "steps" up to the maximum height—use short trunks, deck boxes or "offsets" in the fore and after sides of the highest structure. Generally speaking, it is hardest to group superstructure near the ends of a hull, and this is particularly true in small cruisers. That is why the steering shelter of small cruisers looks so awkward and top heavy in so many instances. This is also seen in motor-sailers and, now that the "doghouse" has become so popular, in sailing cruisers.

Perhaps here it is well to point out that though we may become hardened to ugliness, and thus come to accept it, this fact does not make ugliness beautiful. Ugly and awkward-appearing power cruisers are now accepted, and there are those "advanced minds" who try to convince themselves and others that such craft are beautiful, whereas they are only the visual evidence of ignorance on the part of designers and ignorance on the part of owners.

When the freehand sketch satisfies, the lines in the profile may be drawn in with the assistance of curves, battens and triangles or straightedge. By using a fairly hard pencil, a mark will be left on the paper or cloth which will show after the freehand work is cleaned off by means of art gum or a soft eraser. Professionals usually ink in the lines at this stage, instead of using a hard pencil. If the lines are not inked in, some of the pencil work must be retraced after the freehand work is erased. For this reason time is saved by use of ink and right-line pen.

Choice of Rig

The next step is the design of the sail-plan, and this is another matter that must be thoroughly studied. It has been observed that the choice of rig has been made; not always on the grounds of theoretical "efficiency" but for some practical reason, such as the owner's experience with an individual rig, or mere prejudice. Throughout the history of yachting certain forms of rig have been fashionable for a period of time, and in each case the fad has been supported by contemporary "scientific" reasons. Illustrative of this, the loose-footed mainsail will serve; this type of sail was popular in American schooners until about 1845, after which the foot of the mainsail was laced to the boom. The English cutters retained the loose-footed mainsail far longer and when these yachts were introduced into this country, in the '70's and '80's, this feature in their rig was ridiculed as "unscientific" and "inefficient." The "scientific" arguments against this type of sail appeared to be so well founded, that the loose-footed sail disappeared from the yachting fleets in America and almost went out of use in England. Within the last year or two, however, this type of sail has returned to popularity, since a new lot of "scientific" theories have appeared, indicating that the sailmakers of an earlier generation were not as far wrong as they were claimed to be a few years ago. Other examples could be quoted, such as overlapping headsails, the use of sprits instead of booms, even on headsails, and some matters relating to hull design, but the story of the loose-footed mainsail will serve to indicate that contemporary ideas as to what is either "scientific" or "efficient" are not necessarily correct.

In the light of this past history the choice of rig based on comparative efficiency or scientific correctness becomes something more than difficult. It is heresy to question the advantages of the modern high, narrow rigs now so popular in all yachts, however it does not appear that this design of sail-plan is suited for all types of hull nor that it is preferable to other forms of rig for all usages. The modern staysail rigs, for example, are suitable for few types of hull and are generally too complicated in gear to be satisfactory in cruising. Most of the staysail rigs require a full locker of light sails in order to compare favorably with conventional rigs when off the wind. It seems probable that too much emphasis has been placed on windward ability in cruisers. Racing courses are generally laid out in such a manner that a third of the whole length of the course is a beat to windward. This has put a premium on the ability to work to windward, for this part of the course takes the most time to cover since a sailing vessel travels through the water at a low rate of speed when beating, compared to running or reaching. However, no sailing cruiser spends most of her time at sea in beating to windward as every experienced yachtsman knows; in fact most yachtsmen make particular effort to avoid long beats. The advent of auxiliary engines has enabled yachts to avoid beating when it is necessary to lay a course to windward; countless yachts are to be seen every summer making use of their motors under such conditions, with their sails furled. Curiously enough, many of these yachts have rigs designed particularly for beating, yet their owners will avoid putting the rig to the work for which it is designed! It is apparent, therefore, that the true "efficiency" of a rig is not its windward ability alone, but rather its suitability to the everyday use of the yacht. All yachts having sails should be able to work to windward; there can be no question of this; but sailing and handiness in other courses ought not to be sacrificed to obtain maximum efficiency in beating.

There is little question as to the efficiency of the jib-headed mainsail and the extremely high and narrow sail-plans of modern racers in working to windward, particularly in comparatively smooth water. To assume that this rig is suitable for cruisers, however, may be erroneous. Hulls of large displacement, and this describes a great many cruisers, require rather large sail-plans. To obtain a large area of sail in the high, narrow, modern rigs it is necessary to make the hoist very great, which entails a very tall mast and this in turn creates problems in staying and in hull structure to support it. The use of hollow spars in cruisers has intensified the problem of staying, perhaps the fad for extreme lightness aloft in the construction of the mast has been carried beyond sensible limits. It has been observed by some competent designers that the gain in lightness aloft through the use of hollow masts has been partially discounted by the additional weight of the struts, spreaders and staying that is required to make such masts stand. Furthermore the complicated system of stays, struts and spreaders creates windage to a remarkable degree. It seems possible, therefore, that the limit in the direction of high, narrow rigs has been reached and passed. Probably the high, narrow, modern rig is most efficient in light displacement and heavily ballasted hulls such as are represented in the Thirty or Twenty-two Square Meter classes, and least efficient in the short, heavy displacement cruiser having part of her ballast inside. In wide hulls designed for off-shore cruising the weight aloft of solid spars serves as a counterbalance to slow the rolling, and from the standpoint of comfort the weight of the spars thus becomes helpful.

Discussion of the relative merits of the various rigs could be carried on endlessly and would satisfy none of the adherents of each type of sail-plan. Certain principles of choice of rig can be stated, based wholly on practical considerations, however. The modern high, narrow rigs and the various types of staysail rigs are very expensive compared to the older gaff and leg-of-mutton rigs. Though few would now believe there were any virtues in the old gaff rigs, there are many yachts afloat today that would benefit from the large area and low center of effort that was possible with these rigs. Per yard of canvas, it is cheaper and easier to obtain large area in the gaff rig than in the modern jib-headed rigs. The fact that a hull of large displacement requires a relatively large sail area in order to obtain speed cannot be too strongly stated; this consideration is all-important in deciding the rig of a design or yacht.

Perhaps the best manner of approach to a discussion of the design of sail-plans will be to take up the standard rigs in turn and give the general information required to draw them. Detailed discussion can be left until the drawing of the finished sail-plan is described; this chapter should be referred to when detailing the spars on the preliminary sketch. It is understood that the information given is applicable to cruising yachts, unlimited by the required measurements of any racing rule.

Schooner Rig

The fore gaffsail of a schooner, and all other gaffsails, should not be given hoists greater than two and one half times the length of the boom; otherwise the gaff will sag to leeward and the sail will not stand. Of course, vangs or braces to the gaff peak would correct the sagging of the gaff, but this is extra gear to be handled that ought to be avoided. Small schooners would be improved, so far as speed is concerned, if the fore gaffsail had no boom and was sheeted well abaft the mainmast, the sail being given a good overlap and low clew. This type of foresail, the "lug-foresail," gives the greatest area of "plain sail"; a thing that most small schooners need, but it must be added that the lug-foresail is barred on schooners by existing racing rules. As long as racing rules permit the use of overlapping headsails it is difficult to see the logic of barring the schooner's lug-foresail. It may be stated that cruising schooners under 36 feet overall are not very practical, particularly when rigged with the boom-foresail. The masts of a schooner should not rake the same, for if they do they will appear to be closer together at the masthead than at deck. The mainmast should rake more than the fore; the amount of rake must be left to the designer's judgment. The foremast has the greatest strains placed on it as it not only supports the foresail but also the headsails, and sometimes a foretopsail and jib topsail as well; for this reason it usually should be of slightly greater diameter than the mainmast and might require one or two more shrouds than the main in addition. In order to make the foremast stand properly and not be sprung it is well to place the after lower shrouds well apart even though the boom may not be squared off so much. It should be remembered that the boom cannot be eased off as much as the gaff, as in the event of a jibe the gaff would otherwise be broken against upper shrouds and spreaders. Long mainbooms have gone out of fashion in schooners, as have masts placed very close together, giving big mainsails and very narrow or "ribbon" foresails. Modern practice is a reversion to that of before 1860, making the area of the foresail within 20% of the main. The foremast is usually placed about 20% or 25% of the overall length abaft the stem; the mainmast about 52% or even 60%. This gives mast positions that enable the use of a foreboom equal to half the length of the mainboom, instead of one-third as formerly. By use of the lug-foresail, the area of the foresail could be increased until it was equal to, or slightly in excess of, the mainsail; this would enable a schooner to work under foresail alone in even moderate winds.

Schooners are often rigged with leg-of-mutton sails. The most usual rig employs a gaff foresail and leg-of-mutton mainsail. This produces a rig having a very lofty pole main mast producing an effect not wholly unlike a main-gaff-sail and gaff topsail-in-one. Still another rig was to employ fore and main sails of the leg-of-mutton or jib-header cut. The objection to this is usually the loss of sail area between the masts—which sounds odd if the "increased efficiency" of the leg-of-mutton or jib header is to be accepted. However, leg-of-mutton schooners have long existed in narrow or shoal draft hulls requiring only moderate sail area or having only moderate stability. The rig is an efficient one, no doubt, in an easily driven hull.

Three-masted, or "tern," schooners are not very numerous in the yachting fleet; the rig is usually employed only in very large yachts. Three-masted rigs of this class might well be employed in long, narrow, canoe-like hulls of rather small size for it has many advantages; the rig requires few hands to work it and the heeling effect can be much reduced, compared to the ordinary two-masted schooner. It is practice, in three-masted schooner yachts, to make all masts of equal height, or to lengthen each one foot (the foremast the shortest and the mizzen the longest). This is not particularly graceful and in small craft it could be improved by making the mizzen about 75% of the height of the main, the fore being about 90% of the latter. Such a rig would be practical if leg-of-mutton sails were used, but the staying of the mastheads constitutes a problem with the gaff rig.

The gaff, if used, should be well peaked, schooners usually have less peak to their gaffs than do sloops; if topsails are carried the peak should be less than when none are carried. The fore gaff, in schooners, should peak less than the main; if there is a mizzen its peak is the greatest of all. The booms of all seagoing yachts should be capable of being topped up so that the outboard end of the boom will not be immersed when the vessel rolls in a heavy sea. Unless the boom is very high, as when a roller reefing gear is used, the sails should be cut so that the outer end of the boom is higher than at the mast. Bowsprits should also "cock up" or steeve; in drawing it is well to steeve the bowsprit a little more than is actually desired, for the rigger will pull it down somewhat with the bobstay in setting up the rigging.

"Knockabout" or bowspritless schooners have been common, and if sail area is not lost by omission of the bowsprit, the rig has many advantages—particularly in auxiliary cruisers that must work in crowded anchorages and among wharves.

In general, the schooner rig looses in weatherliness in proportion to the number of sails set. Hence the most efficient schooner rig is one composed of a single jib, a large foresail and a large mainsail, the foresail overlapping the main produces additional area well inboard and low, so is advantageous.

Cutter and Sloop Rig

Cutters and sloops are now almost indistinguishable; the rig-names being now applied with little distinction or accuracy. Correctly speaking, the cutter is a one-masted vessel, rigged with a fore-and-aft gaff mainsail and two headsails and marked by having her mast from one-third to one-half the waterline length abaft the stem. Strictly speaking, a cutter must also have a reefing bowsprit that can be run inboard whenever desired, though this rig is now out of fashion in cutter-rigged yachts. In addition to her lower sails the cutter may carry topsails, square, fore-and-aft and jib; she may set square courses or spinnakers. The sloop has a fixed bowsprit and has her mast placed in the neighborhood of one-quarter the waterline length abaft the stem. She generally has but a single headsail, otherwise she may carry the same sails as a cutter. However, for 75 years the American sloop rig was made up of jib and mainsail; on large sloops there was also a gaff-topsail and jib-topsail. In recent years the gaff mainsail of the cutter and sloop has been replaced by the jib-header and only the jib-topsail of the older topsails has been retained. The earlier remarks on the gaff and boom apply to cutters and sloops and the rigs of both are so well known that detailed description is not required here.

Modern racing sloops or cutters now have a lofty mast well inboard and the headsail stays are usually carried well aloft, often to the masthead. The mainbooms are now short and this resulted in the need for a "kicking strap" or brace to prevent the light boom from cocking up in a fresh breeze. The kicking strap is, in fact, a very necessary piece of gear in the modern rig. The modern sloop rig depends to a marked degree upon light sails when running, due to the use of a high narrow mainsail which sacrifices area when running free. At one time it was common to place the booms very high above the deck, but this is now out of style due to the unhandiness it created when the mainsail was reefed or being furled. It was also once practice to carry the jib or headsail high aloft in a sharply pointed head, but this was a difficult sail to cut and it too is now out of fashion.

Jibs and forestaysails of all rigs should be cut high in cruisers; in many modern yachts these sails are too small and are badly proportioned; as a result they do little work and set poorly. In racing craft it is necessary to carry the heads of the headsails far up the stay to take advantage of the area measured by racing rules, but this is not necessary in cruisers.

Gaff topsails are unpopular except in schooners; in modern cruisers they are often too small to be of practical use. To be effective their area ought to be about one-fourth that of the sail below them. Topsails are light-weather canvas and should be designed accordingly.

Catboat Rig

Catboats should have a great deal of peak to their gaffs and their masts are commonly placed within a foot or two of the fore-end of their waterline. The jib-headed mainsail is rather unsatisfactory in catboats, the balance of rig and hull is destroyed when this sail is reefed and there are no other sails available to correct the shift of centers. The objection to jib-headers might be overcome by raking the mast sharply aft, though this is subject to some objections, the most important of which is the tendency of the boom to swing inboard in light airs. The catboat is the most weatherly of all orthodox rigs. It does not permit efficient use of light sails however, and in large size is considered unwieldy.

Ketch Rig

The ketch rig has become very popular in this country during recent years. Its design may be said to follow that of the schooner except in position of masts and in relative areas of sails. The mainmast of the ketch is usually about one-third of the waterline length abaft the stem and the mizzen about one-sixth the waterline forward of the after end of the waterline. The position of the mizzen depends upon the amount of overhang in the stern, however, for if there is little or no overhang the mizzen must be moved forward; sometimes its position is as much as one-fourth the waterline length from the stern. In this case the main is also moved forward so that its position is in the neighborhood of one-fourth the waterline length abaft the stem. It will be noticed that there is much variation in relative positions of the masts in ketches of the same length due to variations in overhangs and hull types. The distribution of sail-area in ketches follows no rule, except that the mizzen is smaller than the mainsail, the difference ranging all the way from 3% to 50%. In most examples, however, the mizzen is about two-thirds the area of the main. This has become almost a standard rig for cruisers in the United States. Its popularity is due largely to its use in ocean racing, in which the rules favor the ketch.

Yawls

Yawls generally have their mainmasts located about one-fourth the waterline length abaft the stem and their jiggers stepped on, or very close to, the after end of the waterline. In most examples the mizzen is sheeted to an outrigger over the stern. The relative areas of main and jigger vary greatly among yachts, the area of the jigger ranging from one-fourth to one-sixth that of the main. Once a very popular rig, the yawl is now less favored than the ketch rig in ocean racers. In these craft the yawl and ketch rigs are basically rule cheaters, and the trend in design has been to produce a cutter with a small mizzen or jigger attached, to gain a measurement advantage.

Amount of Sail-area

Further discussion of rig design will be found in the chapter on the drawing of the sail plan. Before leaving the subject of rig and sails, however, there is the question of the amount of sail that a design should have. There have been many attempts to fix the proper area of sail by means of mathematical investigation, resulting in proportions based on displacement, stability calculations and wetted-surface, but none of these has proven satisfactory in practice. In recent years graphs have been used, based on a large number of examples, listed by length, beam or displacement; this has also been unsatisfactory. The use of the L.W.L. plane or similar base is the most common basis for comparison, though it too suffers from lack of precision in results. But comparison by any of these mediums must be strictly confined to boats of like model, type and dimensions. Hull form has so much to do with this that the only safe method is to compare the design being drawn with yachts of similar size, hull type and rig that have proven satisfactory in service. In small yachts the sail-area should not be cut up into a number of very small sails for this multiplies the amount of gear required and destroys the power of the sail-area as a whole. In yachts over 40 feet waterline the reverse is true as large sails require large crews and much labor to handle them; therefore some sacrifice in power is desirable. Generally speaking, it is well to canvas rather heavily as sail can be reduced quickly if the rig is properly designed but a very small rig cannot be added to without a large quantity of gear. Simplicity should be the first consideration in the design of the rig of a cruiser; the less rigging required the less will be the cost, work in handling and upkeep; this principle is not at all popular at the present time, apparently. Light sails are undesirable in small cruisers; the working rig should be made so large that they are not often wanted. The wise designer of cruisers avoids extremes, for it is conceivable that a rig that did not function properly at sea might lead to loss of life.

Drawing Sail-plan in Sketch

Returning once more to the sketch, the sail-plan can be drawn. As the first step, the centerline of the mast should be drawn and the bare outline of the sails sketched in. In doing this, allow for the distance between the centerline of the mast and the luff of the sail. The centerlines of other spars that may be required can be drawn in the same way. Do not get booms so high that they cannot be easily reached in reefing; this is a common error. It is very important to draw the sails with the proper spacing of luff, foot, and head, from mast and boom. $1\frac{1}{2}''$ to $2''$ for luffs, and $1''$ to $1\frac{1}{4}''$ for the foot (above the top of the boom) is a good approximation. When this is done, the center of effort and the center of lateral plane (center of lateral resistance or center of lateral area) must be found. The first is really center of gravity of the sails combined and the second is the center of gravity of the profile below the waterline. The balance of the rig and hull will depend, theoretically, upon the relation of these two points; actually, however, both points are based on the theoretical fiction that they are the centers of force of the propulsion of the sails and the lateral resistance of the hull. Unfortunately, the true centers can only be found after the yacht is completed and tested; nevertheless the calculated centers are of practical use if properly applied.

Finding Center of Lateral Plane

The center of lateral plane may be found first. The quickest and easiest, as well as most accurate, method of finding this center is to trace the underbody profile, omitting the rudder, on a scrap of tracing paper; cutting out the profile thus obtained with the scissors and then folding it lengthwise a number of times, giving it a pleated effect. This will stiffen it so that it will not bend when supported in the middle. Make sure that the ends do not droop; fold the figure so that the ends are stiff. Then open the dividers and stick one leg in the drawing-board; bring the other leg up until it is vertical and balance the folded tracing on it, shifting the tracing on the point of the leg until it rests in a level position. This point can be marked by merely pushing it down on the divider point, making a small hole or series of holes in the tracing. Unfold the tracing, lay it over the sketch so that it coincides with the underbody profile and prick the point of balance into the sketch. It will help somewhat if the underbody profile and tracing are marked with coinciding vertical lines, say at the position of the mid-section; in this way the point may be either directly transferred by pricking or scaled off from the tracing to the sketch.

Some designers include one-third or even the whole area of the rudder in the lateral plane; there is much divergence of opinion in this matter. It seems best to omit the rudder in most hull forms, however. In catboats having large outboard rudders of the "barn-door" variety it is practice to include the forward third of the rudder in the lateral plane because of its proportionately great area compared to the lateral plane of the hull.

This method of finding the center of lateral plane may appear less scientific than the method usually recommended in text-books; measuring ordinates and their moments from a chosen point. The latter method is uselessly laborious and unless the ordinates are closely spaced and located with judgment the result will be erroneous. The ordinates must be located so that moments can be taken at such points as the heel of the sternpost and at the angle of the forefoot to properly calculate the center of lateral plane by this method. In view of the fact that the center of lateral plane is only an approximation, practically speaking, it seems best to find it in the quickest and least troublesome manner. It is hardly necessary to pursue this subject further here; those desiring to employ mathematics are referred to the standard text-books of naval architecture. It will be observed that only the longitudinal position of the center of lateral plane need be found by either balancing the underbody profile or calculation; the vertical position is of no importance whatsoever.

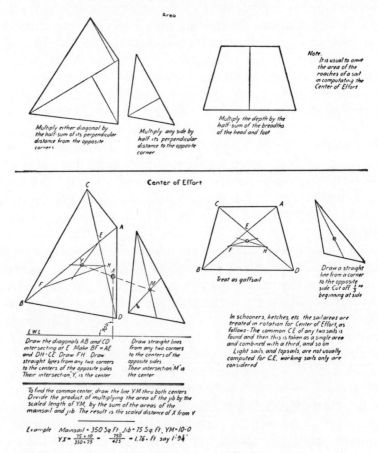

FIGURE 2. *Calculations of sail-area and center of effort.*

Finding Center of Effort

Figure 2 shows the methods of finding the center of effort of individual sails and that for the whole sail-plan. Explanation of each step, including the finding of the areas, will be found in the Figure and so need not be repeated here. It is necessary to calculate for working sails only, those used when closehauled. In yawls and ketches it is important that the centers be found for reduced canvas, as explained in the chapter on drawing the sail-plan. It is customary to omit the additional sail-area produced by the roach (curvature in the outlines of the sail that give it the proper draft or wing-section) in area and center of effort calculations.

Lead

When both the centers of lateral plane and effort have been found they should be squared up and down to the load waterline so that their respective positions can be seen. In modern hull types the center of effort should be forward of the center of lateral plane. The precise amount, however, is subject to many qualifications. In old yachts having a straight or long keel, the center of effort was often well abaft the center of lateral plane. In the schooner *America* built in 1851, for example, the center of effort was .006 the L.W.L. abaft the center of lateral plane. In the noted racing schooners of the end of the last century, keel or centerboard, there were marked reverse leads—as much as .10 of the L.W.L. It has been noted that large schooner yachts having rather short keels also required about 2% of the L.W.L. in reverse lead.

Most keel cruising yachts having the "fisherman profile"— that is, a straight or nearly straight keel of over 50% of the L.W.L. in length—require very small lead, actual practice showing .00 to .10 the L.W.L. in lead of center of effort before the center of lateral plane. However, as the rigs increased in height so did the lead, and modern keel racing yachts have leads of from .10 to .16, calculated with rudder omitted, and having lofty sloop, cutter, yawl or ketch rigs. Probably the average lead employed in modern short keel hulls having a lofty rig is about .12. It is interesting to note that with gaff rigs and short or moderately long keels the lead runs usually .03 to .10, and as little as .015 has been noted. But the range with increasingly lofty rigs is now .04 to .16.

The cause of the increase in lead in the modern rig is un-doubtedly the couple formed by the heeling of the boat. Since the lofty rig gives the greater heeling moment and the high center of effort, or center of drive, apparently moves outboard to leeward, a turning lever is formed with the center of resistance of the hull, which causes the boat to endeavor to come up into the wind increasingly as she heels. This is particularly marked in deep, narrow hulls having high aspect ratio rigs.

In centerboard hulls the lead varies, in general, as the draft. In shoal scows, sharpies, and V-bottom hulls having centerboards but little or no skeg or external keel, only the centerboard and ¼ to ½ the rudder area are usually considered and the lead is usually .02 to .05 unless it is thought the boat is to be sailed at much heel, when the lead should be increased to about .08 to .10. The centerboard, if pivoted, is drawn in "average position," so ⅔ down.

If bilgeboards or leeboards are employed, they are treated in the same manner as a centerboard—only to be used to make the calculations. Because bilgeboards and leeboards are so fitted that they stand vertical, or nearly so, when the boat is heeled to sailing trim, they are more efficient than centerboards and so have less submerged area. As a result, using ¼ the rudder area, the bilgeboard or leeboard is usually placed farther forward than the centerboard to obtain proper balance.

Centerboard hulls having skegs and external keels, or much draft in the body, are calculated in the same manner as keel boats, the whole underbody and ½ the rudder with the centerboard ⅔ down being employed. With dagger boards the center of lateral plane is found as it would be in a fin keel hull.

Various qualifications should be pointed out. One of these is in schooners having leg-of-mutton mainsails and gaff foresails; here the lead is more than when the gaff rig main is used. Hulls having full bows require greater leads than hulls having long easy entrances. Hulls having very full runs usually require reverse leads, as do hulls having long hollow entrances with fine runs. The power of the bow wave or lee surge seems to have a marked effect on the amount of lead required. There can be little question that both the actual center of lateral plane and the true center of effort are in motion when a boat is sailing and the extent of the motion varies with the speed. Hence precise calculations are impractical. The effects of draft or depth, of eddies at centerboard slot, rudder, propellor aperture or strut, and the eddies caused by leeway all affect the center of lateral plane when sailing. There is some reason to suppose that the leading edges of the keel or jib or centerboard play an important part not only in placing the true center of lateral plane but also in determining the efficiency of the lateral plane itself.

The truth is that perfect balance, if obtained by a predetermined lead, is largely a matter of sheer luck. Of course a hull having a very long keel, or one so well balanced in form as not to change longitudinal trim when heeled under sail, may be insensitive to moderate shifts of center, but it does not follow in all instances that this insensitivity produces fast sailing, particularly to windward. As a result of the numerous phenomena found in sail balance, it is usual for designers to draw the rig in such a manner that it can be quickly altered. This is done by fitting the mast so the heel can be shifted easily in the step, thus affecting the rake of the mast, which in turn affects the centers of effort of the sails upon it. To do this the boom sails must have some stive to their booms and there must be some space between the heads of the head sails, and their halyard blocks at the mast head. Also centerboards can be raised or lowered, or the pivots shifted to obtain balance. Sometimes daggerboards are made with cases that permit the boards to be shifted fore and aft. Movable mast partners or variation in size of mast wedges have also been employed. It is well to plan for the adjusting necessary for "tuning up," if a fast sailing boat is intended.

In conclusion it must be said that the question of the proper lead to be employed in designing a rig is subject to over-simplification when an attempt is made to fix leads in proportion to L.W.L. length and mathematical centers of areas. Hence it is very necessary that the design make allowances for alterations in tuning up. Large schooners seem to have reverse lead in nearly every case. It appears that schooners having square foretopsails require more reverse lead than usual.

Modern yachts having short fins and spade, or balance, rud-

ders, with or without a skeg between fin and rudder, are difficult
to balance. Such designs may show longitudinal instability, causing broaching and poor steering characteristics. These are caused
by hull-form and not by rig, though the high, narrow sail plan
must be charged with contributing to the difficulty in design. There is also the effect of depth to be considered; it
may be accepted as an apparent fact that the portion of the
lateral plane farthest submerged is the most effective in creating
lateral resistance; this alone is sufficient to question the accuracy
of accepting the mathematical center of gravity of the underbody profile as the center of lateral resistance. In view of recent
experiments, it seems apparent that the entering edge of the
underbody profile plays an important part in lateral resistance,
both in effectiveness and in the location of the true center of
lateral resistance. It would seem that if the hull were towed
broadside to the line of motion the center of lateral resistance
might not be far from a vertical line through the mathematical
center of lateral plane, or center of gravity of the underbody
profile, but this experiment is wholly useless in determining the
center when under sail, for obvious reasons.

To add to the difficulty in making general rules as to lead,
observation indicates that there is a wide variation in the leads
employed in hulls of the same general dimensions and rig; even
identical hull-types may vary in apparent lead. Many attempts
have been made to analyze this phenomenon. In respect to the
lee-bow wave, it was observed that vessels having full bows required greater lead than sharp-bowed craft; the extreme lead
being required in hulls formed with full bows and long fine runs,
the "cod's head and mackerel's tail model," while hulls having
hollow bows and moderately fine runs required the least. At the
period when hulls had excessively sharp bows such as that of
the famous schooner-yacht *America*, reverse of the lead actually
existed; the center of effort being located about .006 the waterline length abaft the center of lateral plane. These vessels had
rather marked drag to the keel combined with a rather prominent forefoot. Some designers bring the centers of effort and
lateral plane to the same perpendicular or employ a slight reverse

in the lead in yachts exceeding 100 feet overall; this may be feasible because these vessels are commonly reversions to the older hull-forms. It seems apparent that hulls having long straight keels are less sensitive in respect to exact location of centers.

Change of Trim

In observations of the effect of change of trim it was found that the centers of effort and lateral plane should fall very close to, or just abaft, the center of buoyancy (the center of gravity of the hull-form below the waterline); though this is a matter that cannot be properly considered in the sketch, it can be mentioned here. By this means, the tendency of the sail-plan to depress the bow, when the hull is heeled under the force of the wind, is minimized. In centerboarders it was observed that many successful vessels had the center of the area of the centerboard a little abaft the center of buoyancy, though it would seem that this has not been sufficiently well investigated to permit any definite conclusions.

Rake and Stive

Rake in the mast or masts is usually desirable. Changes in it allow slight alterations to be made in the balance of hull and rig, without a major operation or spoiling the appearance of the sail plan. The rake may be slight or marked, as the designer wishes. The extreme rake seen a century ago in American schooners and on Chesapeake Bay craft is no longer common in yachts. Extreme rake in masts causes the booms to fall inboard in light airs but has no other practical objective. It has the same advantage in aspect ratio that swept-back wings have in planes. Whether or not this is important in a sail is probably a matter of opinion.

Stive of the booms is also a matter of appearance. In cruisers it looks well and has no serious objection. In hulls having a stronge sheer, stive to the booms is preferable to horizontal booms, aesthetically. Horizontal and even booms sagging at the after ends have been fashionable in racing yachts, but it is doubtful if there are any scientific advantages.

Stive in a bowsprit is a matter of aesthetics. Normally the bowsprit stives with the sheer. It may slant up from the sheer slightly in large vessels. Normally, the strain set up by the bobstays to counteract the loading of the forestays causes the bowsprit to hog, and the slight extra stive is thus cancelled. But if the bow at rail or deck is rather full and the sheer at all marked, then it is better to set the bowsprit level with (or nearly so) the load waterline. Otherwise there is an illusion of excessive stive or "stick up." It might be said that the stive of the bowsprit should be a continuous line with the sheer forward when the bow is long and fine, and with moderate sheer, but should be nearly parallel with the L.W.L. when the bow is full and much sheered.

Area of Lateral Plane and Centerboards

The area of the lateral plane has been assumed to have been fixed by the draft requirement and the selection of underbody profile. It is plain, however, that there might be too little or too much lateral plane in a design. Comparison is the only effective method of deciding this, but the data thus obtained must be employed only after it has been properly classified. The first generalization might be that the amount of lateral plane has a relation to the amount of area of the sails; it will be found, unfortunately, that this relationship is vague and subject to infinite qualification. Attempts to express this relationship mathematically have been numerous but the results are most untrustworthy. The next generalization might be that the stability of a hull has a definite relation to the area of lateral plane that is required, for it is obvious that a hull which sails upright, or nearly so, receives the full benefit of her lateral area. This will be found very difficult to apply to practice, however, for stability calculations have not proven sufficiently accurate to serve as a basis for computations of this nature. Stability formed by depth and ballast, beam and ballast or by hull-section combined with either or both, varies in its effectiveness in preventing heeling. For example, a narrow, deep, heavily ballasted hull must heel to some extent to obtain the righting lever formed by ballast and its depth below the axis on which the hull rolls over; on the other hand, the shoal, wide and nearly flat-bottomed hull is stable or "stiff" when upright. It is hardly necessary to explain why heeling affects the driving-power of the sails by reducing the area exposed to the wind, and the practical difficulties in expressing these generalizations mathematically or graphically are equally obvious.

Out of these and other generalizations, nevertheless, some rather definite conclusions may be drawn: that hulls having great depth relative to length, or having a large amount of outside deadwood (as a fin), or wall-sided (as in old merchant sailing ships), or hulls that are so stiff that they do not heel a great deal, or whose sail area is so small that its slight heeling tendency produces the same effect as stiffness of hull, require less lateral plane than do hulls whose sections are very rounded below the water-line, or whose stiffness is not sufficient to prevent great heeling, or whose draft is light (shallow keel hulls), or whose sail-area is so large that it produces the same result as a lack of stiffness. In the application of these conclusions it will be found that a center-boarder requires less lateral area than a keel boat of normal hull-form since the centerboard is nothing more than a large fin. It should be observed that keels prettily rounded in section are less effective in preventing leeway than keels drawn with flat sides and angular cross-sections. Any hull-form in which there is a fin or deadwood that has flat sides requires less lateral plane than a V-shaped or U-shaped underbody section hull-form. A deep hull in which hollow garboards are used (with the midsection showing a hollow just above the rabbet) has a more effective lateral plane area than a hull of the same proportions in which there is no hollow at the garboard, assuming that there is not a flat-sided keel or deadwood to be taken into consideration.

Very shoal centerboarders require larger centerboards than hulls in which there is external keel, as a rule. This can be traced to the additional effectiveness of the deadwood to that of the board in the latter type of hull. As an illustration of this, it was observed that while a sharpie (35′ overall, 7′-2″ beam, 10″

draft) had a board 11'-0" long and 3'-0" vertically, a sloop (34' overall, 8'-4" beam, 3'-0" draft) had a board but 6'-0" long and 2'-9" vertically. For small, narrow, very shoal centerboarders the board should be about one-third the waterline in length; small centerboarders having beams exceeding one-fourth of the length of the waterline require centerboards one-fourth or one-fifth the waterline in length. It is now common practice to make the centerboard too small, on the plea that a board of proper size interferes with floor space and footroom to too great an extent. The result of this practice has been to give the centerboarder an undeserved reputation for being lacking in weatherliness. It is useless, however, to argue the point, for an owner who is more interested in footroom than in the sailing qualities of his yacht is not worth consideration. Centerboards placed wholly or partially below the cabin floor have been in favor among inexperienced owners and designers; there are grave structural and practical faults in this type of board when it is employed in a wooden hull, which will receive attention in the chapter on drawing the construction plan.

Two centerboards, one forward and one aft, both on the centerline of the hull, have been used to advantage in shoal cruisers. By means of this arrangement of boards it is possible to obtain a yacht that is very steady on her helm and which is not too sensitive for single-handing; in addition the boards need not interfere with the cabin arrangement to a marked extent. The most serious objection to this method of fitting centerboards is the slowness in stays that its use entails, the alternative of which is the extra work of handling the boards when in stays. Usually the forward board is larger than the after one, the latter being about one-half the area of the former. The combined areas of the two centerboards may be about one-eighth less than the area of a single board, explained, apparently, by the additional effectiveness of the extra entering edge of the second board.

Bilgeboards and leeboards may be one-fourth less in area, compared to the single centerboard of equal efficiency. This is due to the fact that these boards are, if properly designed, about vertical when the hull is heeled to the most common sailing angle and so obtain the full effect of the area of lateral plane which they represent.

The effect of size upon the area of lateral plane requires mention; it was observed that, in practice, large vessels required less proportionate area of lateral plane than small vessels; this seemed to apply to both keel and centerboard vessels. The reason that this is true may be traced, perhaps, to the apparent fact that the stability of a yacht twice the dimensions of another is not twice as great but, rather, sixteen times as great. In practice the amount of area of lateral plane of large craft must be fixed by comparison with successful vessels of the same type, rig, dimensions and hull-form, as far as is possible.

In conclusion, the area of lateral plane is best determined by comparison of the proposed design with boats of similar form, type, rig and size. It is to be noted that in recent years the area of lateral plane in keel ocean racers has been reduced because of the return of the semi-fin with its more marked vertical planes. Nevertheless, rough water requires somewhat more lateral plane then smooth water sailing, in either centerboard or keel hulls. In general, therefore, it is usually better to err in having excess lateral plane than in not having enough. The frictional resistance of excess keel and centerboard area appears to be relatively slight in practice. For rough water use, a boat with a long keel should have marked "drag" in its bottom or shoe; that is the boat should draw more aft than forward. This drag is a helpful check on "broaching" in a heavy following sea.

Stability

It is apparent that the relationship of the sail-area and the area of lateral plane is close, and that both are in turn related to stability, or that quality known as "stiffness." As has been stated, the amount of sail that a vessel can carry with safety depends upon such factors as depth, length, beam, form and ballast of hull; in addition the human factors, the skill and nerve of the crew, must be admitted. The hull factors just mentioned fix stability, and it has been shown that there is a ratio of stability to sail-area, even though it is impractical to express this ratio mathematically. It has been pointed out that the use of stability calculations might be supposed to solve the problem, but unfortunately theory and practice part company here. Because of the difficulty in expressing, mathematically, the forces that influence stability when the hull is in motion, stability calculations are confined to the hull at rest in still water, at given angles of heel. As a vessel actually gains or loses stability when heeled and in motion among waves the error in the calculation is evident. The gain or loss in stability is occasioned by the lee-surge, longitudinal and transverse change of trim, and buoyancy gained or lost in passing through or over a wave. The heeling lever varies as the angle of heel changes; the forces applied to the sails by the wind are not constant. It follows, therefore, that stability calculations are, at best, no more than a very rough approximation of a hull's ability to carry sail unless the findings are checked by model-tank experiments; an expensive operation, and the data obtained must be rechecked with each new design.

Sail-area and Displacement

For high speed under sail there must be a proper relation of sail-area to displacement; a great many modern cruising yachts are deficient in this respect. It has been stated earlier that it is impractical to express this mathematically, but as a generalization it can be stated that an attempt to combine a very heavy displacement with a small sail-area is doomed to produce a relatively slow vessel, even though the lines of the hull be drawn out very fine. It must be apparent that large accommodations, in proportion to hull length, necessitate proportionately great displacement and sail-area; in turn these factors increase the amount of "beef" needed to work the vessel, when compared to hulls of normal accommodation. In all sailing cruisers, designed for extensive voyages, it is proper to sacrifice some accommodation, and therefore displacement, in order to obtain an easy working ship. This is particularly true with shoal hulls; it is very undesirable to combine great beam and displacement for if this is done a tremendous sail-area will be necessary. For cruising, shoal, light displacement centerboard yachts can be designed that are relatively narrow, yet are self-righting; these will work with little "beef" and sail extremely well. It is plain, however, that such craft will have less accommodation than a wide, heavy center-boarder. The same remark applies to keel hulls, insofar as light displacement, narrow beam and small sail-area go hand in hand in the production of an easy working vessel.*

These principles are so easily overlooked or forgotten, in the effort to crowd one more berth or some bit of extra equipment into accommodation plans, that repetition of them is excusable. It is plain, then, that in fixing accommodation the sail-area is also fixed in a general way; it must be remembered that small craft carry relatively greater areas of sail than large craft.

If beam and displacement are both reduced so that stiffness under sail is lacking it is impossible to correct the fault without increasing the designed draft markedly, as has been illustrated in some small English ocean racers.

Single-handers and the Boat Problem

That type popularly known as the "single-hander" offers a particular problem; less intensified in larger craft, but which should be considered in the first steps of design of any cruiser. This problem is how to carry a dinghy. This may appear to be a superficial difficulty at first thought, but when the designer attempts to figure out a method of carrying a boat after he has completed his cruiser he will appreciate that this is a matter that ought to have been considered early in the formation of her design. The smaller the cruiser the more difficult is this problem. In single-handers this problem might conceivably affect the choice of hull-form, accommodation and rig. Illustrative of this, consider an 18 or 20-foot single-hander; it is apparent that she could not stow an 8 to 12-foot dinghy on deck, and the idea of a cruiser of this size towing a boat of such proportionate size is out

---

* This statement does not mean that it is wholly desirable to reduce displacement and beam together, as stability may be reduced too much by such a combination. As beam decreases, it is necessary to increase displacement to carry sufficient ballast to replace the lost stability. An example of this in practice was the old six-beam cutter.

of the question. It must be concluded, therefore, that a practical single-hander of this size must be so designed that she will not only serve as a cruiser, but also as a dinghy; hence she must be of such form that she can be beached and, in addition, maneuvered under oars or a sculling-sweep. It is hardly necessary to pursue the subject further to prove that this matter is one that affects hull-form, accommodation and rig in some cases. It is apparent that miniature yachts of the conventional hull-forms are impractical as single-hander designs. When the hull is large enough to carry a dinghy on deck the problem of stowing the boat is comparatively simple but should not be overlooked. When stern davits are possible they ought to be employed, for they are the most practical means of slinging a boat in a sailing vessel. Side davits, when seen on fore-and-afters, are an indication of lubberliness on the part of owner or designer. It is inconceivable that an experienced seaman would fail to recognize that a boat carried in davits on the side is not only in the way, but also liable to be stove-in when the vessel is heeled in a breeze and rough sea; so far no one has designed a fore-and-after that does not occasionally put her rail under when in a breeze. The problem of getting a boat overside in a sailing vessel is not one that requires the use of davits to solve, as can be proven by the use of masthead or "dory-tackles" on fishermen. Even with sloop rigs, the use of the mast tackles is not beyond ordinary ingenuity.

Ballasting

While these general matters relating to the preliminary steps in the design are being discussed, some mention of the ballasting is necessary. This is an item of design that will receive attention when the lines are being drawn, of course, but since it plays an important part in the design of the underbody profile and in fixing sail-area it requires general discussion now. There has been some difference in opinion as to whether cruisers should or should not have outside ballast; the oft-quoted objection to outside ballast being that its use produced a hull that was an uneasy roller and that was, as a result, very hard on her gear. There can be little doubt that there is much truth to this assertion when large sailing craft are under consideration, but the matter is of comparatively little importance in cruisers under 40 feet overall. In any cruising boat the ballast should not be *all* outside because this craft is subject to change of trim and load brought about by the addition of provisions and gear required in cruising; faulty trim produced by these loads should be capable of being corrected by alteration in the amount and position of some of the ballast, not by having to stow the provisions and gear fore-and-aft nor by having to utilize the cabin as a hold to obtain the proper sailing trim. In a small cruiser the actual deadweight of outside ballast, fitted with these matters in view, is not great when compared to displacement and so does not tend to produce undue uneasiness in a seaway, though in a large cruiser the statement is subject to qualifications. The opinion is offered that the question as to whether or not there should be outside ballast is a matter that is largely dependent upon the choice of hull-form and type, keeping in mind that the lower the ballast the greater the power to carry sail, within reasonable limits. The proportion of ballast outside to that inside, in small cruisers of the keel type, should be about 75% outside to 25% inside. In large cruisers a greater proportion should be inside: as has been mentioned the stability of large hulls is proportionately greater than that of small hulls, varying as the fourth power of the length. Otherwise, the practical considerations in ballasting are that inside ballast is cheapest and that it requires much room below the cabin floor, compared to outside ballast combined with only enough inside for trimming. Outside ballast is of little use in very shoal hulls of the sharpie or scow models unless placed well below the hull by means of a fin or deadwood. It is generally considered that outside ballast is unnecessary in sea-going cruising sailing yachts over 75' overall, of heavy displacement.

Relationship of Hull-form and Rig

As the student acquires experience he will find that certain rigs fit certain hull-forms and that there is a relationship between these rigs and certain forms of underbody profile. These matters should be worked together in order to obtain the harmony between them that is required to obtain a good design. The rig must fit the hull, very rarely will a hull, properly designed to carry one rig, be equally satisfactory under another; a good schooner rarely can be converted to a good sloop, or vice versa.

Relationship of Length and Rig

Before returning to the sketch there is one more point for general discussion: the limits of overall length within which a rig is practical from the point of view of handiness. This is some-what of a matter of individual opinion in many cases, neverthe-less there seem to be rather definite maximum and minimum lengths of hull suitable for each classification of rig. The follow-ing limits are based on a large number of examples of successful application of each.

> Catboat,—12 to 30 feet overall.
> Sloop,—14 to 50 feet overall.
> Cutter,—26 to 60 feet overall.
> Yawl,—26 to 60 feet overall.
> Ketch,—30 to 100 feet overall.
> Schooner, (two-masted),—36 to 130 feet overall.
> Schooner, (three-masted),—70 to 150 feet overall.
> Brig and Brigantine,—70 to 120 feet overall.
> Ships and Barks,—90 to 200 feet overall.
> Four-masted rigs,—145 feet and over.

Yachts have been built outside of these limits but the results have not been very satisfactory. It must be added, however, that hulls having narrow beam in proportion to length and relatively small stability at great angles of heel, such as canoes or sharpies, may have two or three-masted rigs, even though smaller than the minimum lengths for these rigs, since their lack of power does not permit normal rigs being employed. Boats of this class are special types and must be rigged according to the requirements of their hull-forms.

Developing Design

Returning again to the sketch: when the sail-plan is drawn and the centers of effort and lateral plane have been found in rela-

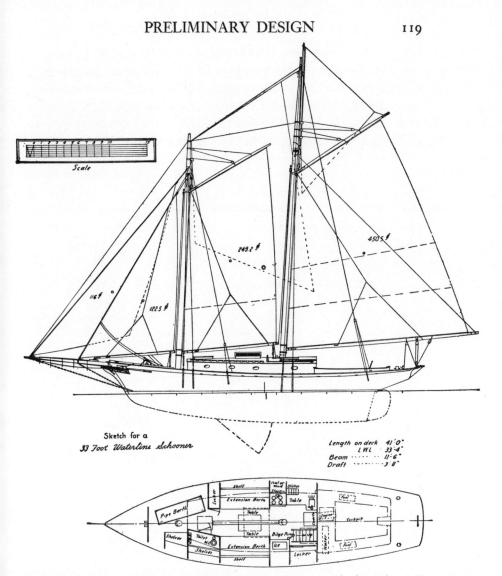

Scale

249.2

450.5

116

122.5

Sketch for a
33 Foot Waterline Schooner

Length on deck 41'0"
LWL 33'4"
Beam 11'6"
Draft 3'11"

Preliminary Sketch of Example. Note how details are worked out here. To a great extent the design is fixed in this drawing. The rig must be balanced before completing this sketch.

tion to one another, it may be necessary to make changes to bring the centers to a proper position. Perhaps the mast should be moved, or the boom, bowsprit, gaff, sails or rake of mast altered to obtain the desired effect. Changes must be made by trial and error, unless the rig can be shifted bodily without causing great difficulties in arrangement; in this case the rig and its center of

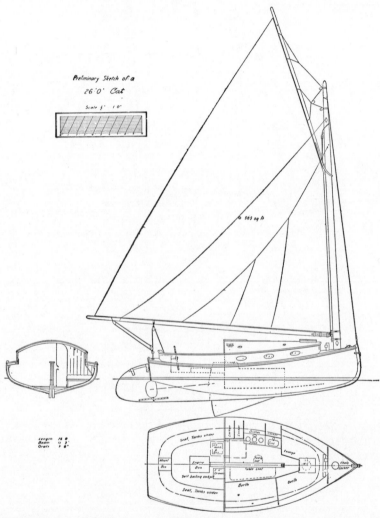

Example of a preliminary sketch, showing midsection worked out to check space available for arrangement.

effort can be traced on a scrap of tracing paper which is placed under the sketch and shifted until the centers suit the designer, after which the sail-plan may be retraced on the sketch. Every possibility ought to be considered: whether it is better to change the underbody profile, shift the rig, alter the shape or size of certain sails; in fact, everything that might procure the proper balance between rig and hull without unduly affecting appearance or arrangement.

When these final alterations are made, the sketch may be "dressed up" with rigging, the outline of the spars, deck fittings, paint lines, shade lines and everything necessary to make a complete picture of the design. When the sketch has been inked-in and hung up on the wall of a room for critical inspection, by standing well away from the drawing the whole picture of hull and rig is obtained and possible improvements in appearance may be discovered; it is well to let the drawing hang for a couple of days as lengthy study may suggest desirable changes. If it is necessary to sketch in a midship section, to see if there is going to be enough headroom or floor space, this should be done before the final study is made. The shape of the midsection is an important detail in the lines and will be discussed at length in the next chapter.

It cannot be too strongly stressed that the sketch should be carefully drawn and worked out in every important detail. To a great extent, the lines are fixed by the details of this drawing, as are the arrangement, construction and sail-plans. No extensive changes should be contemplated when drawing the rest of the required plans. Of course, as the work progresses minor alterations in details may probably be necessary, but the sketch should be as accurate as possible. Comparisons with the plans that have appeared in yachting magazines may lead to new ideas in regard to layout or appearance; these should be tested on the sketch before being accepted for inclusion in the new design; in short, no additions should be made in the later plans that have not been worked out previously in the sketch.

Some designers develop the preliminary sketch to greater detail than suggested in the foregoing. Sometimes a few longitudinal control lines are faired in, say about at the waterline and one above and below, at about half the lowest freeboard and maximum draft, and a single buttock at one-quarter the beam. Then an approximate body plan is drawn which is used not only to check the cabin layout for available space but also to make a number of preliminary calculations for displacement and trim. This practice has the advantage of fixing the design extensively in the sketch stage and, in general, it brings to the attention of the designer many mistakes that would cause extensive revamping of the design at some later stage of development, with all the increased chance of error that that entails. However, for the beginner this is expecting too much and he can confine his sketch to the essentials outlined earlier.

Graphs and "Ideal" Dimensions

One final word in regard to comparison: look upon "graphs" showing "ideal" dimensions, classified by length, or some other dimension, or by a broad general type classification, such as "centerboard," with suspicion. The mere fact that two designs are centerboarders does not infer that they ought to be alike in proportions. The value of graphs depends wholly upon the narrowness of the range of hull-form and general type that was used to lay out their curves. The "average" freeboard, beam, displacement, sail-area and draft of a large number of, say, keel cruising yachts of the same waterline or overall length, is by no stretch of imagination an "ideal" proportion for use in a new design, and such graphs are pseudo-scientific; in fact, they are utterly ridiculous. Graphs formed of a series of examples of Cape Cod Catboats having transom sterns, centerboards, outboard rudders, gaff rigs and inside ballast would be of great use in the design of a catboat of the same type, for example. However, such a graph would be utterly useless and misleading if used as datum for the design of an Inland Lake racing catboat, yet both types might be centerboarders and cat-rigged, having the same waterline or overall length. Another example of the fallacy of graphs based on a number of boats can be given by reference to a graph purporting to give permissible sail-area on the basis of waterline length, or say beam. After what has been pointed out earlier in this chapter, it is hardly necessary to do more than suggest that two boats having the same length or beam would not necessarily be able to carry the same area of sail with safety, since the power to carry sail depends on a number of other factors besides these; yet an inference contrary to this fact would naturally result from the use of such a loosely constructed graph. A graph for permissible sail-area must be founded on a narrow choice such as the Cape Cod Catboats just described: this graph would apply only to hulls of this form that are gaff-rigged but would not serve for those having long overhangs or those having leg-of-mutton rigs. The conclusion is that each designer should make his own graphs so that he is certain that they are based on data correctly classified.

Engine Power

In the preliminary stages of design thought must be given to the engine in an auxuliary or motor boat. It is practice to decide upon the power on the basis of comparison of the proposed design with a known boat or boats of similar design—form, type, rig, draft, size, proportions and speed. It may be tempting to increase the horsepower in the new design simply to obtain more speed. This should be carefully considered. Later, in discussion of the lines, speed-length ratio will be explained but it is sufficient here to emphasize only that boats are efficient in engine operation in relatively narrow ranges of speed. Hence economical and reliable engine performance should be required most at "cruising speed." Therefore it is unnecessary, on grounds of practical usage, to power a boat for more speed than a knot or at most two above the real cruising speed. Such a reserve in speed above the cruising speed also represents the practical limit of reserve in power in an efficient design. It is very important, in designing cruising auxiliaries, to remember that, in most keel and centerboard boats, speeds up to 7 or 8 knots may usually be reached with surprisingly small power, but speeds above this require very powerful engines. It is this that has made the outboard motor in a well effective as an auxiliary motor for sailing cruisers.

The effect of high speed and great power on hull form is very marked; in both V-bottom and round-bottom hulls the sterns must be widened and the run flattened as speed is increased. This has an effect on seaworthiness; hence few small high-speed motor cruisers are safe seaboats in heavy weather. Generally speaking, beam is not harmful in power cruisers so far as speed is concerned. Weight is, however, and for very high speed all hull and accommodation weights must be strictly controlled. Cubic contents in a motor cruiser, as in sailing cruisers, are a factor in engine power selection—the greater the cubic contents, the greater the power required.

Mechanical Layout

The design of the mechanical layout of a boat becomes increasingly important as the power rises. In small auxiliary cruisers having a small engine, the chief difficulty is usually to find a place for the engine and tanks where they interfere least with a mast or with the cockpit and cabin arrangement. As a result, poor installation of the engine and its attendant equipment is common and becomes apparent when inspection and ordinary maintenance are carried out.

There is no simple solution to the question of what engine to select, where to locate it in a boat, how to design its exhaust piping, tankage, fuel, and cooling piping, and proper support for engine and shafting. Each boat design requires a special lot of compromises and the solution of individual design problems.

The preliminary study for a power boat should determine, in general terms, the questions of what number, make, power and drive of engine will be employed. A few remarks on this are in order here, however. In auxiliary yachts twin screws are usually undesirable because of their excessive drag when under sail. Few auxiliaries having twin screws will sail well or tack with certainty in light and moderate winds. The lighter the displacement of the auxiliary the more she feels the drag of her screw or screws with their attendant shafts, struts, etc. Therefore, in light displacement auxiliaries, feathering propellers are indicated; and in small boats of very light displacement, the outboard motor on the transom, or in a well so that the engine can be tipped with propeller and housing out of water when under sail, is by far the most satisfactory installation.

In general, twin-screw installations and twin-outboard engine mountings are very wasteful in power and are costly. In most pleasure craft such installations are therefore difficult to justify. The common excuse for twin-screw installations, or twin-outboard installations is "safety"—if one engine fails the other will get the boat home. This is good in theory but not always so in practice, for in strong winds many twin-screw pleasure craft are unmanageable under one engine and screw, and others lack power to drive the boat against wind and sea with one screw. There are cases, however, where two small engines can be more readily installed than one large engine and so the twin screw has to be used. It should be kept in mind, however, that a boat with twin screws and two 100 hp engines does not have the power of a boat with single-screw and a 200 hp engine of comparable characteristics. In the average small yacht, about 20% of the power in a twin-screw installation is wasted, and the extra weight, maintenance and fuel required in the twin-engine/twin-screw installation are disadvantages. The propeller shafts in twin-screw installations are rarely (but can be) parallel to the hull centerline, but spread out toward the stern; the amount desirable is a matter of hull-form and fore-and-aft position of the wheels. The propellers usually turn inboard to give maximum turning power, with one propeller going ahead and one astern. Theoretically, twin screws should be located as far aft as possible and as near the centerline as possible but with good tip clearance. Experience has shown that, in practice, the twin-screw propellers are not much affected by fore and aft position. Twin skeg boats seem to require screws turning inward. Twin screws should be 0.75 to 1.0 times the screw diameter forward of the fore edge of the rudder. For good steering the transverse distance between screws should be as small as is practical.

In general, the single screw is the most practical installation for yachts; for those having very great power, the twin screw or even triple screw is necessary in order to utilize it at the required draft.

The propeller, to be effective in a small boat in rough water, needs to be as low as possible. But draft is, of course, the practical limitation. In sailing hulls, the question of whether the propeller should be on the centerline or to one side of the stern post is best decided by hull form. The side installation is usually the less costly in a sailing hull. If the wheel can be placed in the tuck, close to the point where the stern post enters the hull, the drag of the wheel is slight, as a rule. Experiments indicate that, placed low and off center, the drag is much greater than when in an aperture on the centerline. But in sailing auxiliaries any fixed-blade propeller placed low makes a heavy drag, and a high position as close to the L.W.L. as is practical is best. In the high position pitching will bring the propeller, or its tips, out of water, but normally the auxiliary is expected to use her engine and propeller only in calms or light airs. It is an exceptional condition to have light airs and severe pitching combined, so it is not usual to design to that requirement and thus to sacrifice speed under sail.

It is always best to have an aperture entirely in the stern post and not to cut into the rudder even partly. Apertures in the rudder cause poor steering under sail, and sometimes under power. This is not to say some of the aperture may not be in the rudder, but it should be minimal.

In outboard-motor boats the propeller ought to be well abaft any keel or skeg, for otherwise cavitation and vibration result.

In motor boats the propeller should be as far abaft the strut or stern bearing as is practical. In an aperture, or in a single-screw boat with balanced rudder, it is better for the propeller to be very close to the rudder rather than close to the stern bearing. It is very important in designing the stern of any boat with power, that there be enough wood outside the post rabbet to permit fairing or "feathering" the trailing edge above the post and below the stern bearing of the shaft. With a skeg there should be no difficulty. Neglecting to fair off the sternpost, and also to fair the stem at and below the L.W.L. increases resistance to a surprising degree, as model tests have indicated.

The propeller is best placed well under the stern, particularly in double-enders. "Hooding" the propeller with squat-boards or a plane placed over the propeller is, of course, no more than a makeshift. In boats with transom-mounted outboard engines, however, squat boards are often made by extending the bottom planks to 8 inches abaft the transom with a semi-circular notch in way of the engine mounting. The plank-ends must be finished and supported by an athwartships piece, edge-fastened to them. These are supplemented by the cavitation plate on the shaft housing of the engine, and these planes are very effective in obtaining proper trim.

It is usually well to pitch the shaft in profile, and indeed this is usually necessary. Many amateur designers feel that the nearer the shaft is to the horizontal the better, but this is not true. The maximum pitch that is safe for any engine is stated in the maker's catalog, or it can be obtained by inquiry to the manufacturer. This pitch should never be exceeded and, in fact, it should be a few degrees below the maximum given to allow for the occasional unexpected trim by the stern. There must be adequate clearance at the blade tips—never less than 1½" in even a small boat.

The use of a reduction gear is often recommended by engine manufacturers. To get maximum propulsive efficiency it is certainly necessary in most cases. Yet in auxiliaries where a small-diameter propeller with fixed blades would be desirable from the standpoint of drag under sail, the reduction gear can be omitted. However, proper precautions to prevent racing the engine or running it at or near its maximum rpm should be taken by use of a governor or stop on the throttle.

In placing the engine, its weight and that of batteries, tanks, etc. must be taken into consideration, as they affect displacement and trim. Next, thought must be given to the space necessary to maintain the engine. The designer who forces the owner to hang over a hatch coaming in the floor of a cockpit too small to stretch out in, with his head below deck in order to adjust the points, clean the generator, or fill the batteries should not be surprised to learn that his reputation is jeopardized! Even if the owner is more interested in getting his motor tucked away out of sight than he is in practical requirements, just remember that this is a passing phase and that he will forget his precise instructions to get the engine stowed as far aft and out of reach as possible and will proceed to damn your soul to all and sundry. Usually the situation is at its worst in auxiliaries, but poor planning for engine upkeep also appears quite often in cruising motorboats in which the owner's main consideration is to have a ballroom floor in his deck house rather than how he is going to keep his engine in condition to run. Hatches over the engine should be as large as possible and there should be room around the engine, particularly for tightening the gland on the stuffing box, cleaning and replacing spark plugs, adjusting and replacing points in the distributor, brushes in the generator, changing lubricating oil with room for pump and oil-catching container, with the latter in a position where it will not fall over from the roll caused by the wake of a passing boat; space to see and attend to the batteries and ventilator blowers and to overhaul fuel strainers and the carburetor—all this is worth thought but rarely receives any at the design stage.

The use of V-drive and reduction gear will also have some effect upon engine position. With regard to the former, the engine can be placed farther aft than would otherwise be the case, yet a good position should be retained for the propeller. But don't forget the owner should be able to get at the gland of the stuffing box without the necessity of lifting out his engine! The reduction gear may require the engine to be raised some inches above the shaft centerline, and this may lead to "headroom" trouble under the cockpit or deck house floor.

It is wise to make an accurate template to scale of the engine profile. Some engine manufacturers, the Lord bless them, actually make such templates or scale tracings of their engines to such common scales as ½, ¾, 1 and 1½ inches. Others, however—and may disaster overtake them—present the troubled naval architect with a drawing lacking dimensions and with no apparent scale. With a tracing or an outline template with centerline of shaft and crankshaft shown, and with the height of the hold-down lugs marked, the designer can locate his engine "snugly" and be reasonably certain it will go in the finished boat where he shows it. In this operation it is well to lay out the engine room in plan. Decide once and for all where the tanks

should be, location of batteries, cooling water inlet and its sea-
cock, or other cooling system requirements, and that always
troublesome matter—where the muffler and exhaust pipe are to
be placed without endangering the fuel tank or setting the hull
on fire if the insulation fails. In large boats there may be an
auxiliary generator or lighting system, lubricating oil tank, water
pressure system, work bench or tool box, and perhaps pumps
operated by the main engine or the lighting plant motor. There
must be room also for wiring and plumbing lines, and perhaps a
switchboard. The more mechanical and electronic gadgets required, the greater the layout problem becomes for the engine
room or engine space. No matter how generous you thought the
allowance for engine space or room was in the preliminary
sketch, you will almost invariably find you are pressed for room
in the final engine layout drawings. This is one of the many
arguments for simplicity in the preliminary design.

The designer has a chance, also, to test his ingenuity in planning steering gear and engine controls, where short leads and
direct lines to the steering position are always desirable but very
rarely obtained.

Tanks are a special problem. They must be located where they
least affect trim. In auxiliaries the favored position—up in the wings
of the engine space under the shelf—while very convenient for
piping, vents and proper securing, has unfortunately much effect upon stability or power to carry sail. The position well aft
for a tank is often practical for power yachts, to counteract
trimming weights forward, but is rarely satisfactory in auxiliaries. Tanks on end at the bulkhead forward of the engine
space, as in cruising yachts, may be worth exploration. Fuel
tanks under berths are not favored for obvious reasons, though
water tanks are often placed there. Water tanks under the cabin
floor, when practical, are handy solutions—but are rarely practical in anything but a deep-bodied heavy displacement auxiliary.

Over-tankage is a common problem in small boat design. This
usually is the case with fuel tanks. Engine manufacturers often
give fuel consumption rates for their engines, and the owner or
designer multiplies this by the number of hours he expects to

operate the engine. The result is excessive because, in fact, the fuel consumption rate given by the manufacturers is for full power output, but in operation this would be ruinous because the power output is only about 60% of the full output; as a result the erroneous estimate may be anywhere from 20% to 40% in excess of needs. And, usually, the specified operational period set by the owner or designer is also excessive. Tankage, therefore, ought to be very carefully considered, and all estimates made with the utmost precision possible, avoiding guesses leading to over-estimates or under-estimates.

In a large boat of the cruiser class it is well to diagram the plumbing lines throughout the boat, including not only water lines—hot and cold, for hand basins and sink—but also salt water lines for toilets, showers, fire pump and deck wash. In addition, the bilge line should be shown if it is necessary to pump water-tight compartments. Usually, in large yachts the engine room is pumped separately from the rest of the boat and is coffer-dammed off to prevent oil working into the bilges outside the engine room.

With installations of combination fire, deck wash and emergency bilge pump driven by power, it is important that the designer locate check valves that will prevent flooding the boat while washing down the deck through the owner's neglect of a closing a valve!

Engine beds and stringers, whether for main engine or for an auxiliary generator, should be carefully designed and, if necessary, well detailed. It is common for amateur designers to "leave the engine beds to the boatyard to worry about" and then to find even they cannot place the engine as shown in the plans because the designer made a mistake in not projecting the beds to see if the after ends will fit as he planned. It is necessary to lay out two or three structural sections in way of the engine beds, then to locate shaft centerline on each, and the engine beds at proper height and width. The beginner will, no doubt, be surprised occasionally to find that the beds run to nothing before the after engine lug or bearer is reached! In that case, of course, the engine *must* be raised or moved forward. Short beds should be avoided with engines above 7 hp, and this creates a problem in carrying the beds well aft of the engine. It is usually desirable, with an engine well aft of amidships, to employ short engine beds and to support these by long, deep stringers. In drawing the stringer, however, examine the engine drawings carefully to allow access to any part of it; it may be necessary to notch the stringer on one or both sides to permit removal of the distributor or a hand-plate.

In former years it was considered good practice to place a metal pan under the engine in a boat; into this the lubricating oil for the base was drained and then pumped or bailed out of the pan. These pans are no longer used extensively, for they produced noise and deteriorated rapidly from bilge-water and acid in the pump. It is now practice to pump the engine base in modern engines. But if a draincock is used then a pan is generally necessary. The designer should check the intended engine regarding this matter.

In placing the engine, the designer must be certain no part of the base casting of the engine rests on a floor, frame or plank; it must rest only on the engine beds, and there ought to be at least 1¼ inches clearance minimum under the engine base casting. It is also desirable to give thought to the possibility of arranging the boat so the engine can be lifted out bodily without tearing the boat (or its superstructure) to pieces, or without extensive disassembly of the engine. This is sometimes academic, however, because of the owner's insistence upon some cabin arrangement that will prevent engine removal; indeed, owners are generally unrealistic about the relative importance of a pet cabin arrangement and easy maintenance of a boat.

The propeller shaft should receive attention in a design and the location of the engine *must* allow 4 inches in the clear between the after end of the shaft-to-engine coupling and the forward face of the stuffing box, so that the gland of the latter may be backed off to repack. When the shaft is relatively short, as in an auxiliary yacht with engine aft of amidship, it is sufficient to support the shaft with a stuffing box inboard and a strut, or a stern bearing in the port, aft. Trick installations such as having the propeller abaft the rudder blade and a "shark's mouth" in the rudder blade to allow it to swing, or bearings abaft the propeller are best avoided if possible.

When the propeller shaft must be long, it may require support of bearings along its length. This may be decided by reference to handbooks or by the simple boatyard scale: the maximum span of unsupported shaft for up to 1 inch diameter shaft = 4 feet 6 inches;

$$1\tfrac{1}{4} \text{ inch} = 5 \text{ feet } 9 \text{ inches}$$
$$1\tfrac{1}{2} \text{ inch} = 6 \text{ feet } 3 \text{ inches}$$
$$1\tfrac{3}{4} \text{ inch} = 7 \text{ feet } 3 \text{ inches}$$
$$2 \text{ inch} = 8 \text{ feet } 3 \text{ inches}$$
$$2\tfrac{1}{4} \text{ inch} = 8 \text{ feet } 6 \text{ inches}$$
$$2\tfrac{1}{2} \text{ inch} = 9 \text{ feet } 3 \text{ inches}$$
$$2\tfrac{3}{4} \text{ inch} = 10 \text{ feet } 3 \text{ inches}$$
$$3 \text{ inch} = 10 \text{ feet } 6 \text{ inches}$$

In practice, the spacing of intermediate bearings should be determined not only by the length and diameter of the shaft but by structural members available, on hardwood blocks spanning two floor timbers, with the bearing between the floors, wherever possible. But as a rule the span of unsupported shaft should be within the range given here.

The desirability of "flexible couplings" in a propeller shaft is determined by two factors—the total length of shaft required and the probable rigidity of the hull. Lightly built and long, shallow hulls about 40 feet length, with an engine well forward, often require one flexible coupling. The couplings available for the required horsepower range may be selected from the marine hardware catalogues, and in the process the need for a thrust bearing astern the flexible coupling will also be determined. The flexible coupling will permit deflection of hull and shaft without damaging the engine bearings or shaft bearings. The location of the flexible coupling should be between two support-bearings and at the point where maximum deflection may be expected. This is often close to the engine, because of its weight, and therefore it is common practice to place the flexible coupling a few feet abaft the engine coupling. The flexible coupling is also useful where, for some reason, precise alignment of the engine may be impractical. In locating all shaft bearings and the flexible coupling it should be remembered that these need periodical inspection and servicing, so it should be easily reached without a carpenter being required.

In designing a boat for power it is necessary not only to place the propeller to the best advantage but also to select the proper diameter and pitch. The selection of propellers is difficult and requires experience and calculation. In practice, many designers consult the engine manufacturer and accept his recommendations. Handbooks and text books on yacht design and naval architecture give methods of propeller selection, but without more data than is generally available for a small boat, the results are rarely precise, and as a result propellers are often replaced after trials are run on a boat. It is important, therefore, that there be room enough to allow the propeller diameter to be increased slightly should the selected or estimated wheel be unsatisfactory. There are times in which this is not possible, but a design so restricted is usually the result of careful development in which comparison data is available in sufficient scope to allow a very precise estimate.

The exhaust pipe and muffler should usually be shown in the plans, particularly for cruisers. When the exhaust line must pass through a cabin there is need for careful detailing and projection in the construction sections. In sailing hulls the danger of flooding the engine through the exhaust must never be forgotten. But in any boat this is always a possibility, to be avoided by proper design. The author's book, *Boatbuilding*, shows details of power installations. A designer soon learns that he should begin thinking about the exhaust pipe, steering cables, piping and engine problems when he is drawing his preliminary studies for a design, since that is when he often creates problems that will plague him in the final drawings, if he is not foresighted enough. He plans on which side he will place the exhaust line, and where the steering cables will be, and marks his sketch as a memorandum. In laying out exhaust lines, the rule is not to make 90° turns in a short radius but rather in a series of 45° turns, appreciably separated by straight nipples or short lengths of pipe—in any case, as few bends in the line as is possible. Protect the occupants of the boat from contact with an exhaust pipe, even when "lagged." Use hose or corrugated lengths of pipe for flexibility and as a protection against failure through fatigue due to vibration. Cool the exhaust as soon as possible after it leaves the engine. If a "dry" exhaust is employed it must be very short indeed. Leave the engine "high" and the boat "low." Using a loop, or a "standpipe," prevent flooding of the engine through the exhaust line. Have the exhaust line so it can be quickly drained either of water or condensate. Common black iron pipe and fittings are usually specified. Steam hose is used for flexible pipe after the line is cooled, corrugated flexible unions before.

Corrugated flexible unions should be placed at engine in a well-designed exhaust line of any marked length, but this is rarely done and, as a result, cracked manifold flanges are common. Usually cooling water is entered into the line before the muffler receives the gas. The muffler can be omitted and a quiet exhaust, within reason, obtained. One way is to have a short length of inner tube over the outboard end of the exhaust, long enough so that it folds across the outlet when no gas is passing through. This is a check valve against flooding as well as quieting the exhaust—an old bootlegging trick. The standpipe also acts as a muffler to some extent. Large quantities of cold water passed through the exhaust pipe also quiets the exhaust. The outlet of an exhaust should be close to the L.W.L. at rest, as stain will appear and cannot be avoided. Exhaust lines must be well supported, otherwise noise will result. Supports should be 2 to 4 feet apart. Never support exhaust lines from deck, as this causes drumming. The muffler should be supported independently of the rest of the line and should never be supported only by the line. Water-jacketed exhaust pipe is very expensive. Copper exhaust lines are also very expensive but have the advantage of light weight, and some advantage over iron in length of usefulness. In cruisers, exhaust pipes should have insulation where they pass through woodwork even when "cooled." Common "lagging" or insulation of exhaust piping is done by mixing ground asbestos with a little plaster of paris (a teaspoon of the latter to a pound of the former), and plastering the pipe with the mixture. The mixture is held by iron chicken wire wrapped around the pipe as reinforcing, or with a sheet metal jacket in small boats with canvas sewn over the lagging.

Steering cables should run as directly as possible; the more "bends," the more sheaves—and the more power required to operate a steering gear. In many designs it is the custom to employ a quadrant at the head of the rudder port. This requires careful lining up of the quarter sheaves, and if the post is not plumb there may be lead difficulties. In general it is more practical and less expensive to use a tiller and blocks at the quarter that adjust themselves to the changing lead. By placing a single-sheave block on the tiller, and leading the bitter-end of the cable to a becket on the quarter-block, or to an eyebolt nearby, the power is increased. Turnbuckles for adjusting tension in cables should be located where they can be easily reached. It is usually desirable to lay out the steering cable in a rough sketch in order to write a specification; if the lead is long, it should be drawn to scale in order to place fair-leaders and blocks properly. There is no need here to describe every type of steering gear, for the requirements for each are established in marine hardware catalogs, or in manufacturer's brochures. It is necessary, however, to warn the amateur designer that strains on steering gears mount rapidly, with the speed of the boat. Therefore a strong, simple and easily repaired or adjusted steering gear should always be the objective.

Electrical layouts are employed only in designs for large yachts. They would be useful, however, if a small boat has a number of electronic devices requiring individual circuits. The designer should be guided by the manufacturers specification for each electronic device. Only marine cables should be used for mains, and all wiring should be placed where it can be inspected. Specifications of the classification societies are sound guides.

Ventilation is very important in yacht design. Normally, in small craft, it is of the natural type and is accomplished by correctly opening hatch and skylights or by cowl and clam-shell vents. The ventilation by natural draft in a boat is from the openings at the after end of a cabin to the fore end openings, particularly when at anchor, no matter what the wind direction. Therefore hatches and skylights are the most effective since their areas are so large. Vents less than 3 inches diameter are of little value.

Powered mechanical ventilation is usually restricted to the use of blowers in the engine compartment or engine room in compliance with legal requirements. Non-sparking motors are a must and the electric blowers must be placed so that air in the engine-space bilge is exhausted quickly. There are usually intake and exhaust blowers, both leading to the bilge with sheet-metal exhaust pipes. These pipes should be as straight and as direct as possible. Elbows, bends and horizontals slow down the rate of flow very sharply.

Fire prevention equipment should be specified for cruisers of any size, of course. In his plans the designer should show where extinguishers are to be placed—and place them as effectively as possible with due regard to local fire dangers in the boat. Thus there should be a fire extinguisher near the galley stove, at the companionway or galley door—*not over* the stove! Similarly, there should be a suitable extinguisher at the engine-space hatch or door, or near the engine box. No cruiser having an engine of any kind should be without a fire extinguisher. Mechanically operated fire extinguishing systems must meet legal safety requirements now being enforced by the U. S. Coast Guard.

The drawings of the "lines" is the next step in the production of the design of a yacht.

III. The Lines

Relation of Preliminary Sketch and Lines

THE shape of the hull of a vessel is shown in the drawing usually referred to as the "lines"; old-time shipbuilders called it the "draught" or "sheer draught." In this plan the shape of the hull is represented by a series of sections taken through the hull at locations chosen by the draftsman; these sections are longitudinal, transverse, horizontal and vertical, in order that the hull-form may be strictly defined. The drawing of the lines is the operation of determining the shapes of these sections and of bringing them into proper relation to one another.

The preliminary sketch has fixed, to a great extent, the form which the lines must represent. It is obvious that the lines must enclose and distribute space to suit the desired arrangement; this is the first practical consideration. The example chosen to illustrate the consideration of design, in the first chapter, encompasses a number of problems met in practical yacht design. The specifications laid down by the owner do not require repetition; it is sufficient to point out that these requirements are the designer's aim, rather than the obtaining of an ideal hull-form for speed or some other sailing quality with accommodation a mere afterthought, as some amateurs seem to think. This may seem an obvious proposition, but text-books and magazine articles relating to yacht design have approached the subject of the lines as if it were merely a matter of obtaining an ideal hull-form for speed or other sailing quality.

Calculation and Design

Some writers and students claim that hull-form, in the lines, can be determined by the use of some mathematical formulae based on a theory of resistance; others resort to the pseudo-scientific "average proportions" as expressed in graphs and co-efficients. These methods seem to simplify the problem but, as sole guides for forming the lines, they are wholly false since they do not take into consideration the exacting requirements of hull-type, rig and accommodation. It is important that it be understood that there are no "scientific facts" in regard to the form that lines should take; there are some rules that seem to be useful but they must be accepted as "theories that seem to work in practice with but minor qualifications."

Methods of hull-formation based on calculation or mathematical expression assume that there is some fixed proportion or inflexible rule of form that will apply to all types of craft, without regard to hull-type, rig, size or intended employment. It would be bootless to waste time detailing the error of such an assumption; even the most casual inspection of a number of successful yachts shows wide variations in elements of form. The inability of mathematical methods to express more than a single element in hull-form, such as the amount of displacement or center of gravity, leaves the designer but one alternative: to resort to graphic exploration by means of trial projections, assisted by a limited number of simple calculations, when drawing the lines. From the foregoing, it is apparent that the forming of the lines is far more of an art than a mere engineering problem, to be solved by calculations alone.

In spite of the obvious error of assuming that there are fixed proportions or inflexible rules of form, many mathematical methods of hull-formation have been in vogue, in the past, among the so-called "scientific" yacht designers. Among the many theories of this class, Chapman's theory of mathematically constructed diagonals, Scott Russel's "wave-line" form of waterlines and Colin Archer's similarly formed "curve of area" theory have been hailed as the most "scientific." These are now considered obsolete and an explanation of their construction and application would be only of historical interest. Mechanical methods of forming the lines also deserve mention; these are usually based on a single form of curve constructed mechanically or mathematically, such as the parabola. Obviously, mechanical methods of hull-formation limit all hulls to one form, regardless of size or other considerations. Theories of these types fascinate amateurs because they employ involved calculation, the logic of which few understand. The more involved and difficult the calculation, and the more difficult the logic of such a calculation is to understand, the more "scientific" the result is considered, apparently. Before wasting time in the development of such theories, the beginner should consider the practical rule that no one hull-form will be suitable for all conditions, types, rigs, dimensions or speeds.

Limitations of Considerations

The matters that enter into the designer's operations in the drawing of the lines are limited, for most of the hull requirements have been fixed in the preliminary sketch. The matters that concern the lines, however, are of the utmost importance in such matters as seaworthiness, balance and speed. Seaworthiness is decided by form, to a great extent, as is speed. Both of these matters are, therefore, considerations in the shaping of the various sections that make up the lines. Balance is a matter of distribution of such factors as structural weight, displacement and area; this is the element that is most easily expressed mathematically.

Speed and Resistance

Generally speaking, speed is the most interesting technical element to the designer, when he is considering the lines, for it is far more elusive than seaworthiness or balance. Since speed is a comparative quality, a standard of measurement is necessary. The most popular is the speed-length ratio mentioned earlier, found by dividing the highest observed speed, in knots, by the square-root of the waterline length. The result is the speed-length coefficient, an index of comparison. The highest speed in knots of a sailing yacht, of the rather heavy displacement type represented by seagoing keel cruisers, may be expressed by multiplying the square-root of the waterline length by the coefficient 1.25, *i. e.*, $\sqrt{\text{L.W.L.}}$ length $\times$ 1.25. In exceptional cases the coefficient has been as high as 1.455; the theoretical limit of speed of a given length of hull of this class being expressed by the coefficient 1.50. In practice, however, few sailing yachts show greater speed-length ratios than 1.25, except in the cases of hull-forms that tend to plane when traveling very fast, such as the scow and sharpie types. These types have been observed at speeds greater than expressed by the coefficient 1.50. Catamarans, flying proas, and other light displacement types having abnormal power to carry sail, also develop speeds whose coefficients are greater than the theoretical limit. The importance of waterline length in a comparison of the speed of yachts is illustrated by this standard, however. The only practical value of this ratio, outside of being an index of comparison, is that it indicates the maximum speed that can reasonably be expected on a given waterline length. It must be understood that mere possession of extra waterline length does not indicate a fast hull; few yachts can reach their theoretical speed-length ratio, since some are of improper form for speed, others lack power to carry sail in a breeze that would enable them to reach their maximum possible speed, or have hulls or rigs that will not stand the structural strains of such conditions.

Speed-length ratio in power boat design shows a greater range than in sailing craft, of course. Auxiliaries of the cruising type rarely exceed 1.0; burdensome motor cruisers of the fisherman type, and utility boats, commonly run in a range of .9 to 1.3; fast cruisers and open boats of the round bottom displacement models operate in a range of about 1.2 to 2.6, while semi-planing and planing hulls run in the range above 2.5. Few pleasure boats, excepting out-and-out racers, operate in speed-length ratios above 3.5. Speed-length ratio has little usefulness as a means of comparison in planing models and is therefore usually resorted to only when comparing displacement-hulls.

So far as the lines are concerned, speed is governed by the resistance the hull encounters in moving through the water. Resistance is made up of a combination of factors; the most important are skin friction, eddy-making and wave-making. Skin friction is created by the adhesion of particles of water to the submerged skin of the hull; skin friction is of importance at low speed. Obviously, the ways that the effects of skin friction can be combated would be to make the submerged skin, or wetted-surface, as smooth as possible and to reduce the area of wetted-surface as much as displacement will allow. In recent years much has been made of the desirability of reducing wetted-surface to a minimum, hence the cutaway underbody of modern yachts. It must be observed, however, that some of the reputed reduction of wetted-surface claimed for modern yacht hull-forms is purely imaginary when comparison is on the basis of actual displacement. The wetted-surface of the hull that is required to enclose the cubic contents of a given displacement is large, compared to that required for the deadwood, rudder, or centerboard, as a rule. Theoretically, the hull with the least wetted-surface should be the fastest in light weather, but in practice it is found that drifting ability is not to be obtained by the simple expedient of reducing wetted-surface. It seems reasonable to suppose that the skin friction is not equally effective at all portions of the wetted-surface; thus wetted-surface in the forebody might be less objectionable than that in the afterbody, but as yet no acceptable theory in regard to this appears to have been developed.

Eddy-making and wave-making are the disturbances of bodies of water caused by the movement of the hull. In creating these disturbances, force is expended that would otherwise be adding speed to the hull. The visible effects of these disturbances are the wake and bow wave, as well as the disturbance alongside, seen when a hull is being driven at high speed. These visible effects, by their violence, indicate in a general way the amount of energy consumed in wave and eddy-making. Both forces are difficult to measure or analyze accurately, but are the most important factors in resistance when speed is high. Eddy-making and wave-making are controlled to some extent by the shapes of certain sections in the lines, such as the buttock lines and waterlines, and by the shape of all entering and trailing edges. The distribution of displacement in the hull may also influence resistance created by these forces; these matters will be treated in detail when the operations of drawing the lines are described.

These simple explanations of resistance cannot be considered as completely covering this complicated and only partly-explored subject. Those who wish to investigate the subject further are referred to standard text-books on theoretical naval architecture and to the reports of technical societies. In spite of the many years of experiment and study of resistance, it is still impossible to calculate which of two hulls, alike in dimensions but differing slightly in form, will develop the less resistance (and therefore the greater speed). For this reason it is necessary to resort to towing scale-models in specially constructed tanks before the most satisfactory form can be chosen. Unfortunately, this is an expensive operation and, as a result, this experiment is practical only with large and expensive vessels. Still more unfortunately, the towing tests must be repeated after every minor change in model, for no other means of obtaining accurate information is possible.

Trim, "Boat Sense" and Proportion

The Colin Archer theory of "wave-line" form of curve of areas has been mentioned; this was an attempt to fix the distribution of displacement by a predetermined limitation in which the submerged area of each station or cross-section was fixed before the lines were drawn. This method seemed to have some advantage but it was found that strict adherence to the theory was impractical in all forms of hull, with the result that the "exceptions" became so numerous that the theory lost form. In modern practice, therefore, the distribution of displacement is rarely predetermined; the designer depends wholly on his judgment of hull-form to obtain the desired results. An observant designer soon develops a sense of proportion so accurate that he can judge by eye alone whether or not the lines show the proper distribution of displacement. In fact some designers can make a very accurate estimate of displacement shown in the lines; judging whether or not there is a sufficient amount shown without resort to calculation. This does not mean that they omit any useful calculation necessary to check their judgment, but that their sense of proportion is sufficiently accurate for guiding the first steps in the formation of the lines. This sense of proportion is not an inherited gift; it is obtained by long study of lines, models and completed yachts. It can only be compared to the similar sense of proportion that aids the sculptor, the painter and the architect in creative work. There is no mechanical method nor mode of calculation that can replace this feeling for "form"; and the student should use every opportunity to study hull-form in order that he may obtain what is best described, perhaps, as "boat sense." The use of cardboard half-models will be found helpful to the beginner in the study of form. (See Appendix.)

There need be no calculation prior to drawing the lines; unless the design is for an unballasted type, or unless the ballast is to be *wholly* outside. In either of these two cases, a trim calculation should be made to ascertain the approximate center of gravity so that the ballast and the displacement may be properly distributed in drawing the lines. For the sake of clarity, in the example chosen, the lines will be drawn and hull-form discussed in detail, then trim and other useful calculations will be explained.

The lines will solve, as far as the owner's requirements and the designer's skill will permit, the problems of speed, seaworthiness and weatherliness; the calculations will enable the amount and position of the ballast to be determined, the amount of displacement to be obtained and other matters that are necessary in order that the hull may float on her designed waterline. It must be observed that there are no methods of calculation that will give certain information about the performance of a yacht under sail; this matter is the acid test of the designer's "boat sense."

Working Up Sketches for Lines

The hull profile developed in the preliminary sketch must be reproduced in the lines. The first step, therefore, is to divide the waterline length of the hull, on the preliminary drawing, into equal parts, say ten, and to erect perpendiculars. It is customary to use ten equal parts, but this varies with the method employed in the calculation for displacement; for the present it will suffice to say that the Simpson Rule requires an equal division, or an odd number of stations, while the Trapezoidal Rule may be used with either an even or an odd number of stations or ordinates. The last-named rule works best if the stations or ordinates are fairly close together; it also requires less numerical work. There is no great difference in the accuracy of the two rules, but since the Simpson Rule is commonly used in this country it will be employed in the example.

Dividing the waterline in the sketch into ten equal parts, eleven stations or ordinates are obtained. The length of the waterline is 33'-4"; dividing this by 10, the spacing of the ordinates is found to be 3'-4", or 3.325' exactly. The fore and aftermost stations or ordinates are located at the extremes of the load-waterline as a rule; when the lines are to be faired to the rabbet, instead of to the face of the stem and to the trailing edge of the sternpost, many designers take the length of the load-waterline as being from rabbet to rabbet. At the proper intervals on the load waterline in the sketch the ordinate or station lines are drawn in pencil on both elevation and plan views. These station lines, it is understood, are perpendicular to the load-waterline in the elevation and to the centerline in the plan view. It is not uncommon to find that the ordinate spacing works out at some inconvenient dimension, say 3.9' (3'-10¹³⁄₁₆"). In such cases the ordinates should be spaced at the nearest "convenient" dimension which should be in even feet and inches; or feet, inches and fourths. The excess or shortage of length caused by this arbitrary spacing is thrown into the end spaces. Example: calculated spacing 3.9' (3'-10¹³⁄₁₆"), proper spacing 3'-11", with the end spaces 3'-10". In the calculations, however, it is proper to assume the stations to have been located at the calculated distances apart.

Next a series of lines are drawn parallel to the load-waterline, above and below it, on the elevation in the preliminary sketch. The distance these lines should be apart should not exceed 12". If the hull is to be "hard-bilged" the spacing should be closer in the vicinity of the turn of the bilge (the turn of the bottom

into the side of the hull seen when the cross-sections are projected). These lines are the "waterlines" and will be developed
as horizontal sections in the lines. While the scale to which the
lines are to be drawn may be considered in spacing the waterlines, the size of the hull is the best general guide. The following
spacing suggestions will follow general practice. Boats under
16 feet, waterlines spaced 3 or 4 inches (or half the draft of
water); boats up to 24 feet in length, waterlines spaced 4 to 6
inches apart; larger hulls, waterlines spaced 6 to 12 inches. It
is good practice to space the waterlines in even inches; if intermediate waterlines are to be used, as suggested at the turn of
the bilge, their spacing ought to be half that used above and
below.

As an illustration, the example to be drawn will have waterlines spaced 12" apart except that there will be intermediate
waterlines 6" apart above and below the load-waterline; making
three waterlines above the load-waterline and three below, seven
in all. The designer must decide, in all cases, whether or not
additional waterlines should be drawn on the sketch in order
that enough measurements may be obtained to correctly en-
large the profile; the same consideration should apply to the
spacing of ordinates.

Scale of Lines

The lines drawing may now be started. The first question is
that of scale. The scale to which the lines should be drawn depends upon the size of the boat, and also upon the size of the
drawing-board that is available. Subject to the last condition,
the scale of the lines may be decided from these suggestions—
the lines drawing should be drawn to as small a scale as accuracy
permits; it is easier to judge the shape and fairness of a set of
lines on a small size plan than on a large size plan. The actual
length of the hull in a lines drawing of a yacht under 60 feet
should not exceed 40 inches. Large scale lines are liable to show
undesirable proportions or distribution of elements when seen
reduced in size because of the impossibility of the eye being able

to see a large drawing as a whole. With these considerations as a guide, a proper scale for a set of lines may be chosen. For very small boats a scale of 1½″ equals one foot will serve; while hulls up to 30 feet in length may be drawn on 1″ equals one foot. Larger hulls can be drawn on ¾″, ½″, ⅜″ or ¼″ scales. Builders prefer drawings to the ⅜″ or ¾″ scales since measurements on such drawings may be lifted off with an ordinary carpenter's rule (using ¹⁄₁₆″ as 2″ on the ⅜″ scale; and as 1″ on the ¾″ scale). The example used to develop the drawing of the lines in this chapter was drawn to ½″ scale.

Starting the Lines

A piece of drawing paper of suitable size is now tacked to the drawing-board and a horizontal line, to represent the load-waterline, is drawn. At the distances determined on the preliminary sketch, the perpendicular ordinates are erected: great care being taken that these ordinates are accurately spaced and that they are perpendicular to the waterline. The ordinates may be extended the full height of the paper. Next, the waterlines, above and below the load line, are drawn at the spacing determined in the preliminary sketch. Here again great accuracy is necessary; the spacing must be accurate and the waterlines must be parallel. Then, at a distance below the load line equal to or greater than the draft of the hull, another line parallel to the load line is drawn; this may be used as a base line for spacing frames and from which offset heights may be measured or may be used as the base line for laying off diagonals. Next, at a distance below this last line, a little greater than half the greatest beam of the proposed hull, another line is drawn; parallel to the load waterline also. This last line will be used as the center-line for the "half-breadth" plan or plan view.

In spacing lines for stations and so forth, it is most accurate to add the distance between lines progressively and set the sums off along the base or vertical by means of a long scale rule.

Example:
Station   0 to 1 = 3-4

0 to 2 = 6-8
0 to 3 = 10-0
0 to 4 = 13-4
etc.

It is not practical to achieve accuracy by spacing with dividers or repeated scalings of the single spacings. A pricker can be very useful in spacing off stations and waterlines with the scale rule.

Laying Out Deck Line

Referring to the sketch, scale off the greatest beam and note it. In the example the greatest beam is about 11'-4". Take one-fourth of the greatest beam (2'-10" in the example); lay off a line parallel to the lowest line (centerline of the half-breadth plan) on the new plan and above it; the distance between the two lines to be equal to one-fourth the greatest beam. This new line will represent the "quarter-beam buttock" in the half-breadth plan. The spacing of the quarter-beam buttock from the centerline should be arbitrarily fixed at even feet and inches, nearest the calculated distance. Now other buttock lines may be drawn, all parallel to the centerline and quarter-beam buttock in the half-breadth plan. The spacing of these can be decided by the space between the quarter-beam buttock and the centerline. The number of buttocks required should be decided by the degree of flatness in the bottom; the flatter the bottom of the hull the more buttocks required. The spacing of the buttocks ought to be in even inches, and need not be less than that of the waterlines, and the buttock farthest from the centerline need not be at a point greater than three-quarters the distance between centerline and point of greatest beam. Three buttock lines, 1'-5" apart, are considered sufficient for the example. The buttock lines will be developed as longitudinal sections, perpendicular to the line of flotation. If the ordinates have not been drawn clear across the paper they should be projected down to the lowest line on the drawing.

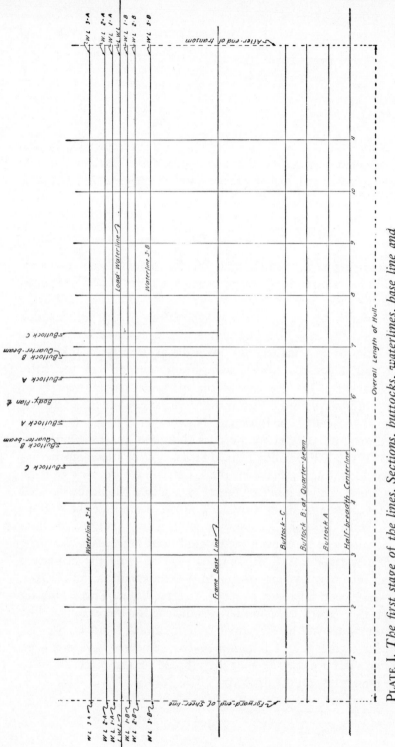

PLATE I. *The first stage of the lines. Sections, buttocks, waterlines, base line and centerline drawn.*

Body-plan

Numbering the ordinates from the stem, choose station #5 or #6 as the centerline of the "body-plan," which will be super-imposed over the profile or elevation. Draw lines perpendicular to the waterlines and parallel to the chosen ordinate, to each side of it; these will represent the buttock lines and must be spaced from the centerline as in the half-breadth plan just de-scribed. The "body-plan" will show the cross-sections, or trans-verse sections, of the hull; these are planes cutting the hull per-pendicular to the waterlines in the elevation and perpendicular to the centerline in plan.

Accuracy

Plate I shows the drawing at this state of development and the lines just described may be identified by reference to it. The importance of locating these lines with all possible accuracy cannot be too strongly emphasized; errors in spacing waterlines, ordinates or buttocks will make it impossible to fair the lines correctly. It will be found desirable to ink in all these lines and it may help if colored inks are used; say the load-waterline is drawn in black, other waterlines in blue, the buttock lines in red and the ordinate or section lines in black. The centerline of the half-breadth plan should likewise be drawn with black ink; also the base line. All lines must be sharp and fine to insure ac-curacy of measurement.

After these lines are inked in and the whole has been checked for accuracy in spacing, the profile of the hull may be drawn, carefully scaled and enlarged from the preliminary sketch. Since the stations and waterlines have been reproduced on the sketch, the profile of the hull can be laid down accurately on the lines, to scale. Great care is necessary in order to reproduce exactly the curves of the bow, stern, keel and sheer. It may prove de-sirable to employ temporary ordinates and waterlines at the ends of the hull, drawn in pencil, in order to obtain exactness in the enlargement. From the preliminary sketch the sheer line (use the underside of the rail-cap as the sheer in the lines), the bottom of the keel (and usually the rabbet as well), and the profile of the bow and of the stern are reproduced on the lines, in the elevation. The outline of the deck is reproduced in the half-breadth of the lines, laid down from measurements lifted from the deck plan in the preliminary sketch. It is understood that the same line used as the sheer line in the elevation must be used as the sheer line in the half-breadth plan, or plan view.

Half-breadth of Keel and Posts

Now the half-breadth of the keel must be decided upon. The breadth or thickness of the keel is not only a consideration in the lines but also a matter of great importance in the construction plan. It is impossible to lay down any rule for fixing the thickness of the keel; this matter can only be decided by the type of hull and the method of construction to be employed. Perhaps the best guide for the beginner is the clipping file, where he can see what is generally done in the particular hull-type he is using. It will be found that when outside ballast is used in quantity the keel must be wide enough for strength and to allow the keel bolts to be staggered. In centerboarders, the keel is usually wide enough along the centerboard case to allow room for fastening the frames to it in a secure manner. It is usual to taper the keel fore-and-aft; the stem and sternpost having less thickness than the keel. Very often the stem and sternpost taper as well, the heads being thicker than the heels. Sometimes, however, the keel in centerboarders is narrow and the centerboard slot is placed alongside, in one garboard. This does not harm sailing qualities and is economical, in large craft particularly. The example shows the tapered keel and tapered stem and sternposts as well. The width of the keel, in any hull, should not be more than 12″ if possible. Timber exceeding 12″ in width is usually very expensive and the specifying of timber of greater width will add to the cost of construction. On the other hand, the keel should not be so narrow as to be weak; a narrow keel combined

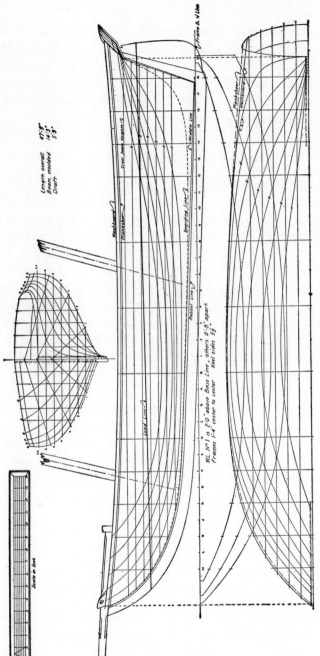

Length overall 47'5"
Beam, moulded 14'3"
Draft 5'3"

Scale in Feet

Lines of a schooner-yacht, the Dream, built at New York City, in 1833, by Isaac Webb; showing lines drawn to inside of planking, old-fashioned upper and lower transoms, flaring topsides, straight rise of floor, greatest beam for'd of mid-length and straight keel. Ballast all inside. Sawn frames. Note that "cross seam" is the bottom of the lower transom at rabbet of post.

with even a moderate amount of outside ballast may result in leaky garboards. Only in hulls having no ballast outside should very narrow keels be employed; in such craft a hull of 45 feet overall may have a keel of but 5″ thickness (or "siding") but a hull of similar size having outside ballast would require a keel siding at least 8″, usually more.

Inside and Outside of Plank

It is now the custom to draw the lines to the outside of the planking; in former times the lines were drawn to the inside of the planking. The latter type of drawing is the best from the builder's point of view but makes calculation difficult and requires a knowledge of loft work that few amateurs possess. It is also a custom, in yachts at least, to fair the lines to the face of the stem and sternpost; the rabbet line being projected to the sheer plan from intersections obtained in the half-breadth plan. Except that it is the fashion, there is no advantage in fairing the lines to the face of the stem over fairing to the rabbet. In clipper-bowed craft, and most full-ended hulls, it is better to fair to the rabbet in order that there be enough wood outside the rabbet to give the proper appearance to the stem and to protect the ends of the planking at the rabbet. The example is to be faired to the rabbet, the method of fairing to the face of the stem and of projecting the rabbet will be explained later. If the lines are to be faired to the face of the stem and sternpost, in the modern fashion, it is usual to fair the sections in the body-plan to the bottom of the keel; if this is done the rabbet (line of intersection of the outside face of the planking with the outside face of the keel, stem and sternpost) is not drawn until the rest of the lines are projected and fair.

Locating Greatest Keel Half-breadth and Rabbet

Returning to the example, the width of keel was fixed at 11″ and the half-breadth of the keel was laid down, using the lowest line (centerline of the half-breadth plan) as the centerline of the keel. The location of the widest part of the keel was fixed

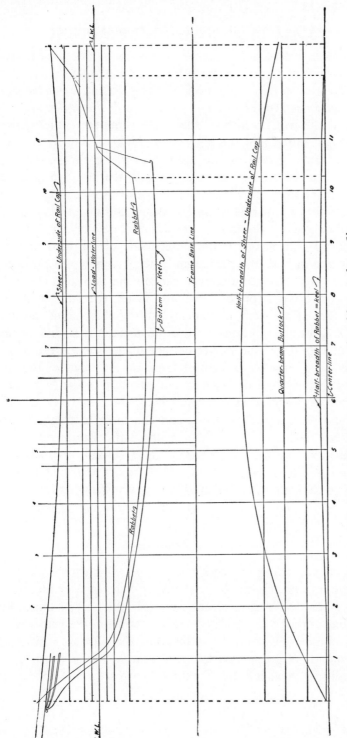

PLATE II. The second stage of the lines. Sheer, bottom of keel, rabbet, and profile of stem and stern drawn in the Sheer Elevation; the half-breadth of the sheer and rabbet in the Half-breadth Plan.

by the location of the centerboard on the preliminary sketch. The taper of the keel was fixed by eye, care being taken not to have the keel so thin at the heels of the stem and sternpost as to cause weakness. In the example the half-breadth of the keel was taken as the half-breadth of the rabbet line; were the sections of the hull faired into the bottom of the keel, the latter would be laid down instead of the rabbet, assuming the bottom and sides of the keel to meet at an angle until the keel can be faired off on the body-plan sections. When the profile, deck-outline and half-breadth of rabbet are laid down and inked in with fine lines, the drawing should have the appearance of Plate II. It will be noticed that the sheer line (underside of rail-cap) and the rabbet line in both the profile and the plan view are projected to their "fair" intersection, even though the bulwarks are to be cut away forward for the bowsprit. When the lines are faired to the face of the stem, the half-breadth of the face of the stem and the sheer line intersect in the same manner. It is obvious that the half-breadth of the rabbet or face of the stem at the height of the sheer must be decided at the time the taper of the keel is fixed. It is not out of place to call attention to the fact that it is highly improper to assume the face of the stem to be a knife-edge and to fair the waterlines and the sheer to points on the centerline in the half-breadth plan; the half-breadth of the face of the stem and sternpost *must* be fixed (usually not less than ⅜″ full width to take a stem band) before the lines may be faired to the face of the stem in the now popular fashion.

Shape of Midsection

The next steps in the design are to lay down the midsection and the transom (in the body-plan), and the quarter-beam buttock aft and the load-waterline forward (the quarter-beam buttock line in the profile and the load-waterline in the half-breadth plan). These will control the shape of the hull, to a great extent, and are of great importance. Hereafter, the forward half of the hull will be called the "forebody," the after half the "afterbody." The midsection is drawn in with the ordinate chosen as the centerline of the body-plan as its centerline. The shape of the transom, viewed from dead astern, is also drawn on the same centerline, only one-half of the transom being drawn. The quarter-beam buttock is next drawn, on the sheer elevation (profile). Then the load-waterline, from the midsection to the stem, is drawn on the half-breadth or plan view. Plate II shows the appearance of the drawing when these lines are completed. So much for the general directions, now for the specific explanation of each step.

First, the midsection must be discussed and drawn. The shape of the midsection is governed, to a great extent, by the type of hull and the system of ballasting to be employed. It is difficult to detail every conceivable shape of midsection; the best guide for the beginner is comparison with plans in his clipping file. In such comparison, the designer should ask himself certain questions:

1. Does the new design require greater or less displacement than the design in the clipping file?

2. Is there to be greater or less sail area in the new design than in the one it is being compared with?

3. How much cabin floor space (width) is required amidships; deducting the thickness of planking, frames and ceiling?

4. Is the ballast to be all outside, partly so, or all inside: will the quantity in any case be greater or less than in the design used for comparison?

5. Has the new design more or less beam than the old design: has it more or less depth?

In making comparisons of this nature it is important that the general dimensions of the new and old design are reasonably similar and that the hull types are of the same general form, of course.

Answers to the foregoing questions will give an idea of the form of midsection required. The procedure is something like this—

1. If more displacement is required, the midsection may have a harder turn at the bilge; less rise to the floor (that is, less sharpness to the bottom in cross-section); less hollow near the rabbet; or greater beam at the load-waterline (using tumble-home topsides perhaps), thus increasing the submerged body. If the displacement is to be less, the rise of floor may be increased; the hollow at the garboards greater; the turn of the bilge softened; or the breadth of the load-waterline decreased (using flaring topsides if desired), thus decreasing the submerged body. Any one of these methods of increasing or decreasing the submerged area of the midsection may be employed, or any combination of methods, in order that the designer's needs may be met. It is as important that over-displacement be avoided as it is that under-displacement should not exist; therefore the designer ought to use the greatest caution in deciding this question.

2. If the new design is to carry a greater sail-area than the one it is being compared with, it is usually best to harden the bilge, fill out the garboards so that more ballast can be carried inside, or to increase the beam at the load-waterline. If less sail is to be carried then the procedure may be the opposite, of course.

3. Let the cabin floor width, required by the arrangement, fix the breadth of the hull at the depth of the cabin floor below the load-waterline.

4. If the ballast is all inside, the hollow at the garboard (lowest plank of the skin of the hull; at the rabbet, in other words) should be very slight, as a rule, in order to allow enough room below the cabin floor for the ballast and for the necessary construction members of the hull. If the ballast is to be partly inside the hollow may be fairly marked, unless the proportion of ballast inside is to be great. If the ballast is all outside or nearly so then the hollow of the garboards may be as great as the designer thinks best. Further, it should be observed that the bulk of the area of the midsection (and therefore the bulk of the displacement of the hull as a whole) should be near the waterline since in this way stability and power to carry sail are increased.

The deep U-section form of midsection is always undesirable since it creates hulls lacking in these qualities. If the rise of floor (deadrise) is to be very great, it is well to employ a little hollow in the garboards in order to keep the vertical "bulk of area" as high as possible. Straight rise of floor, as represented in V-bottom hulls, does not seem to be satisfactory if the deadrise exceeds 30° from the horizontal. Extremely thick keels and marked full-ness at the garboards are undesirable features in the midsections of deep draft sailing craft.

5. If the beam is to be greater in the new design than in the one it is being compared with (supposing the depth and sail-area to be about the same) it is plain that the displacement must be kept from increasing. This may be accomplished by employing very flaring topsides or by the use of slack bilges. On the other hand, if the beam is to be less the bilges should be harder and it may also be necessary to obtain more room for ballast, if it is to be inside, or to increase the hollow at the garboard (thus de-creasing the sharpness of the rise of floor) if the ballast is to be outside in order that stability may not be lacking. If the depth is less in the new design, then the bilges may be harder (usually this increases the beam at the load-waterline somewhat), but if the depth is to be greater then the bilges should be slacker, pro-viding the displacement is to be approximately the same.

It is necessary to call attention to the fact that it may be de-sirable to add to the displacement of a design in order to obtain additional stability through increased ballast. In cases where such procedure is necessary it is most satisfactory if the addi-tional displacement be obtained by the hardening of the bilges or increase of beam at the load-waterline; in short, the increase in displacement should be as near the load-waterline as possible. It should be noted, however, that the element of size has some im-portance in this consideration; large craft, such as the big cruis-ing schooners exceeding 70 feet in length, should have rather easy or slack bilges in order that they may not have a snap at each end of their roll. Hard-bilged craft of this size not only have a jerky roll, but also such designs usually have a quick roll as well; either of which is uncomfortable to crew and guests as well as hard on spars and rigging.

Some compromises in the foregoing considerations will undoubtedly prove necessary; usually the designer may draw his midsection by means of the reasoning just outlined, then he modifies the shape of the section as his judgment directs. If he is following some particular type of hull, such as the Cape Cat, Friendship Sloop, or other local model, the choice of midsection becomes strictly limited and the range of alteration or compromise slight. In reference to sailing V-bottom hulls, the greatest speed is developed when the deadrise is comparatively slight; therefore such midsection forms should be limited to centerboard or fin-keel types of light displacement. A round, barrelshape or U-section midsection should be avoided at all costs; there should be some straightness to the rise of floor between the rabbet or hollow of the garboard and the turn of the bilges. The length of straight line shown in the rise of floor of the midsection need not be very great; it might be observed that the greater the stability required the longer the straightness of line in the rise of floor should be. In shoal hulls there is usually little or no hollow at the garboards; the topsides often flare a great deal. When the midsection is designed it is not uncommon to draw both sides to show the full section, the idea being that it is easier to fair the lines by so doing. This is largely a matter of opinion and the beginner may do so or not, as he thinks best.

Location of Midsection

It has been assumed that the location of the midsection was fixed by the placing of the greatest beam on deck in the preliminary sketch. It is common practice to use the point of greatest beam on deck as the midsection, though there are numerous exceptions to this custom. It is desirable, therefore, to discuss this matter in some detail since it was barely mentioned in Chapter II. In many modern yacht types the midsection has been arbitrarily located at some point between 52% and 55% of the waterline length abaft the stem. Here, sometimes, a false ordinate is drawn, to represent the designer's midsection in the body-plan. This station and its cross-section, used as the actual midsection, is employed only in the fairing of the lines, not in the calculations or in the construction; it is not always necessary to lay it down on the mould-loft floor or to give offsets for it. The designer should decide for himself whether or not such a section is necessary or helpful in his particular hull. Another method of treating the midsection is the use of what is known as the "raking midsection." This is designed, or rather, developed, by making the greatest breadth on each successive waterline a little farther aft than on the one below, when the hull is well cut away forward as in modern yacht hulls. In old-fashioned craft having the greatest beam on deck very far forward, the greatest beam on each successive waterline usually moved forward, coming up from the keel toward the deck. It will be seen that, in the case of the raking midsection, the point of greatest beam on deck is not the true location of the greatest actual beam, necessarily, though it is common practice to locate the midsection on the plans at the point of greatest beam on deck or at the rail.

The midsection of a power boat is treated in much the same manner as that of a sailing hull. However, the forms of motorboat midsections are limited in number, and in the majority of designs the floors are straight and rising amidships. The stability obtained in the midsection form of sailing hulls is not usually so important a consideration in motorboat hulls, for in the latter, particularly in the high speed models, the wide and usually rather flat afterbody gives ample stability. The raking midsection has been used in the example and it will be seen that either station #6 or #7 or a false station between might have been used as the midsection for fairing the lines. When the example is fully developed the raking midsection will be seen and its development understood. Station #7 is considered as the midsection in the example, for the purpose of fairing the lines. Displacement power boats usually have the midsection abaft the mid-length of waterline, usually about 51% to 55%, though the greatest beam on deck is well forward.

Drawing Midsection

Now for the actual drawing of the midsection; measure with the dividers or tick strip the depth from load-waterline to rabbet at the midsection in the sheer plan or elevation. Transfer this measurement to the centerline of the body-plan (if these do not coincide in the drawing). Then measure the freeboard, load-waterline to sheer line, in the elevation at the same station, and transfer this to the centerline of the body-plan also. At the points thus obtained on the centerline of the body-plan, square out the half-breadths of the sheer and rabbet lines as measured and transferred from the same station in the half-breadth or plan view. These measured points in the body-plan will be exactly the same in width from the centerline and in height and depth from the load-waterline as they are in the half-breadth and sheer plans. The points thus obtained are the fixed points of the midsection; between these two points of measurement the shape of the midsection may be drawn in to suit the eye of the designer and in accordance with the suggestions previously made.

Next, on the half-breadth or plan view, sweep in a curve, with the compasses, or with curves and sweeps, to represent the top of the transom in plan view. The amount of curve it is given is a matter of taste, but only a little is necessary; large vessels of 100 feet overall often have no more than nine or ten inches, measuring from the chord to the center of the arc. Now, project upward the point where the sheer line and the arc forming the top of the transom intersect in the half-breadth plan to the sheer line in the sheer elevation, or profile. This projection locates the after end of the sheer line in the profile, assuming the rake of the transom and its top to have been taken from the sketch at the centerline of the hull, since this is the extreme after end of the overall length. This projection will also fix the amount of freeboard at the intersection of the sheer with the transom, in the profile, though the amount should agree very closely with that shown in the preliminary sketch.

Transom

The next step will be to draw the elevation of the transom in the body-plan. The top of the transom is not drawn in this step. All that is needed is the outline of the transom, bottom to sheer or rail. It is understood that this is the apparent shape (not the true or expanded shape if the transom is raking); that is to say, the shape of the transom, as seen from dead astern, is drawn.

The shape of the transom is another detail where judgment must rule. Transom shapes might be roughly classed as being hard or soft bilged; that is, having a hard or an easy turn at the joining of sides and bottom. Usually hard-bilged transoms have rather flat bottoms, though this is not always true. As in the case of the midsection, the transom might have both deadrise and hard bilges. If the bilge of the transom is both hard and close to the waterline (as might be the case if there were little deadrise in the bottom of the transom, for example) it may cause a disturbed wake when the hull is sharply heeled; this condition represents increased drag or resistance. On the other hand, a transom lacking in bilges might represent a lack in bearings aft as well. Bearing, or stability, is much affected by the hardness of the bilges of the transom (which also represent the hardness of the bilges in the afterbody or "quarters"). Many modern yachts lack power to carry a press of sail in a breeze because their quarters are weak; that is, their afterbodies have been formed with overly slack bilges (particularly in the after quarter of the overall length) with regard to their models and proportions.

It follows, then, that these subjects, model of hull and hull proportions, are very important considerations in the design of the transom shape. It would be impossible to make hard and fast rules, but the following is offered as a guide to the beginner. Hulls having beam equal to or greater than one-fourth their overall length rarely sail at great angles of heel and hence may have "heavy" quarters; that is, hard and low bilges in the afterfourth of the overall length. For the same reason, shoal centerboarders and wide, shoal keel hulls may also have rather heavy quarters. In any case, however, the bilge of the transom should not become deeply immersed until the "average" sailing heel (say, deck-to) is passed. Hulls that are narrow and deep should have slack bilges in the afterbody since they sail at great angles of heel. The shape of the midsection and length of the stern overhang can be considered to advantage in the design of the transom; the latter's rake also influences appearance and should be reckoned with.

Lack of deadrise in the transom may lead to pounding, even in a short overhang, since the shape of the transom indicates the heaviness or lightness of the quarters to a great extent. In sea-going craft, flat-bottomed transoms or U-shaped ones are to be avoided, as a rule. There are some designs in which the transom is merely a reduced copy of the midsection; such designs might, in some cases, result in hulls that are lacking in power to carry sail in a breeze.

Double-enders

In the case of double-enders there is no transom to be considered, but the design of the quarters are of very great importance and an effort must be made to obtain bearing aft by use of the very full deck-plan aft combined with a very hollow load-waterline in the half-breadth plan and flat, rather straight buttock lines in the sheer plan, the drawing of which will receive attention in later pages.

Power Boat Sterns

Power boat sterns are determined by the speed-length ratio, for the faster the boat the wider the transom and the harder its bilge. The extreme is reached in planning round-buttom outboard motor boats, where the transom is often the largest section and the boat's maximum beam at the transom bilge.

Drawing Transom

To draw the transom, measure the height of the bottom of the transom and the height of the sheer line at the transom (after end of sheer line in the profile as just projected) in the sheer elevation and transfer them to the centerline of the body-plan, using the load-waterline as a base line, if so used before in laying off the midsection. Measuring the half-breadth of the sheer in the half-breadth plan (measuring the half-breadth of the deck- or rail-plan, whichever the sheer line represents, at the point where this line intersects with the top of the transom, and square to the centerline), and also the half-breadth of the rabbet (or bottom of keel); transfer them to the body-plan, squaring out from the body-plan centerline at the heights previously marked. See Plate III and Figure 3.

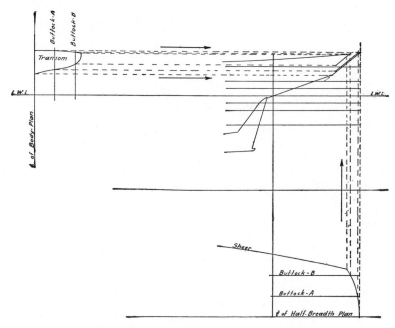

FIGURE 3. *Projection of Transom, first stage, shown by dotted lines; projections made in directions shown by arrows.*

Deck Crown

The deck crown must be laid out next. The diagram of the deck crown is shown on Plate III under the half-breadth plan, at the bow. To construct this, lay off the greatest half-breadth

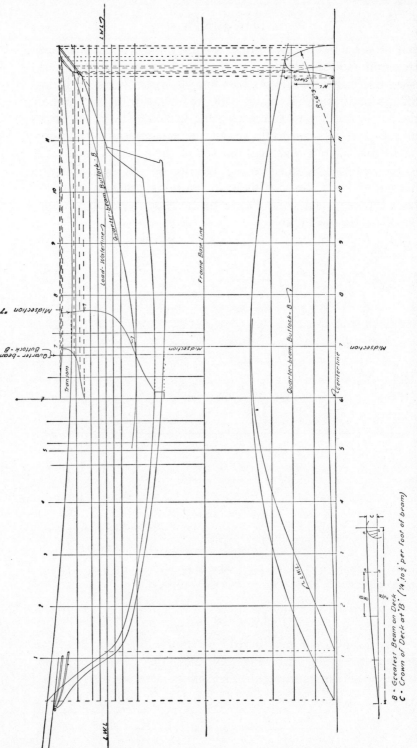

PLATE IIi. *The third stage of the lines. Midsection and transom drawn in Body-Plan, quarterbeam buttock in Sheer Elevation; L.W.L. in Half-breadth Plan. The second stage of the projection of the transom is shown by dotted lines, likewise the method*

of the deck as a base line and erect perpendiculars at each end. Using the intersection of one of these perpendiculars and the base line as a radius point, and with a radius equal to the amount of crown in inches, sweep in a quadrant as shown in the diagram. Divide the radial line (part of the base line inside the quadrant) into four equal parts and then divide the quadrant into four equal parts also, by use of the dividers. Draw lines connecting these points as shown in the diagram on the plate. Divide the base line (greatest half-breadth) into four equal parts and erect perpendiculars. Then, using the base line, lay off heights on each of these perpendiculars equal to the length of the lines just drawn inside the quadrant; measuring from base to quadrant along each line so that aa equals aa (see diagram on Plate III). With a batten or sweep, run a curve through the points just found on the perpendiculars; this curve will be the typical curve of the deck crown. The diagram is usually drawn on a scale twice that of the lines. The amount of crown that should be given the deck depends largely upon the size of the hull; it is usual to use more crown in the deck of small hulls than in large, in proportion to beam. The crown is usually fixed between ¼″ and ½″ per foot of beam. Once the sweep of the crown is designed, it is customary to use it for all deck beams; the height at the centerline of the deck will vary with the amount cut off the ends by the reduction in breadth of the deck, fore and aft.

The top of the transom should have the same, or a greater, amount of curve as that of the deck crown, when viewed from afore or abaft the transom. Using the deck crown curve, draw in the top of the transom in the body-plan, making sure that it does not have less curvature than the deck crown.

Next, project the points, where the centerline and each of the buttocks in the body-plan intersect the top of the transom, to the stern in the profile, making light pencil lines parallel the load-waterline. Then project upward the corresponding points on the half-breadth plan so that intersections are made on the sheer elevation. A curve drawn through these intersections and to the after end of the sheer line in the profile plan is the top of the transom viewed broadside on. Now, the transom, if curved, should be a portion of a cylinder; therefore the buttock lines on the face of the transom are parallel to the centerline of the hull in all views, including the sheer elevation. Hence, it is evident that lines drawn on the transom in the sheer elevation parallel to the centerline through the intersections of the buttocks at the top of the transom are really continuations of the buttock lines downward on the face of the transom. Now the heights of the points where the buttocks intersect the bottom of the transom in the body-plan can be projected to the sheer elevation where intersections are obtained on the buttocks that were projected downward on the face of the transom. A curve drawn through these points of intersection will be the side and bottom of the transom as seen in the profile or sheer view. The points of intersection of the buttocks just mentioned are then squared downward to the half-breadth plan, to fix the shape of the bottom and sides of the transom in that view. See Plate III and Figure 3.

A waterline may pass through the transom, as in the example (3-A). This can be projected from the sheer elevation to the half-breadth plan by squaring downward the points of intersection of the centerline and buttocks with this waterline in the sheer elevation, to their equivalent lines in the half-breadth plan. The half-breadth of the transom on this waterline must be taken from the transom outline in the body-plan. The intersection of the side of the hull and the transom at this waterline is now squared down from the profile to the half-breadth plan and this half-breadth measurement laid off on the projection. A curve swept through the various points thus obtained on the half-breadth plan will represent the appearance of the transom when viewed from underneath the keel. Plate III shows the completed projections.

The general procedure may be repeated. First, draw the curve in the top of the transom in the half-breadth plan. Second, lay off the deck crown. Third, draw the lower portion of the transom in the body-plan; decide the curve of its top in this view by reference to the curve of the deck crown. Fourth, project each buttock intersection at top of transom onto the sheer elevation from the body and half-breadth plans. Fifth, project the intersections of the bottom of the transom with the buttocks from the body-plan to the sheer plan, thence to the half-breadth plan, Sixth, project any waterlines in the transom, shown in the body-plan, to the half-breadth plan through the sheer elevation in order to obtain the correct fore-and-aft intersections. This is the direct method of designing the transom and is based on one fixed line—the transom top in two views. The advantage of this method is that the appearance of the completed transom is designed directly without the use of the false section often employed. The latter is favored by some designers, however, and consists of a false fairing section drawn at the extreme after end of the proposed transom, perpendicular to the same baseline as the other stations. When the buttocks and waterlines have been all faired into this section, the transom is finally projected at the proper rake and curve; the radius of the transom being arbitrarily fixed. The objection to this method is that the actual shape of the transom cannot be seen until much work has been expended on the plan; after which it may be found that the transom is too large or is taking an ugly shape, due to the form of the quarters, rake and overhang. In the method proposed in place of the use of the false section, it is sometimes necessary to use the top of the deck at the transom in lieu of the top of the transom itself in making the projections, as the actual top might be of some arbitrary form having no similarity to the deck crown. Flat transoms are less difficult to draw as the projections necessary are those used in the rest of the sections in the body-plan, even though the transom rakes in profile. When the transom is flat it is not necessary to predetermine the top of the transom or the deck crown.

Quarter-beam Buttock

The quarter-beam buttock of the afterbody must be next drawn on the sheer elevation. The shape of this curve seems to have much effect on the speed of a sailing hull insofar as it indicates hull-form. It was first suggested by Dixon Kemp, the noted English naval architect and writer on the subject, that observation indicated all fast-sailing hulls, shoal or deep, large or small, to have a quarter-beam buttock of a certain general

form. By comparison of a large number of fast hulls, Kemp concluded that the proper form of curve for the quarter-beam buttock aft was nearly that of half of a parabola. It was evident, however, that a mathematically constructed parabola need not be assumed to be the proper form; rather it was sufficient to assume that the form of the quarter-beam buttock in the afterbody need only be similar; that is to say, the curve should flatten markedly as it rose from below to the load-waterline. In some very fast hulls, the quarter-beam buttock is actually straight from a point well below the load-waterline to above it. It is evident, however, that there can be excessive length to this straightness of quarter-beam buttock, particularly in yachts having deep, full midsections and cut-away profiles, forward. This type of hull is represented in many modern racing yachts; when the buttock's straightness has been carried too far forward in these hulls, the buttock takes a marked V-shape in the sheer elevation. This indicates that the displacement is too concentrated amidships for either speed or easiness in a seaway. In any form of hull, it seems highly advisable to employ some straightness to the quarter-beam buttock, just forward of where the buttock intersects the load-waterline; in most hulls, however, the length of the straightness need only be between one-sixth and one-tenth the length of the load-waterline. In no case does it seem necessary to extend the straightness of the quarter-beam buttock beyond one-fourth the load-waterline length. It is to be noted that the location of the midsection longitudinally, and its rake, will play a great part in the determination of the length of the straightness in the quarter-beam buttock. Some vessels have been designed with reverse curve in the quarter-beam buttock but this not only produces a rather ugly stern overhang (unless the overhang is very short) but also may develop undesirably heavy quarters.

There are two improper forms of quarter-beam buttock: the one that takes a V-shape in the profile (showing a quick, hard turn amidships, where it changes direction) and the one that sweeps up round and full to the load-waterline, aft. The latter type of buttock is to be seen in the lines of too many so-called "seagoing cruisers" and deep-bodied double-enders. When this form of quarter-beam buttock is seen, it may be concluded that the hull has a run that is too short for speed and that seaworthiness is probably impaired. The shorter the run, the more liable a hull is to being pooped in a heavy following sea. As far as has been learned, the explanation of this seems to be that the large quarter-wave, created by hull-forms having full quarter-beam buttocks, has a tendency to disturb the surface of the following sea and to make it break, sometimes with fatal results to vessel and crew. When a vessel is running in a heavy sea, wind and wave conditions are often such that the hull moves at abnormally high speed; it is then that the quarter-wave, hardly noticeable formerly, becomes large and produces great disturbance in the wake. It is plain, then, that a short, full run is not indicative of seaworthiness and that the quarter-beam buttock must be shaped in such a way that this form of run is avoided.

The quarter-beam buttock in fast power boats may be long and straight. The higher the speed-length ratio, the longer the straightness in the buttock. It is not uncommon to see the straightness carried forward ⅝ to ⅔ the waterline length or even more in very fast motorboats, and this is very marked indeed in planing hulls.

It might be laid down as a rule for good hull form that the quarter beam buttock must show some straightness in the run and that the straight portion must always cross the after load-waterline and extend some distance forward of the intersection. In deep draft hulls, power and sail, with relatively short runs, this may produce a slight hump in the buttock just abaft amidship. There seems to be no harmful effect in this if the buttock does not rise sharply forward of the hump, at least in the speed-length ratios commonly met with in heavy displacement hulls.

Projection of Buttock

To project the quarter-beam buttock on the sheer plan, measure the depth of this buttock at the midsection on the body-plan and transfer it to the equivalent station on the sheer plan. It is assumed that the load-waterline is being used as the base line in measuring depths and heights, but the frame base line may be used or the lowest waterline if desired. The elevation of the quarter-beam buttock has already been found on the sheer elevation at the transom. With these two points fixed, the curve of the quarter-beam buttock is sketched in the sheer elevation. The appearance of this line in the drawing can be seen by reference to Plate III. The buttock, it will be seen, is drawn in the afterbody profile only, for the present.

Shape of Load-waterline

Now the shape of the load-waterline of the forebody should be laid down in the half-breadth plan. First, however, the shape that should be given this line must be decided. This varies widely in different types of sailing craft. Perhaps the best method by which the beginner can decide upon the proper shape is to refer to his clippings. It will be seen that some types have hollow waterlines, some convex, some are sharp and some are full; it will also be seen that there is a certain relationship between the shape of the load-waterline and the shape of the stem in profile. This might be expressed thus: if there is a marked forefoot, as there is with a clipper or straight stem, then the load-waterline in the half-breadth should usually show some degree of hollow just abaft the rabbet of the stem; as near to the stem as possible, in other words, to avoid too marked a reverse curve or "shoulder" as the line approaches the change of direction amidships. With overhang bows, the load-waterline forward rarely shows any hollow, usually being convex in the half-breadth plan. In any case, the hollow or convexity may be fixed by the profile of the stem; the amount of either, however, must be left to the designer's judgment and to the requirements of the individual type he is designing. It might be added that shoal hulls usually have fuller load-waterlines than deep hulls, but this statement is not an inflexible rule, by any means.

To illustrate, catboats are shoal, but usually have hollow in the load-waterline just abaft the stem, due to their marked forefoot. On the other hand, shoal yachts having overhanging bows show much convexity in the load-waterline forward. If the forefoot is deep and if an attempt were made to employ a convex or full load-waterline the result might be very full lines when heeled. This would appear when the diagonals were faired; the forebody buttocks (properly called "bow lines") will develop very round and full and may show hard sharp curves, or knuckles, abaft the curve where stem joins keel, in the profile.

It is evident from what has been said that the shape of the load-waterline is not a matter of using a given form of curve but rather of employing fair curves, that is, curves without shoulders, and of obtaining a proper distribution of area within the limits of the load-waterline. This last subject cannot be wholly developed here since we were drawing only the forebody waterline, not the whole. In this, the best guide is comparison with other designs in addition to careful consideration of the interior arrangement worked out in the preliminary sketch. Naturally, the designer's first thought will be to obtain enough room inside, in the forebody, to permit the use of the proposed arrangement. As a matter of fact, in some boats this must be carefully considered, not only in the fore but in the afterbody as well. Power boats usually have straight or slightly convex waterlines forward; hollow is not usually considered necessary.

Projection of Load-waterline

To draw the load-waterline, drop a perpendicular from the sheer elevation at the point where the load-waterline intersects the face of the stem or the rabbet of the stem (whichever is used to fair the lines to in your particular drawing) to the half-breadth of the face of the stem or rabbet in the half-breadth plan. The point thus found in the half-breadth plan will be the forward end of the load-waterline in that plan. Then, measure the half-breadth of the load-waterline of the midsection, in the body-plan, and transfer this to the equivalent station in the half-breadth plan. Through these points the load-waterline must be drawn with sweeps or battens. Plate III shows the example at this stage, station #7 having been taken as the design mid-section, it will be recalled.

Principles of Projection in Lines

The principles of projection used in drawing the lines of the hull must now be taken up. They are: 1—the heights of the sheer line and buttock lines on the stations in the body-plan must conform exactly with the heights of the sheer line and buttock lines on the corresponding stations in the profile; 2—the locations of the rabbet and bottom keel on the stations in the body-plan must also correspond exactly with those of the equivalent stations in the profile; 3—the half-breadths of the sheer, rabbet, all waterlines, the bottom of the keel, etc., must conform exactly with those of the corresponding stations in the half-breadth plan; 4—the intersections of waterlines and buttocks in the profile (or elevation) must conform with those in the half-breadth plan; that is, the corresponding intersections of waterline and buttock line in each view must be exactly in the same perpendicular (the same distance from the nearest station lines, in other words); 5—the ends of the sheer line, all waterlines, buttocks, etc., in the elevation must be in the same perpendiculars (or the same distance from the nearest station line) in the half-breadth plan. The diagonals will be treated the same as waterlines, and will receive attention later.

Accuracy in the transfer of these measurements from elevation, body-plan or half-breadth plan to another portion of the drawing is *absolutely necessary;* all projections and intersections must likewise be accurately transferred. The lines cannot be properly faired unless the work is done with extreme accuracy. There is no such thing as "near enough" in fairing lines and in transferring measurements or intersections.

Shaping the Body-plan

If the plan is inspected at this stage of development it will be seen that there are three control points for each station yet to be drawn in the body-plan. These are the sheer line (height in the elevation, and half-breadth in the half-breadth plan), the rabbet line or bottom of the keel (depth in the elevation, and half-breadth in the half-breadth plan), the height of the quarter-beam buttock in the afterbody (shown in the elevation) and the half-breadth of the load-waterline in the forebody (shown in the half-breadth plan). Laying off these control points in the body-plan for alternate stations, say #1, #3, #5, #9 and #11 (#7 being already drawn), sketch in, freehand, the shape of each of these sections. The shapes given these must have a certain similarity to one another but their general form must be decided by the type of hull employed and the ideas of the designer. It will be discovered that the underbody profile will have a marked influence on the shape of the sections, particularly in the ends of the hull. The shape of the topsides, in the sections sketched in, must receive as much study as the immersed portions since sea-

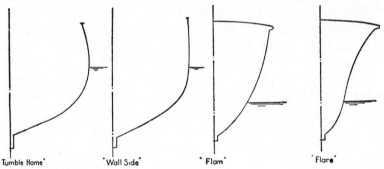

Basic Topside Sections.

worthiness and power to carry sail are governed by the former to a great extent. In most hull forms some "flare" or "flam" is highly desirable, to give the excess or margin of buoyancy that will prevent diving. Excess buoyancy gained by the shape of the topsides in the afterbody increases the power to carry sail, as a rule; also enables the stern to lift quickly in a following sea. Wall-sided sections should be avoided in nearly all hulls. If the hull being designed is of such a form or type that she will sail at marked angles of heel, "flam" instead of "flare" should be used in the forebody. The hollow side, formed by flare, may cause trouble in a hull that habitually sails well-heeled, either through a tendency to cause "tripping" and wild steering or through excess wave-making effecting speed. "Tripping" may be described as capsizing or knocking down in a quartering direction ahead, better known perhaps as "broaching-to," caused by a sudden and terrific increase of resistance forward and the related lifting of the stern. In extreme cases of "tripping" hulls have actually capsized end-over-end; this is known as "pitch-poling" and is a fault of lofty-sparred hulls poor in form and deficient in length, also of catamarans having hulls too sharp forward. In shoal hulls there may be a tendency to sheer wildly off the course, following this with a knock-down or complete capsize. While other features of hull or rig design may cause "tripping" or "broaching," the most common cause is undoubtedly errors in the shaping of the topsides.

The shape of power boat sections is, too often, fixed more by fashion than by sound practical considerations. We see excessive and exaggerated flare at the extreme bow and tumble-home at the extreme stern for no good reason. Some flare or flam forward is certainly desirable, of course, but excess represents not only dead weight but cost in construction, neither which is a functional requirement. Likewise excessive tumble-home aft serves no purpose. In fact in boats there is no sound reason why the flare or flam should not be carried to the stern, indeed in planning boats there is some reason why there should be flam right aft as well as amidships and forward. Streamlined after-bodies do not work well with the known limitations imposed by seaworthiness so far as topsides are concerned, and the designer must never allow his desire for a modernistic appearance to overcome his good judgment regarding seaworthiness.

Plate IV shows the sections sketched in, freehand, on the drawing. When these sections are drawn, they must be faired up by adding the rest of the waterlines and buttocks. The usual procedure is to draw in every other waterline and to complete the buttocks progressively. If the buttocks and waterlines are faired in together much erasing and changing can be avoided. After transferring the half-breadth of a waterline from the body-

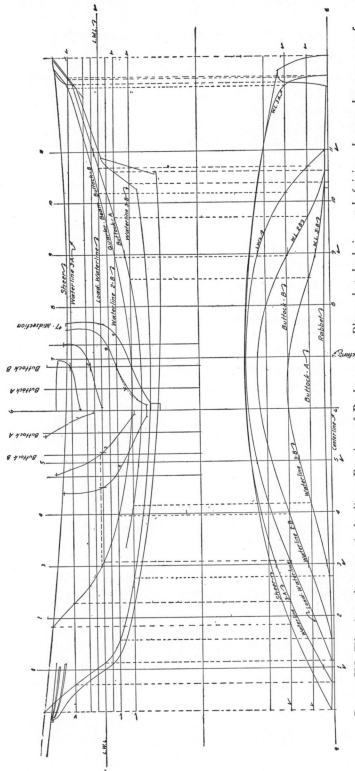

PLATE IV. The fourth stage of the lines. Portion of Body-waterlines and buttocks. Projections of intersections of buttocks and waterlines indicated by dotted lines. Lines marked √ are those being faired. Plan sketched in, and fairing begun by means of

plan to the half-breadth plan, it should be possible to sweep in a curve that will touch all the control spots thus obtained, yet which will be fair. If this cannot be done, then the offending section must be changed in the body-plan to agree with the half-breadth obtained in fairing a waterline in the half-breadth plan. Probably the beginner will find more than one section out of fair; sweep the waterline through the majority of the control spots and make the remaining sections agree by redrawing them in the body-plan. The same procedure must be followed in the buttock lines, of course.

Art of Fairing Lines

There is an art to fairing lines that is difficult to describe. This is true because the sole judge of fairness is the eye; neither mechanical nor mathematical means will produce a fair set of lines without this assistance. Turn to a completed set of lines which show some hollow at the load-waterline. Note that there is a gradual progression in the degree of hollow in the waterlines above and below, in the half-breadth plan. The waterline just below the load-waterline has slightly more hollow, the one above slightly less. Lay a long curve or sweep on the half-breadth plan so that a portion of it coincides with the waterline; then move it to the nearest waterline above or below, shifting the sweep or curve slightly fore or aft. It will be found that the sweep or curve also coincides with a certain portion of this waterline too. This can be done on other views, profile and body-plan. It can be done on the buttock lines in the former and on the sections in the latter. Try this on the body-plan by finding a curve that will fit the curve of the topside of the midsection, bilge to sheer. Now shift the curve to the next section toward the bow. It will be found that the curve may be made to fit a portion of each section progressively, toward the bow, by shifting it constantly in one direction, up or down. Try this in the sections of the afterbody and the same condition will be found to exist; usually the shift will be in the opposite direction from that when moving toward the bow. If there is a marked change in curves, as between the tumble-home topsides amidships to the flare at the foremost stations in a body-plan, it will be usually found that there is a point at which the curve being used should be reversed rather than a new curve chosen. The shift, from section to section, or curve to curve, is usually very slight, unless the stations are very far apart. The similarity of curves in a fair set of lines is always very noticeable; another point is that the greatest beam on each waterline or section is on a straight line or a slight, single curve that may be drawn through the points of greatest beam in either body or half-breadth plan. It might be possible to have fair waterlines, sections and buttocks, so far as mechanical fairness is concerned, yet have an unfair set of lines. This would be apparent to the trained eye because of the fact that the greatest beam of the waterlines in the half-breadth plan violated the foregoing; in other words, it would be necessary to draw a reverse curve, or series of reverse curves, in order to draw a line athwartships that would pass through the greatest beam on each waterline and through the greatest beam on the sheer half-breadth. Obviously, the draftsman must practice and observe to obtain the necessary skill. There is one more detail in fairing lines that needs particular mention here. This is the art of drawing reverse curves, particularly in waterlines. It will be found that there is a small portion of a reverse curve (where the direction of the curve reverses) that is straight; in waterlines this straightness should be exaggerated in order to avoid "shoulders."

Projecting Waterlines and Buttocks

Now, the actual projection of the waterlines and buttocks must be described. In the example, sections #1, #3, #5, #9 and #11 were sketched in, on the body-plan, after the heights and half-breadths already fixed by previous drawing were ticked off. Then the waterlines 2-A, the after part of the load-waterline, 2-B and 3-B were faired in, and the fore portion of the quarter-beam buttock was completed. Next, buttock-A was drawn in the afterbody. The plan then appeared as in Plate IV.

The projections of the ends of the waterlines and buttocks, likewise of the intersections of waterlines and buttocks, are shown by dotted lines on this plate. It will be observed that the ends of the buttock lines in the profile are obtained by squaring up their intersections, with the sheer line forward and transom aft, from the half-breadth plan; their ends at the transom being found as directed for the quarter-beam buttock. The ends of the waterlines are squared down from the sheer elevation to the half-breadth plan similarly to the directions given for locating the fore-end of the load-waterline. The intersections are worked up and down, as the plan's progression allows; it is not unusual to have to do some erasing and checking in order to get the intersections to agree on the profile and half-breadth. This is particularly true where the intersections take place at acute angles. The projection of the intersections are as important as any other on the lines and must be done with great care.

Diagonals

The next step should be the drawing of some diagonals. There has been a good deal of careless talk on the importance of diagonals as guides for hull design; sometimes reference is made to some particular shape of diagonal as indicating this or that about a design. A little consideration will prove that the shape a diagonal shows is largely dependent upon where its location is in the body-plan; that is, its angle to the centerline and where it crosses the midsection. In practice it is common to locate diagonals in such a manner that they are "normal" to as many stations in the body-plan as is possible and so that they pass through those portions of the stations or sections that are not fixed or faired by either waterlines or buttocks. By "normal" is meant "nearly at right angles." The ideal diagonal, in practice, should nearly represent a batten bent around the moulds or frames of a hull prior to planking. Such diagonals usually develop as fair, easy curves, with perhaps a slight hardening of the curve at the ends, particularly at the stern. In the example six diagonals have been used. It will be noticed that the uppermost, diagonal-L, and the next, diagonal-M, show a slight hardness at the stern, when laid off. This is due to the fact that they are not normal to the sections in the counter as can be seen in the body-plan. It is a good rule, therefore, not to cross the bilges with any diagonal in the body-plan, though one diagonal ought to run through the bilges of all the sections if possible. It would be better, perhaps, if diagonals-M and L, in the example, were raised somewhat at the centerline in the body-plan, particularly in the afterbody. The method of doing this, leaving the forebody diagonals as they are, will be explained later with diagonal-L as an example. Generally speaking, it is best to lay off the diagonals on the body-plan in such a way that they meet the centerline at wide angles. It is usually poor practice to place diagonals so that they cross low in the midsection and very high at bow and stern; such diagonals will often show a "hump," even in a fair set of lines.

Some writers have recommended that all diagonals cross the centerline of the body-plan at the same angle. While this gives a "pretty" appearance in the drawing, it destroys what value a diagonal has as a fairing line and in picking up offsets. It will be found that diagonals that meet the body-plan centerline at an acute angle are not useful; this is also the case with diagonals that cross sections at very acute angles. Such intersections cannot be accurately fixed for offsets, though unfortunately they often occur not only in diagonals but in waterlines and buttock lines. The aim, then, in placing diagonals, is to avoid as many of these acute intersections as possible.

As long as the curve of the projected, or expanded, diagonal is fair, with no "humps" below the waterline, the shape of it does not matter greatly. In shallow scow-like hulls that are designed to sail on their side, the "normal" diagonals should be fair, easy curves below the heeled waterline (as fixed on the body-plan); the amount of curvature should be slight. In normal hulls (either keel or centerboard), however, the shape of the diagonals is subject to so many conditions that it is considered satisfactory if the diagonals are merely fair when projected. It should be observed that the amount of beam employed in the hull will affect the amount of curvature of the diagonals (excepting those diagonals that are very low in the body-plan, of course) just as the same element will influence the amount of curvature in the upper waterlines.

The important uses of the diagonals are their fairing qualities and their aid in taking off measurements (offsets) from the lines for the mould-loft. No lines, with the possible exception of the quarter-beam buttock and the forebody load-waterline, will be as much help to the designer as the diagonals when it comes to obtaining a fair set of lines. The diagonals will often show the designer an unfair spot in his hull that could not be discovered from use of buttocks and waterlines. It is not unusual, therefore, for a designer to change waterlines and sections in order to obtain fair diagonals. The fairness of the diagonals in the forefoot and in the after deadwood and run is very important; the hollowness or convexity of the waterlines may be very great, but the diagonals running through the hull below the load-waterline must be fair, smooth curves. It must be stated again, however, that there is no form of curve that might be employed in all diagonals that would indicate anything about the performance of the completed hull, except in the case of hulls of the scow-form.

The influence of the angle with which a diagonal meets the centerline in the body-plan can be illustrated. A waterline represents, in the half-breadth plan, the outline of a horizontal plane obtained by cutting through the hull at right angles to the centerline shown in the body-plan. The buttock represents the outline of a longitudinal plane vertical to the waterlines and parallel to the centerline shown on the body-plan. A diagonal, when projected in a plan, represents the outline of a plane obtained by cutting the hull longitudinally but at an angle to the waterlines and to the centerline in the body-plan. It is obvious, then, that the nearer the plane formed by the diagonal comes to the planes of the buttocks, that is, the nearer the diagonal is to the vertical in the body-plan, the closer the shape of the diagonal, or outline of the plane, approaches that of the buttocks. By the same analysis, the flatter the angle of the diagonal in the body-plan, the closer the shape of the expanded diagonal approaches the shape of the waterlines. It will be seen, then, that it would be highly improper to say, for example, that reverse curves should not appear in diagonals; or that full, convex ends should never been seen, without extensive qualification.

Projection of Diagonals

With the value of the diagonals explained, it is time to draw them on the plan. Referring to the example, the first diagonal to be drawn will be the bilge diagonal-M which is drawn on the body-plan as nearly normal to the sections as conditions permit. This is drawn in such a manner that it cuts through the turn of the bilge of each section, or at least the majority. The angle to the centerline in the body-plan is incidental to the foregoing but if possible the diagonal should intersect the centerline within the body-plan and should not cross the sheer line of that plan. Sketch the diagonal in lightly at first, then check the height of the intersection of diagonal and centerline from waterline or base line to see if it cannot be made to measure an even distance in feet or inches without great alteration. It should also be checked to see if it could not be made to cross some waterline at an even distance, in feet or inches, from the centerline in the body-plan. These two matters are practical considerations in laying down, where it is desirable to avoid fractions of inches in measurements whenever possible. The aim of the bilge diagonal is to discover whether the turns of the bilges shown in the sketch sections of the body-plan are fair. If the diagonal crosses many sections between waterlines, in the body-plan, so much the better.

When the proper angle and position for the diagonal has been decided, the line should be inked in on the body-plan, with a thin red or green line. Great care must be taken that the intersection of both sides of the diagonal (representing the diagonal in the fore and in the afterbody) is exactly on the centerline; also that each side intersects the same waterline at exactly the same distance out from the centerline; by this means it is certain that both sides are alike. Now, another diagonal may be drawn in the body-plan; take diagonal-P in the example as an illustration. This was laid off nearly "normal" to the floor or deadrise amidships and to the hollow or "tuck" in section #9. Other diagonals may be drawn in a similar manner, some to pass through portions of sections that are not faired by waterlines (as in the topsides forward in the example, which are faired by diagonal-L or through similar portions in the underbody, faired by diagonal-R). Though there is no diagonal that passes through the sheer in the body-plan in the example, let us assume that one does since diagonals of this description occasionally appear necessary.

Imagine that you have a solid block, shaped like half of the hull divided longitudinally along the centerline as represented in the body-plan in the drawing, and that you sawed this block along the lines indicated by the diagonals on the body-plan. If you laid each of the freshly sawn faces on the drawing and traced their outlines you would have the shapes of the diagonals as they are to be projected on the lines.

Now, let us proceed to expand the diagonals of various types. First, take the imaginary diagonal just mentioned, one which crosses the sheer line in the body-plan. Before we could lay off this diagonal, however, the sheer line in the forebody portion of the body-plan would have to be established. The height of the sheer at the rabbet of the stem is projected from the sheer elevation or profile to the body-plan, and its half-breadth (taken from the half-breadth plan) laid off at this point. Next the height of the intersection of the quarter-beam buttock and the sheer, on the profile, is projected to the quarter-beam buttock in the forebody portion of the body-plan. In the example there would now be six control points through which the sheer could be drawn in the body-plan; the stem or rabbet, sections #1, #3, #5 and #7, and the quarter-beam sheer height just found. The sheer, drawn in, is shown in the body-plan in Figure 4.

Now, project the intersection of the diagonal and sheer line in the body-plan (in our case the imaginary diagonal since the supposed line is not required) to the sheer elevation so that the

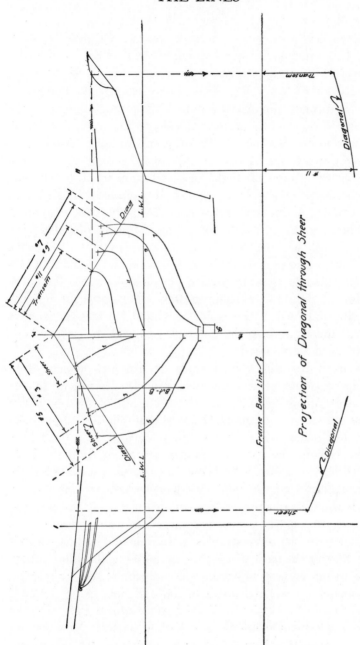

FIGURE 4. *Method of locating ends of this type of diagonal shown by dotted lines. dimensions show how half-breadths are obtained.*

height above the base line or waterline is the same. Where this projected height intersects the sheer line in the profile make a mark. From this point, square down to the base line (just below the keel in the example) and make a tick. This is the fore end of the diagonal when expanded. The after end is obtained in a similar manner; the height at which the diagonal intersects the transom in the body-plan is projected to the profile where an intersection is obtained on the transom outline. This is then squared down to the base to be used for expanding the diagonals and thus the after end of the diagonal is obtained. Should the stern be sharp and should a diagonal cross the sheer in the body-plan, the end of the diagonal is obtained in the same manner as described for the forebody, of course. Measure off, *along* the diagonal, the half-breadths in the body-plan from centerline to the intersection of the sheer, each section and to the transom; transfer these to their respective positions measured from the base line. It should be possible to draw a fair curve through the ticks thus obtained. If this is not possible it is necessary to alter some of the sections in the body-plan so that the proper half-breadths can be obtained.

So much for this special form of diagonal, which often troubles amateur (and some professional) draftsmen. In the case of diagonals that intersect the centerline of the body-plan within the view, as diagonal-M in the example, the rabbet half-breadth of the stem is drawn on the body-plan, as is the rabbet half-breadth of the sternpost. These are taken from the half-breadth plan; measurements being taken at each waterline there and transferred to the corresponding waterline in the body-plan. If the sides of the stem are parallel, obviously fewer measurements are required in this operation. The intersection of each diagonal with the half-breadth of the rabbet (or half-breadth of the face of the stem when lines are faired to this line) is projected to the corresponding line in the profile; the intersection thus obtained is squared down to the base line, fixing the ends of the expanded diagonals. Where the diagonal intersects the transom, its end is obtained as already described. Now we are ready to expand the shape of these diagonals. As before de-

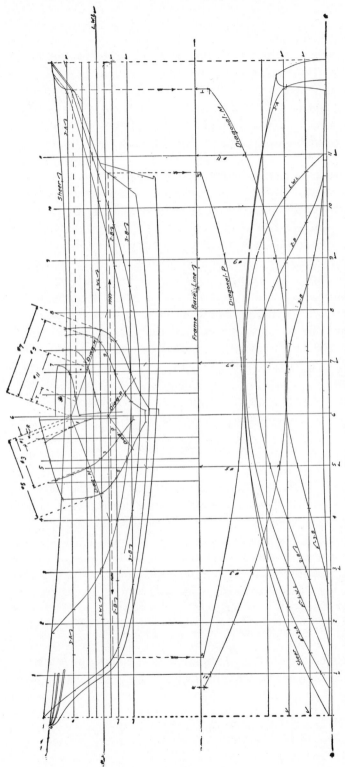

PLATE V. The fifth stage of the lines. Fairing the diagonals. Dotted lines and arrows show the direction and projection of the ends of the diagonals. Dimension lines indicate how half-breadths of diagonals are measured. Diagonals "M" and "P" are faired in this illustration.

scribed, measure, *along* each diagonal, the half-breadths in the body-plan, from centerline to the rabbet (or face of stem) half-breadth and to each section and to the transom. Lay off these measurements at their corresponding positions along the base line and sweep curves through the points thus obtained. The appearance of the diagonals can be seen in Plate V, representing the example.

The projection of the ends of the diagonals should be done with great care and all measurements of half-breadths, from centerline to sections, transom and rabbets, must be accurate. It is a regrettable fact that there are professional designers, as well as amateurs, who do not know how to project and locate the ends of diagonals, resulting in serious errors in fairing. In passing, it should be noted that fairing the sections by means of the diagonals may lead to numerous changes in sections, in the body-plan, with resulting alterations in waterlines and buttocks. Care should be taken, however, that the quarter-beam buttock is not altered by the diagonals, below the load-waterline. Plate V shows diagonal-M with dimension lines in the body-plan which are duplicated in the half-breadth plan in order to show the treatment of the measurements just mentioned.

False or Twisted Diagonal

There is another method of treating diagonals that requires explanation. This method has been referred to in the reference to the diagonal-L. It will be recalled that this diagonal crossed the bilge in the afterbody, as was indicated in the body-plan of the example. It was then suggested that it might be well if the diagonal in the afterbody were raised at the centerline without changing the forebody portion as well. This can be done by means of a false or "twisted" diagonal. See Figure 5. Suppose we wish to draw a false diagonal at diagonal-L in the example so that a fairing line may be run along the turn of the bilges in the afterbody. The diagonal-L would first be drawn in the usual manner (as illustrated in the plates). Then, in the afterbody, the point where the midsection (section of greatest beam

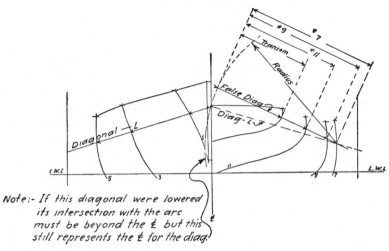

FIGURE 5. *Projection of a "False" or "Twisted" Diagonal. Note how corrected centerline is obtained.*

at diagonal) intersects the diagonal-L is used as a radius point, and with the length of the diagonal from this point to the center-line (measured along the line of course) as the radius, an arc is swept in; upward if the diagonal is to be raised, downward if the diagonal is to be lowered. Now the false diagonal-L can be drawn; it must pass through the point used as the center or radius-point (the intersection of the original diagonal-L with the midsection) but may intersect the arc at any place which may be required in order to run the false diagonal through the desired portion of the body-plan. The intersection of the new diagonal with the arc is used in lieu of the centerline in measur-ing half-breadths taken along the false diagonal in order to fair. If by chance the midsection or largest section on the afterbody side of the body-plan does not happen to be the point of great-est beam on the diagonal as a whole, the radius-point may be obtained by transferring this intersection from the forebody to the afterbody; or vice versa if the false diagonal is to be em-ployed in the forebody. It is rare to see the false diagonal em-ployed today, but it is useful in some hull forms.

Completing the Lines

Next, the incomplete buttock should be faired in, and with a hard drawing pencil and curves, the sketched sections in the body-plan should be cut into the paper, making certain that each section agrees in heights and half-breadths with its corresponding section or station on the profile and half-breadth plans. Now, points have been obtained so that the shape of the remaining sections may be fixed, #2, #4, #6, #8 and #10 in the example. Also, more stations may be drawn at bow and stern so that the builder will have enough control points in laying down to avoid any possibility of error in the entrance, or run and counter. These sections are drawn in the sheer, half-breadth and body-plans; the heights and half-breadths being lifted from the waterlines, buttocks and diagonals already faired in, at their intersection with each station or section in the sheer elevation and half-breadth plan. In the example, a station, 1-A, was placed at the bow, spaced halfway between #1 and #2. Stations #11-A and #12 were also added to the afterbody, spaced at half the distance between the original stations. When these stations were drawn on the sheer elevation and half-breadth plans (and across the expanded diagonals and their base as well), the half-breadths and heights of each were transferred to the body-plan so that the sections might be drawn out. When this has been done, the rest of the waterlines, buttocks and diagonals may be faired in. The height of the deck and waist lines (if these do not coincide with the sheer) should be drawn on the profile and their heights on each station projected to the body-plan (to corresponding sections) in order that half-breadths of each may be obtained; these are transferred to the half-breadth plan and faired in the same manner as waterlines. These lines, along with the undrawn portion of the sheer, should be added to the body-plan. The heights at which these lines intersect the buttocks in the profile, as well as at which they intersect the stations, should be transferred to the body-plan. By this means a large number of control points for each of these lines is obtained in the body-plan and the lines are easily drawn in. In hulls having no bulwarks, the center of the deck is usually laid off in the profile, using the crown curve employed in designing the transom. This is applied to each section in the body-plan; the narrowing of the half-breadth of the sheer line fore and aft will fix the amount of crown at each section or station. Finally. the half-breadth of the face of the stem and bottom of keel may be laid off on the body'and half-breadth plans, if this has not already been done.

Rudder

The rudder, its shape and area, may now be considered. The area, to some extent, is subject to the outline of the rudder and to the area and distribution of lateral plane in the hull. Generally, the area enclosed in the outline of the rudder blade amounts to about $\frac{1}{15}$ of the area of lateral plane in boats up to 45 feet on the waterline; in large vessels, however, the proportion may not be more than $\frac{1}{40}$. The width of the rudder, fore and aft, may be about $\frac{1}{15}$ the length of the load-waterline in small craft, and from $\frac{1}{20}$ to $\frac{1}{25}$ on large. These proportions are very general, however; the best guide is comparison with boats of similar type, underbody profile, and dimensions.

Actually, the rudder area is controlled by the actual speed-length ratio of the hull; fast motorboats, for example, have less rudder area than slow craft. Hence a planing boat may steer well at high speed and very poorly at low speed, illustrating another reason why the selection of the actual cruising speed desired in a power boat is so important.

The shape that should be given a rudder is a matter of great importance. The idea that the rudder should have a graceful profile, fairing daintily into the underbody profile, is not well-founded. The profile thus obtained adds nothing to the speed or steering qualities of a yacht. Invariably, such rudders are narrow at the bottom and wide near the load-waterline. The most efficient portion of the rudder is the lowest third, however, so it can be seen that such outlines are most inefficient. The best outline for rudders seems to be one that is wide at the bottom and narrow at the top, the reverse of the "pretty" rudder so beloved by yacht designers in the past. Rudders having the most efficient outline require far less area than the other, to obtain the same results.

The placing of the propeller aperture must sometimes be considered in designing the rudder in auxiliaries. Formerly it was not uncommon to cut the greater part of the aperture into the rudder. It has been found, however, that this often produces undesirable steering effects, and now it is considered good practice to have the aperture almost entirely in the sternpost if possible.

The features of rudder design that are of importance, next to shape and area, are the trailing edge (tail of the rudder), rake of rudder-post and the balance. The tapering of the trailing edge of the rudder (streamlining) is done to reduce eddy-making. While it is well to streamline the rudder in very deep hulls, the taper should not be carried to extremes, as the resulting tail will be so thin as to be weak. It is rank disrespect to the modern fad for streamlining to call attention to the fact that the eddy, caused by the square trailing edge of rudders that are not streamlined, is an aid to steering. The added resistance of the eddy is counterbalanced by the reduction in wetted-surface that is possible by means of the reduced area (or rudder size); about 5% reduction is permissible in the non-streamlined type. In shoal draft hulls, in particular, the square-tailed rudder is superior to the streamlined design.

Rake

The rake of the rudder-post appears to have some effect upon the steering qualities of a hull, but this is due to the resultant distribution of lateral plane in the hull rather than to the effect of rake upon the rudder itself. The rake should never exceed 45°, measured from the perpendicular, and observation suggests that hulls having deep, full midsections combined with fine runs (as is the case of modern racing sloops, for example) are better for having very moderate rake to the rudder-post. This seems particularly true when these features are combined in a hull that sails at wide angles of heel. Keel hulls having relatively shoal midsections, such as are employed in hulls having all ballast inside, seem to receive some benefit from extreme rake to the rudder-post, however. Very light displacement hulls should not have raking rudder-posts as a rule, for the rudder when hard over and raking becomes a very effective brake.

Balance of Rudders

The balancing of the rudder is the distributing of area fore and aft of the rudder-post. Rudders of this type are therefore known as "balanced rudders"; these have been found to be of use only in shoal hulls of the scow or sharpie type, and in power-boats. Experience has shown that the balanced rudder is not practical in keel craft of any description. The design of the balanced rudder has become standardized; about ¼ to ⅓ the area of the whole rudder blade is placed before the rudder-post. The turning qualities of this design of rudder are great and little area is required to achieve satisfactory results in shoal craft. In keel hulls, however, the objection to this rudder seems to be that it is made ineffective by the eddies formed in the wake of the keel; these have marked effects on the fore end of the balanced rudder and cause wild steering. In racing scows twin balanced rudders are used, one on each side, sloping outward at the bottom in line with the bilgeboards. In using the balanced rudder it is necessary to take precautions to have the post very strong and well-supported inside the hull, and the post should have no rake. Outboard rudders, balance type, are objectionable in light displacement craft, for the reason mentioned earlier.

Relationship of Rudder to Hull

It should be noticed that the shape of the rudder is sometimes a matter of hull type, as in the catboat, for example. In drawing the rudder it will help the builder if the centerline of the rudder-post is shown and dimensions given to fix its rake accurately. The rudder should not drop below the bottom of the keel; should it do so it would be liable to damage and to unshipping when the vessel grounds. In most craft it is an excellent plan to support the heel of the rudder-post by means of a strong casting at the bottom of the sternpost or by the ballast casting, if this is of iron and if the distribution of ballast will permit. Where the rudder-post passes through the counter or overhang, it is sometimes necessary to swell the rabbet athwartships in the way of the stock so that the rabbet seam is not cut. If the stern overhang has much deadrise this should show not only in the half-breadth plan but in the profile. Enough room must be left between the top of the rudder blade and the overhang or counter to allow the rudder to be lifted enough to unship at the heel casting, when being removed for repairs.

It is not wise to place a balance rudder close abaft a fin or skeg, for this sometimes results in wild steering, in both power and sailing hulls. If a balance rudder is desired in a finkeel sailing hull, with a short fin nearly amidship, the safest plan appears to be to hang the rudder outboard on the transom, at the end of a reasonably short counter.

Generally speaking, the rudder is most effective when it is placed as far aft as possible, in both power and sailing hulls. It is also most effective, as has been stated, when its largest area is well submerged and as near to the maximum draft as possible. It is effective in backing only when it is abaft the propeller. In power boats it should be in the wake of the screw, when manoeuvering ability at low speed is desirable. Contrary to common belief, a long keel power hull of marked draft, moderate drag and nearly angular forefoot can be made to steer very well and turn in a reasonably short circle by a rudder of proper area and design. The most common error is to employ too small a rudder, the next most common error is to locate it improperly and the third is to shape it incorrectly. In fact in power boats there is certainly some objection to making it too large as it then produces overly quick steering and requires very low gearing to handle it, manually, with a steering wheel. But in the heavy displacement cruiser and auxiliary there is no such objection.

There is a wide difference in professional opinion as to the proper calculation for rudder area. It is notable that the area of rudder, in proportion to lateral plane, is not a constant proportion to size of vessel. Small craft have relatively greater area than large vessels. A lateral plane of 3% to 4% is sometimes taken as a good proportion for rudder area in heavy displacement hulls. Balanced rudders are usually slightly less in area than unbalanced rudders, the reduction being about 10%. In fast motorboats the centerline of the stock in a balanced rudder is usually 20% to 21% abaft the leading edge, and the leading edge ought to be sharp. There is no advantage, apparently, in very thick rudders heavily streamlined. Moderate thickness is preferable in all streamlined rudders.

Shoal draft sailing craft, and more rarely power boats, sometimes have a drop blade rudder which can be lowered or hoisted by a lanyard to give maximum steering qualities in deep water and also to allow the rudder draft to be reduced in shoal water or in beaching. Rudder blades fitted with what in effect is a centerboard is an old idea for the same purpose. A third method is to have the rudder stock so fitted that it can travel up and down on its pintles or in its tube.

The metal stock diameter can be determined by formula if desired, though usually fixed by comparison in small craft. The most common formula is:

$$D = 0.2 \sqrt[3]{A \times R \times V^2}$$

D = dia. of stock in inches
A = Area of rudder in sq ft
R = Average length of trailing edge
 of rudder from centerline stock
V = max. speed of boat or 8 knots
 whichever is greater.

This formula gives a heavy service stock and is suitable for large yachts having heavy displacement, and steel or bronze rudder stocks. Metal rudder stocks should always be of ample diameter and even in small sailing boats should not be less than 1" or 1¼" diameter.

Projecting the Bowsprit

If there is a bowsprit, its intersection with the bulwarks in the profile may be found by laying off its half-breadth on the half-breadth plan and projecting its intersections with deck, waist or sheer to the profile; if the bowsprit is round where it passes through the bulwarks only one intersection is projected as the opening would appear to be an ellipse in the profile and can be sketched in freehand. If the bowsprit is rectangular, however, its intersections in the half-breadth plan should be projected from both deck and sheer, since the bowsprit will join the bulwarks in a straight line, the rake and position of which ought to be established. The importance of this matter is not great but the careful designer will make these projections in order that the actual appearance of the upper portion of the bow can be seen and ugliness avoided, should trial projection show any.

Scrolls

The bow and stern scrolls, and the ends of the rail-cap, should be drawn in the profile as these details improve the appearance of the plan and enable the builder to locate these properly in relation to one another.

The bow and stern scrolls, if any, and the ends of the rail-caps, the waist and guards lines, should now be drawn, as these enable the builder to see what is required in finish and to locate them properly in relation to the sheer and end profiles.

Scrolls are not as common today as they were in the past, and it is a pity. The modern use of chromium mouldings and wing form applied-castings or stampings, or the use of what the critics call "radiator cap decorations" do not give the finish that was obtained by simple cove and bead lines, and by artistic use of scrolls. With the clipper bow, scrolls filled an aesthetic need, and they still survive. However, decadence is often apparent. The rail scroll near the bow can be used with almost any stem profile. If combined with a cove—as indicated in the sketch of the straight stem, page 58, the stalk of the vine or of the plant represented should be abaft the scroll and there the carving is compact and accentuated, carried forward in lighter carving and spread out. If the scroll is not connected to a stalk or line it may be reversed and the lighter and wider foliage carried aft. If there is a hawse casting, two plants are usually represented with stalks entwined around the hawse lip and the flowering ends running each way, fore and aft. In the clipper bow the stalk of the vine or plant was always at the outer or billet end (or figurehead) and the carving was carried aft on the side or on the trailboards in gradually lengthening and spreading "growth" so that the flowering end was *always* aft. So too, the trailboards and headrails spread as they go aft. Quarter carvings are usually like those of the straight stem, but with stalk forward and flowering end aft. Stern carvings are of a variety of form. Sometimes a medallion or figure is placed centrally on the flat transom of a counter stern. On a round stern this is often done but with carved vines or design, wing fashion, on either side and brought around almost to the quarters on either side. Various forms of mouldings, false windows and stars, etc. can be employed, in addition to a carved and ornamented name-and-trailboard, as long as the carvings are not too massive and florid (a modern failing, curiously enough, in yacht carving) or excessively large (which is also a modern tendency).

The use of carved and painted decoration adds much to the appearance of a yacht or small boat, either sail or power. Carved work should usually be shown in the lines plan, or if that causes too much confusion, it should be shown in a separate drawing to the same or larger scale. Carving is best shown in a separate sketch, drawn over small squares, say at 3″ x 3″ at the given scale, to enable accurate reproduction.

Figureheads should be shown in the same manner and much care should be given to designing such carvings to the proper size and rake as well as to an appealing design. The easiest mistake is to make figureheads *too large*. It is better, by far, to have them a bit too small than overly large. And never, never should a figurehead just be nailed onto the stem; it must be a part of it and fair into the stem profile. Some of the most awkward and ugly figureheads have appeared on modern yachts, apparently just added and not "designed into" the stems.

Billet heads are the most common endings of clipper bows. These are a tight scroll or wound-stalk of spiral form, growing into the flower abaft. The profile of the billet then is like the head of a fiddle—fiddle-head—with the hook of the fiddle-head down. It is true that, in the early and middle part of the eighteenth century the fiddle-head, or hook, turned up, and it is sometimes done in modern designs. But since the fiddle-head had the "hook" turned down for over 200 years we have come to accept that as traditional and therefore it is perhaps better to follow tradition in this respect.

The trailboards should be rather narrow at the after ends; the width should be about ⅐ or ⅛ the freeboard. The after end of the trailboards should be, abaft the rabbet, a distance equal to nearly ⅓ the length of the head, from rabbet to billet, outboard.

In small craft it is an excellent idea to draw and dimension the profile of the cabin trunk, coaming, hatches, skylights and bitts for the same reasons. When the position of the masts has been established and checked in the construction and sail-plans, this should be drawn on the lines and carefully dimensioned as to rake and position. It is always desirable to fix exact locations, widths, heights and lengths for the builder, and the lines plan is an excellent place to do this with dimensions, or by use of offsets as well as scale drawings. This insures that the boat can be built as designed.

Expansion of Transom

Next the radius to which the builder must bend the transom may be found. In the sheer elevation of the transom, at the point where the transom appears widest (or reaches farthest forward), erect a perpendicular to the centerline of the transom. This is the radius line, of course, since the face of the transom is a portion of a cylinder. Measure the distance along the perpendicular, from the centerline to the point where it crosses the outline of

Procedure

1. Lay off radius of transom as described in the text, using ₵ of the Half-breadth Plan as the ₵ of the arc. Square out the radius line in the profile to form the "stretchout" line. See sketch.

2. Bend a batten around the arc of stretchout" in the Half-breadth Plan, tick off the distances from the ₵ to the buttocks and edge of transom. Transfer batten to 'stretchout' line in the profile and tick the line. It will be seen that by this means the distance x y on the "stretchout" is equal to the expanded arc between buttocks A and B on the "arc of stretchout", in the sketch.

3. On the "stretchout", (expanded "arc of stretchout") draw in buttocks parallel to ₵ of transom; and then square out the intersections of each buttock with top and bottom of transom in the profile to the corresponding buttock on the "stretchout"

4. If a waterline crosses the transom, project its intersection with edge of transom, parallel to the buttocks, to the arc of stretchout", in the Half-breadth Plan. Measure arc to ₵. Square out intersection of waterline with edge of transom in the profile (dotted line in sketch) and lay off the expanded arc just found. Do same with the Sheer.

5. Through the points thus found, draw outline of the expanded transom. Add buttocks and waterlines if more points are required

Note :- The projection used is the "developed surface of cylinder".

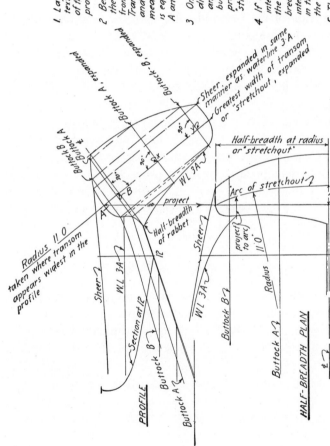

FIGURE 6. Method of expanding transom after radius is ascertained.

the transom in the profile. Now, project the height of the point of intersection of the perpendicular with the outline of the transom in the profile to the body-plan and measure the half-breadth. At some convenient place, lay off a base line and erect a perpendicular at its right-hand end. Measure off the half-breadth just found on this perpendicular and make a tick. Now, draw a line through this tick, toward the left, parallel to the base line, and then lay off the distance found on the profile, along the perpendicular drawn there, from the centerline to the outline as first measured, and make a mark. This mark, it is understood, is above the base line and to the left of the perpendicular last drawn. Now, by trial and error, find the radius that will sweep a curve through the intersection of the perpendicular with the base line and the last tick (on the line parallel to the base line and above it) that was made. The radius point must be on the base line. When found this radius is the one on which the transom is bent and should be recorded on the plan as shown in Plate VI.

By expanding the arcs between each buttock the true shape of the transom could be found. Some designers expand the transom on the lines plan and give the expanded offsets, but it is better to omit the latter. It is safe practice, however, to expand the transom in order that its shape may be properly visualized by the loftsman. In designing the transom, when the stern overhang is very short, some designers expand the transom shape upright in order to study its form, however.

Projection of Rabbet in Faired Keel

The lines are now complete, so far as projection and fairing are concerned in the example and may be inked in. Plate VI shows the drawing of the lines of the example at this stage. A graphic scale has been added in the example but this is rarely done in actual practice. There remains one more projection that must be described though it does not appear in the example. This is the projection of the rabbet in hulls that are faired to the face of the stem. Plate VII shows the lines of a small keel catboat with the lines faired to the face of the stem and bottom of the keel in

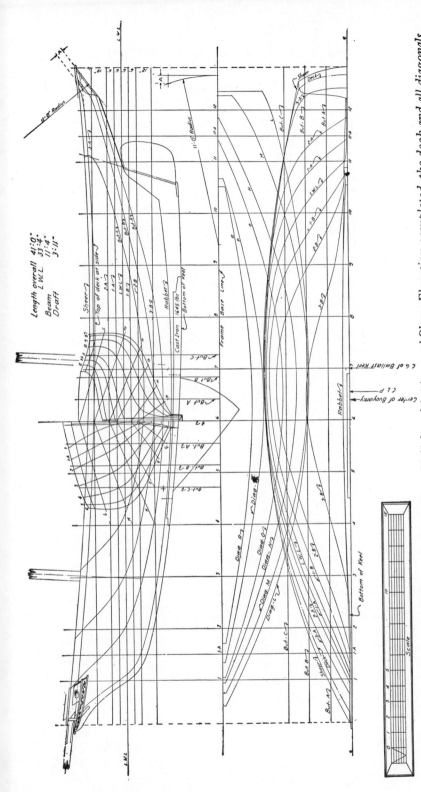

Length overall 41'·0"
L.W.L. 33'·4"
Beam 11'·4"
Draft 3'·11"

PLATE VI. *The sixth stage of the lines. Body-Plan, Half-breadth Plan, and Sheer Elevation completed, the deck and all diagonals faired in, and the rudder designed. Method of finding radius of transom is indicated. This illustration represents the lines and calculations completed; the ballast keel calculated and located. Transom expansion omitted.*

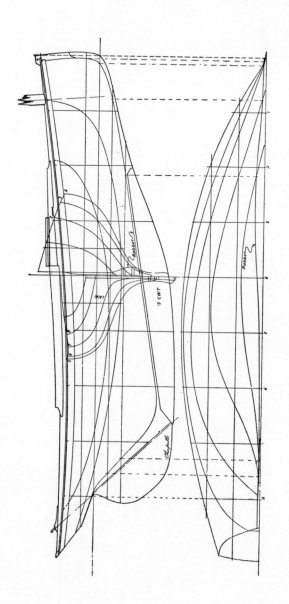

PLATE VII. *Lines of a Keel Cat. This shows the method of projecting rabbet when the keel is faired into the hull. Plan shows tumble-home bow and short counter, orthodox sheer and "wine-glass" midsection.*

the modern racing yacht fashion. For the moment we will assume that the lines of this boat have been drawn and the outside
ballast calculated and drawn in. Now the rabbet must be established on the profile, half-breadth plan and body-plan. The
first step is to lay off the rabbet line along the top of the ballast
shown in the profile, allowing a little space between the two lines
so that there will be some wood to caulk the rabbet against in the
completed hull. Usually the top of the ballast would be straight
and so a portion of the rabbet would be straight, perhaps. At any
rate, the rabbet may be arbitrarily established in the profile at
the midsection. Project the height of this to the body-plan and
obtain as many half-breadths as the length of the straight rabbet
on the profile will permit. Transfer these to the half-breadth
plan (even though only the half-breadth of the rabbet at the
midsection has been established) and lay off the half-breadth of
the rabbet, establishing the half-breadth of the rabbet on the
stem and sternpost arbitrarily as in the previous example (the
schooner). Now the points of intersection of the rabbet with the
waterlines, sheer, deck and waist lines in the half-breadth plan are
squared up to the corresponding waterlines, the sheer, deck and
waist in the profile. The half-breadths of the bow and stern rabbets are now picked off from the waterlines in the half-breadth
plan and transferred to the body-plan; the rabbets being drawn
in the end sections. The heights of the rabbet in these sections
are now transferred to the profile. If there are not enough control points on the profile to draw in the rabbet there, more may
be obtained by lifting half-breadths from the half-breadth plan
and obtaining intersections of corresponding sections in the
body-plan, the heights of which may be transferred to the profile. It will be observed that the method of projection of the rabbet in this case is not unlike that used to lay off buttock lines on
the profile, the only difference being that the rabbet is not a
straight line in the half-breadth plan. If, for any reason, the ballast has not been drawn in the profile, the available timber widths
permissible in the keel will serve to indicate the maximum half-
breadth of the rabbet; this angle of the problem should receive
consideration in any case. The projection of the rabbet, as illus-

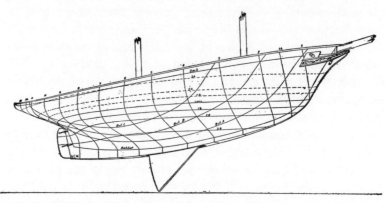

Perspective of lines showing cutwater and appearance of lines of the example viewed from afore the bow.

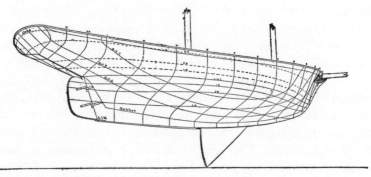

Perspective of lines showing transom and appearance of lines of the example, viewed from abaft the stern.

trated in Plate VII, is too often omitted in modern designs with the result that extraordinary keel sidings are found to be necessary when the builder lays down the lines on the mould-loft floor; the result is usually added expense to the owner in the way of "extras" and delay while the builder searches the market for suitable keel timber, all of which might be justly charged against the designer's laziness or ignorance.

Calculations

The calculations are the next step. The amount of displacement must be known, from which the amount of ballast can be reckoned. The center of buoyancy (center of gravity of the submerged bulk enclosed in the lines, *i. e.*, displacement) and the center of gravity of the ballast must not only be found but these two centers must be brought into such relation to one another that the hull will trim as desired in the lines. The weight of the hull and fittings, and their effect upon the fore-and-aft trim of the hull, must be studied. These, in addition to the calculations employed in finding the centers of lateral plane and of effort in the sail plan, constitute the calculations most commonly used in professional practice. As the calculations are discussed, an attempt will be made to investigate the possibilities of using them to foretell the performance of the actual boat, as far as recent research will allow.

Displacement

There are a number of methods of finding the displacement, all based on the immersed area of the sections shown in the body-plan multiplied by the common interval between them that is shown in the other plans (sheer and half-breadth) making up the lines. The "builders' method," used by many builder-designers of the past generation, was to divide each section into a series of triangles so arranged that their combined area appeared to equal the area of the section. Multiplying the base of each triangle by half the altitude to find the area of each, and then totaling the areas of all the triangles, the area of the section was very closely approximated. Using what is known as the "trape-zoidal rule," the areas of each section were added together, half the area of the end sections subtracted from the total and then the result was multiplied by the common interval between the stations. This gave half the displacement in cubic feet. The weight of a cubic foot of salt water is assumed to be 64 lbs., that of fresh water, 63 lbs.; actually there is some variation in the weight of water according to temperature and locality. Multiplying the half-displacement by two and the result by 64 (or 63 as required), the displacement in pounds was found. It is customary to convert this to tons in all but very small boats. The ordinary ton of 2000 lbs. is not used, however, but the "long ton" of 2240 lbs. A long ton contains 35 cubic feet of salt water and 36 cubic feet of fresh; at least that is the assumption generally employed. Therefore, the displacement in pounds is divided by 2240 to convert to long tons. The short-cut of dividing the displacement in cubic feet by 35 or 36 is naturally followed in practice, of course. Sometimes, in making comparisons, it may be desirable to convert the displacement into short tons of 2000 lbs., assumed to contain 31.23 cubic feet of salt water and 31.75 cubic feet of fresh water.

The area of the sections may be found also by use of either the "trapezoidal" or "Simpson's rule." This is rarely done in practice, however, because of the labor involved. The "trapezoidal rule" is the most practical of the two for this purpose. The half-breadths are measured off on the waterlines in each section, half of the load-waterline and of the lowest waterline are found and added to the sum of the other half-breadths. The total is multiplied by the common interval between the waterlines. The area in the sections between the lowest waterline and the rabbet (or keel bottom) may be calculated as a trapezoid (half the sum of top and bottom, multiplied by the altitude) or series of trapezoids. The area of these added to that already found gives the area of the whole immersed section. Every immersed section is put through this calculation and then the series of sections are treated as outlined in the "builder's method," Figure 7. If there are stations at the end of the waterline that are not spaced at the common interval, these may be treated separately, using the areas of the waterlines in the half-breadth plan between the end stations and the rabbets as sections. Ordinarily, however, the waterline is divided into stations having a common interval.

Theoretically, "Simpson's rule" can be used but this usually necessitates drawing special ordinates for each section (since an odd number are required) having a common interval.

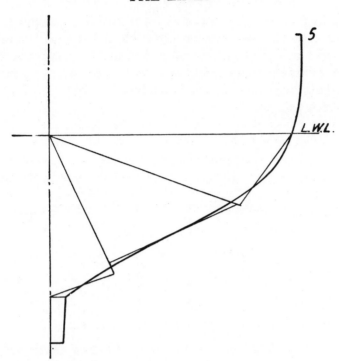

FIGURE 7. *"Builders' Method" of calculating sectional areas for displacement.*

Most professional designers use the planimeter for finding the area of the sections as this instrument is both accurate and time-saving. When such an instrument is not available the beginner should use the "builder's method" or the variant of using a piece of paper laid off in square feet to the scale of the lines, checker-board fashion; on this pencil tracings of each half-section are laid and the number of square feet contained in the area counted, the fractions being estimated. This is somewhat less accurate than the old "builder's method" but if done with care gives sur-prisingly satisfactory results.

The "Simpson rule" has been referred to many times hereto-fore and must now be described. The area of figures bounded by a curve may be found by this rule. Figure 8 shows the formula; in words the rule is: divide the base line into any *even* number of equal parts and draw ordinates or station lines as shown. To the sum of the end ordinates add each of the even-numbered ordinates multiplied by four and each of the odd-numbered ordinates multiplied by two. The sum thus obtained, multiplied by one-third the common interval or spacing of ordinates, gives the area of the figure.

Figure 8 also gives the formula for the "trapezoidal rule"; in words, divide the base line into any *convenient* number of equal spaces and erect perpendiculars or ordinates. Then, to the half sum of the end ordinates add the sum of the others; the result

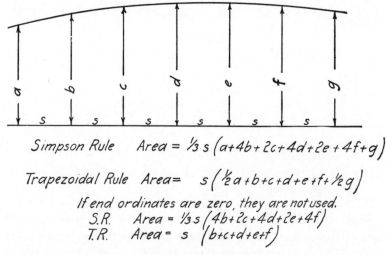

Simpson Rule   Area = $\frac{1}{3} s (a + 4b + 2c + 4d + 2e + 4f + g)$

Trapezoidal Rule   Area = $s(\frac{1}{2}a + b + c + d + e + f + \frac{1}{2}g)$

If end ordinates are zero, they are not used.
S.R.   Area = $\frac{1}{3} s (4b + 2c + 4d + 2e + 4f)$
T.R.   Area = $s (b + c + d + e + f)$

FIGURE 8. *Formulae of Simpson's Rule and Trapezoidal Rule.*

multiplied by the common interval of the ordinates gives the area. If the end ordinates are zero, the area will equal the sum of the other ordinates multiplied by the common interval, of course. The "trapezoidal rule" is often preferred to "Simpson's rule" in displacement calculations because any number of ordinates can be used.

In the calculation of the sections the area in square feet is obtained; in the calculation of the displacement the ordinates are the areas of each section and the result is the displacement in cubic feet. Ordinates placed between stations spaced at common intervals need not be considered in this calculation as the original number of ordinates will give sufficient accuracy for most purposes.

Should it be necessary to calculate the displacement of lines drawn to the inside of the plank, in the old style, some allowance must be made for the added displacement of the skin or planking. This allowance may be expressed in an equation:—the moulded displacement (calculated to the inside of the plank) will be to the true displacement (measured to the outside of the plank) as the cube of the moulded beam at the load-waterline is to the cube of the beam at the load-waterline with the plank on. Or, with a representing the moulded breadth, b the beam with the plank on, c the moulded displacement and d the displacement with the plank *on*, the equation is $a^3:b^3::c:d$ and therefore $d = \dfrac{b^3 \times c}{a^3}$.

Center of Buoyancy

To find the center of buoyancy, lay off a base line equal to the load-waterline in length, erecting ordinates perpendicular to it at the same intervals as used for the stations in the lines, and at the same scale, of course. Measure off, on each perpendicular, a distance equal to the area of the corresponding immersed section in the body-plan. The measurements for these may be on any convenient scale, say one inch equals five square feet, using an engineer's scale to measure with. There is another way—divide the area of each section by some common divisor, say 5 or 10, and lay off the result by use of the same scale as the lines, using the architect's scale. A curve drawn through the points so located is the "curve of areas" and should be a *fair* line. In practice, the curve of areas is drawn before the displacement is calculated as the fairing of the curve gives a check on the accuracy of the sectional areas. If it is impossible to draw a fair curve through the measured points it indicates there is an error in the calculation of the area of one of more sections, except when curve of area includes fin keel or ballast keel, in which case "bumps" or

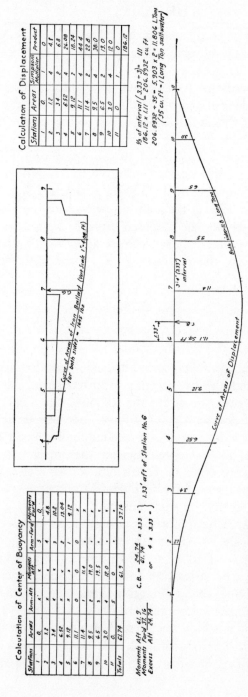

Calculation of Displacement

Stations	Areas	Simpson's Multiplier	Product
1	0	1	0
2	1.2	4	4.8
3	3.4	2	6.8
4	6.52	4	26.08
5	9.12	2	18.24
6	11.1	4	44.4
7	11.4	2	22.8
8	9.5	4	38.0
9	6.5	2	13.0
10	3.0	4	12.0
11	0	1	0
			186.12

⅓ of interval (3.33 ÷ 3) = 1.11

186.12 × 1.11 = 206.5932 cu. ft.

206.5932 ÷ 35 = 5.903 × 2 = 11.806 L. Tons

(35 cu. Ft = 1 Long Ton saltwater)

Calculation of Center of Buoyancy

Stations	Areas	Arm-Aft	Moments Aft	Arm-Ford	Moments Ford
1	0				0
2	1.2			4	4.8
3	3.4			3	10.2
4	6.52			2	13.04
5	9.12			1	9.12
6	11.1	0	0	0	
7	11.4	1	11.4		
8	9.5	2	19.0		
9	6.5	3	19.5		
10	3.0	4	12.0		
11	0	5	0		
Totals	61.74		61.9		37.16

Moments Aft 61.9
Moments Ford 37.16
Excess Aft 24.74

C.B. = 24.74/61.74 × 3.33 = 1.33' aft of Station No. 6

or = 4 × 3.33 =

FIGURE 9. *Illustrating method of calculating the displacement and center of buoyancy of the example. The curve of areas and center of gravity of the ballast keel are also shown.*

unfairness should appear. The curve of areas may be traced and cut out, then balanced, as was done with the underbody profile to find the center of lateral plane. The point where the curve of areas balance is the center of buoyancy. Figure 9 shows the curve of areas of the example.

The location of the center of buoyancy may also be calculated, by multiplying each ordinate by the number of intervals from a given station, and then dividing the difference of the sums of the moments forward and aft of this station by the sum of the areas. The quotient multiplied by the interval spacing gives the distance to the center of buoyancy from the station chosen as the pivot-point. The end, bow or stern, which has an excess of moments, is the direction in which the center of buoyancy falls, fore or aft of the pivot station.

Center of Gravity

It is evident that the center of gravity, or center of the weights of the hull, fittings, spars, engine, etc., combined, must be exactly over the center of buoyancy in order to procure the designed trim fore-and-aft. If this condition is not obtained the vessel will have deeper draft at bow or stern than called for in the lines. Hence, the problems of ballast and hull weights are of great moment. It is possible to calculate each item of weight in a boat's structure, and to find its center of gravity and also its moment from the center of buoyancy with some degree of accuracy. With this information it is possible to fix the position and weight of the ballast in accordance with the hull weights so that the designed trim could be maintained. However, this is a laborious task and in practice the short-cut to be outlined is followed.

As a "rule of thumb" it is assumed that the center of gravity of the hull structure (planking, keel, deadwood, stem, sternpost, frames, floors, deck-beams, decking, bulkheads, cabin trunk, cabin floor and cabin joinerwork) is at the middle of the overall length. As a matter of fact this assumption is not over an inch or two out in normal sailing hulls, excepting deck-

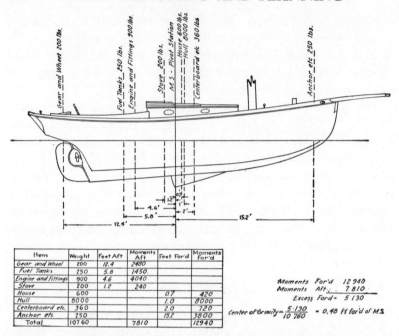

Item	Weight	Feet Aft	Moments Aft	Feet For'd	Moments For'd
Gear and Wheel	200	12.4	2480		
Fuel Tanks	250	5.8	1450.		
Engine and Fittings	900	4.6	4040		
Stove	200	1.2	240		
House	600			0.7	420
Hull	8000			1.0	8000
Centerboard etc.	360			2.0	720
Anchor etc	250			15.2	3800
Total	10760		7810		12940

Moments For'd   12940
Moments Aft.:   7810
Excess For'd = 5130

Center of Gravity = $\frac{5130}{10760}$ = 0.48 ft for'd of M.S.

FIGURE 10. *The method of calculating the center of gravity of a design, as carried out in practice.*

houses (such as are used in motor-sailers) from consideration. Since this is the case it is customary to calculate on this basis and to reckon on the heavy weights, such as the engine, full tanks, lighting plant, batteries, icebox, stove, winches and windlass, chain and anchors, spars and large deck structures, as the items of weight controlling trim which must be counterbalanced by ballast. Figure 10 shows the method of finding the center of gravity by this method and the result is accurate enough for cruiser design at least. Only in designs in which comparison is impossible should extensive weight calculations be necessary; the importance of trim calculations becomes very great in unballasted hulls and in designs having all the ballast outside. In such cases every item of construction, fitting and gear should be calculated or estimated; the greater the number of items, the more accurate the result is likely to be as the errors in estimates usually balance in practice. However, neither type is suitable for cruising and should not be attempted by the beginner until he has had experience with the more practical designs. In obtaining weights of fittings for this calculation it is usual to employ catalogue weights when these can be obtained; measurements for the location of fittings from the pivot-point are taken from the preliminary sketch. It will be seen that the method of calculating the center of gravity is similar to that employed in calculating the center of buoyancy, weights and moments being calculated about a pivot-point.

Ballasting

The ballasting of keel yachts, particularly those with part of their ballast outside, is likewise a "rule of thumb" procedure in practice. The proportion of total ballast weight to displacement varies with the type and size of hull, of course. Deep, narrow keel craft have the largest proportion, 50% to 67% of the total displacement being the weight of ballast; shoal hulls and large craft, such as schooners, have a smaller proportion of ballast in relation to displacement, say from 30% to 50%. Most modern cruising keel yachts have 40% to 50% of their displacement in ballast, as a general proportion. In cruising craft the proportion of ballast outside is often small. Many craft of this class have but 10% of the total weight of ballast outside; though some reach as high a proportion as 75%, particularly among the small keel "racer-cruiser" types.

Many designers of small and moderate size auxiliary keel cruisers arbitrarily fix the amount of ballast outside somewhere between 40% and 55% of the total displacement, an additional 10% going inside as trimming ballast. The range in percentage is due, usually, to the variation in engine and fuel weights. The smaller these weights, the larger the percentage of ballast, of course. The best guide for fixing the proportion of ballast outside is comparison. There is one important consideration that is too often overlooked, however; that is the weights added in cruising gear and provisions. As a generality it might be said that the longer the cruises to be made by the proposed yacht, the less the ballast outside should be; that is, until the low percentages (10% to 25%) are reached.

The modern tendency has been to put all the ballast on the outside, even in cruisers. Various specious reasons have been given for doing this, largely on the assumption that such a method was "most scientific." This has led to some startling results. The small, light-displacement, heavily ballasted ocean racers developed in Britain and copied in the United States in recent years will serve as an illustration. Having been built to a rule which did not require the boats to be measured to their actual displacement for a given ocean race of specified length but rather permitted measurement in "light" condition, they had very small displacements on a given range of waterline lengths with a very high proportion of fixed ballast. As a result, in actual ocean racing trim, they were loaded far beyond their designed displacement and so are dishonest designs for "light displacement ocean racers." Because of their narrow margins of stability their displacement cannot be lightened by removal of fixed ballast to allow them to approach their designed displacement when fully loaded for sea.

It is evident that the only sensible method is to design to the actual racing or cruising displacement. Since it is plain enough that for ocean races of different distances the necessary loading will not be the same, then a narrow range of displacement can be obtained only if the ballast can be altered—and equally obvious is the necessity that load and ballast changes must not cause severe variations in sail carrying power. It follows then that ballast in a cruiser or ocean racer never should be all outboard, and at best outside ballast never should be more than 85.90% of the total ballast required. Only in day boats should the outside ballast be at 100% to the total—and even here "tuning up" often shows it desirable to have some ballast inside for trimming purposes. Indeed, scientific reasons (or if preferred call them "facts") indicate that the boat with ballast all outside, if designed and built to strict measurements, must be inefficiently designed for part of her career, or as an alternate, must cheat. Boats grow heavier as they age—they soak up water, paint accumulates, etc., and so, if a fixed displacement is to be had at "average" they must be "light" as launch and ballasted accordingly. The result is they are usually never at their really best sailing trim. Common sense surely indicates the need of tuning up in any sailing racer and cruiser not being applied to trim by ballast alternation where possible.

Since there should be a fairly large amount of trimming ballast inside, in cruising craft, there is much leeway in locating the center of gravity of the outside ballast in reference to the position of the center of buoyancy. For that reason, many designers place the outside ballast well aft in order to get its weight as low as possible so that the full effect of its righting tendency may be had. Ordinarily the trimming effect of this is easily counteracted by trimming ballast, unless there are exceptionally heavy fittings or equipment aft.

As a matter of common practice, however, the following is a safe guide:—if the bow has little or no overhang, and if the counter or stern overhang is very long, then the center of gravity of the outside ballast is a few inches forward of the center of buoyancy. Under nearly all other conditions, including the use of the clipper bow, it is customary to locate the center of gravity of the outside ballast a little abaft the center of buoyancy and to obtain the designed trim through additional ballast inside.

The ballast, whether inside or outside, should not be concentrated amidships in a cruiser. On the other hand it should not be too spread out, fore-and-aft. In the first case the yacht will be so lively in rough water that she will be most uncomfortable, in the second case she will have a tendency to dive and pitch heavily in rough water and to be very wet. It is impractical to attempt to give a minimum proportion, but the maximum that outside ballast can be carried fore-and-aft is about 60% of the load-waterline, but such percentage would be possible only in long-keeled hulls. If the outside ballast is moulded to the shape of the hull, as in the keel cat in Plate VII, its weight and center of gravity are calculated by use of the curve of areas and the trapezoidal rule. This was done in the example also since the centerboard slot prevented the use of the trapezoidal rule alone.

The method of using the curve of areas is the same as that employed in calculating displacement. In drawing the ballast in the lines, its position and length are best fixed by trial and error: drawing, calculating, redrawing and calculating again until the required position of the center is obtained or until the weight is brought to the proper amount. The ballast must first be drawn by eye (as the builders say "by Guess or by God") so that its position in reference to the center of buoyancy looks right. Then the position of the center of gravity and the weight must be checked by calculation and the drawing changed until the results are satisfactory.

The question of ballast material enters into this calculation, of course. Practically, the matter is one of cost and concentration of weight. Lead weighs 707 pounds or 708 pounds, as most keels are made of second-hand lead per cubic foot, but it very expensive; cast iron weighs but 442 pounds per cubic foot and is far less expensive than lead. If the outside ballast must be heavy and must be compact, then lead should be used. In most cases, however, cast iron will be found satisfactory in cruisers. Sometimes other materials are employed for outside ballast, such as concrete (mixed with scrap iron or boiler punchings), but these are not very satisfactory because of the bulk necessary to obtain weight and because of the cost. The problem of inside ballast, so far as material is concerned, does not enter into the lines to any great extent. The matter of bulk is of some moment, of course, but this is something that must be allowed for in the midsection design, as has been mentioned. In this country most cruisers use scrap iron or boiler punchings and concrete as inside ballast, though occasionally some owner insists on lead. In very cheap craft of the "fisherman" types the inside ballast often consists of shingle, gravel or stone. The use of pitch to secure inside ballast is to be considered because, unlike concrete, it does not encourage rot.

In the example, the proportion of ballast outside is very small compared to the displacement, the general hull form being one suited for inside ballast.

In drawing lead and iron keels on the plans the difference in shrinkage of these materials should be kept in mind. This applies to shape only; not to weight or dimensions, it is understood. In iron keels, the fore and after ends should not be drawn with single square corners, but should be scarph-shaped in profile, unless the ballast keel is very shoal. If an attempt is made to cast an iron keel having square ends, there is danger of cracking at the ends of the casting. This trouble does not appear in lead castings, however, and these may have ends that are without scarphs.

It is often asked why professional designers use "rule of thumb" methods as much as they do. The answer is that calculation carried to the extent suggested in text-books is most laborious and requires a great deal of time. Where the designer of large steamers may have four vessels to design in a single year, which will furnish him sufficient income to maintain his staff, pay his expenses, and produce a profit, the yacht designer may have to produce forty designs, to accomplish the same result. Therefore, the yacht designer must conserve time and must shorten his methods as much as possible yet still obtain reasonable accuracy in results. Furthermore, the weights of wooden yacht hulls are practically impossible to calculate within 5% of actual weight. The amount of moisture, the kind of timber, the place where the timber was procured, texture and the weight and number of fastenings, all govern the weight of a wooden hull and are impossible to estimate with the accuracy possible in hulls constructed of steel or bronze.

Calculation and Performance

There is but little chance of using calculation for predetermining performance. The only practical calculation of this kind is to draw curves of areas at different angles of heel, using the same displacement as when upright. By superimposing these curves it will be possible to see at once whether the hull will change trim longitudinally as she heels in sailing. A change of trim, theoretically at least, would be indicated by a gain in the curve of areas forward or aft, when heeled, as compared with the curve of areas upright. However, most normal shaped hulls will show a tendency to gain in displacement aft and lose forward as they heel, the theoretical result of which would be to raise the stern. However, it has been found that the effect of the wind in the sails and the lee-surge seem to overcome a great deal of this tendency to change trim. It is impossible to place a proportion on the permissible gain in displacement at the ends, in heeling. The only proportion that will be practical must be obtained by comparison with similar hulls, which are not subject to change of longitudinal trim when under way.

While various theories on the design of hulls balanced longitudinally have been advanced, it seems generally agreed by experienced designers that some weather helm is desirable in windward sailing. The practical advantage of the investigation of longitudinal balance in form is that it will prevent an excessive lack of balance. It does not appear that perfect balance is desirable, on the other hand. It is therefore apparent that the use of curves of area upright and heeled as suggested are adequate guides for the limited purpose.

The beginner who desires to experiment in mathematical research will find much material for study in the standard textbooks of naval architecture. Calculation can be carried to great extremes, though the results are hardly worth the effort in normal designs.

Offset Table

When the ballast has been drawn in, on the lines, the drawing may be traced. The offsets are then taken from the original drawing. These measurements are made in feet, inches, and eighths. The height of sheer, deck, rabbet and the bottom of the keel are taken off the sheer plan; the half-breadths of the sheer line and rabbet line are taken off the half-breadth plan; the half-breadths of waterlines and diagonals and the heights of buttock lines are taken off the body-plan. These measurements are taken off at each station and at the bow and stern profiles.

Offsets of bow and stern profiles must be taken from the sheer plan, of course, and it may be necessary to add dimension lines to accurately fix the profiles, as in the example. These measurements are set down in a Table of Offsets as shown in Plate VIII. The offsets are used by the builder to lay down the full-size drawing on the mould-loft floor. The offsets should be so complete that the lines can be redrawn from them without requiring additional measurements from the lines.

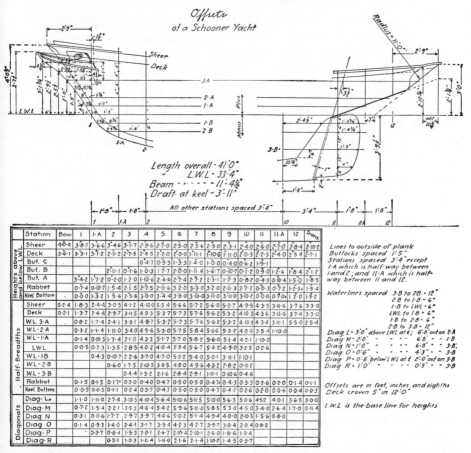

Offsets
of a Schooner Yacht

Length overall · 41·0"
L.W.L · 33·4"
Beam · · · · · · 11·4½"
Draft at keel · 3·11"

	Station	Bow	1	1·A	2	3	4	5	6	7	8	9	10	11	11·A	12	Trans.
Heights above and below L.W.L.	Sheer	4·0·4	3·8·7	3·6·6	3·4·6	3·1·7	2·9·6	2·7·0	2·5·0	2·3·6	2·3·0	2·3·1	2·4·0	2·6·0	2·7·0	2·8·4	2·10·2
	Deck	3·6·1	3·3·1	3·7·2	2·11·2	2·7·5	2·4·5	2·2·0	2·0·0	1·11·1	1·10·6	1·11·0	2·0·3	2·2·3	2·4·0	2·5·4	2·7·1
	But. C						0·4·7	0·9·3	1·3·3	1·4·0	1·0·0	0·4·0	0·6·2	1·9·1			
	But. B				2·11·1	0·1·6	1·0·3	1·7·7	2·0·0	1·11·4	1·6·7	0·10·7	0·1·2	0·9·0	1·2·6	1·8·4	2·1·2
	But. A		3·4·2	1·7·2	0·2·0	1·2·0	1·10·6	2·4·6	2·7·4	2·7·2	2·3·1	1·7·3	0·8·2	0·4·3	0·10·4	1·5·0	1·8·5
	Rabbet		0·7·4	0·10·7	1·5·4	2·1·5	2·7·5	2·11·6	3·2·0	3·3·0	3·2·0	2·11·3	2·7·2	0·0·3	0·7·2	1·2·3	1·5·4
	Keel Bottom		0·0·0	1·3·2	1·9·6	2·5·6	3·0·0	3·4·4	3·8·0	3·10·0	3·11·0	3·11·0	3·10·2	0·0·0	0·7·0	1·2·0	1·5·2
Half-Breadths	Sheer	0·2·4	1·8·3	2·4·4	3·0·5	4·1·2	4·10·0	5·3·4	5·6·6	5·7·2	5·6·0	5·2·7	4·9·5	4·3·3	3·11·6	3·7·6	3·3·0
	Deck	0·2·1	1·3·7	2·4·4	2·9·7	3·11·5	4·9·3	5·3·7	5·7·3	5·7·6	5·6·2	5·3·2	4·10·3	4·3·6	3·11·6	3·7·4	3·3·0
	WL·3·A		0·8·2	1·7·4	2·4·7	3·9·1	4·8·7	5·3·7	5·7·3	5·7·6	5·6·2	5·3·2	4·10·3	4·3·4	3·11·1	5·5·0	2·5·4
	WL·2·A	0·3·2	1·1·4	1·11·0	3·4·0	4·5·6	5·3·0	5·7·5	5·8·4	5·6·6	5·3·2	4·8·0	3·5·4	1·10·0			
	WL·1·A	0·1·4	0·10·3	1·7·4	2·1·0	4·3·3	5·1·7	5·7·0	5·8·2	5·6·0	5·1·4	4·2·1	1·10·0				
	LWL	0·0·5	0·5·3	1·3·5	2·8·5	4·0·2	4·11·4	5·5·4	5·6·7	5·4·2	4·9·0	3·2·5	0·2·6				
	WL·1·B		0·4·3	0·10·7	2·2·6	3·7·0	4·7·0	5·2·2	5·4·0	5·0·1	3·11·1	1·10·1					
	WL·2·B			0·6·0	1·7·5	2·10·5	3·11·5	4·8·0	4·9·6	4·3·2	2·8·2	0·11·2					
	WL·3·B				0·4·4	1·3·2	2·1·6	2·8·4	2·9·1	1·11·1	0·10·6	0·4·6					
	Rabbet	0·1·5	0·1·5	0·1·7	0·3·0	0·4·0	0·4·7	0·5·0	0·5·0	0·4·7	0·4·3	0·3·3	0·2·6	0·2·0	0·1·4	0·1·1	
	Keel Bottom	0·0·5	0·0·5	0·1·1	0·2·4	0·3·7	0·4·7	0·5·0	0·5·0	0·4·7	0·4·2	0·2·6	0·2·0	0·0·6	0·0·4	0·0·3	
Diagonals	Diag· L	1·1·0	1·1·0	1·11·0	2·7·4	3·10·5	4·10·4	5·6·4	5·10·6	5·11·5	5·10·0	5·6·3	5·0·6	4·5·2	4·0·1	3·6·5	3·0·0
	Diag·M	0·7·2	1·5·4	2·2·1	3·5·3	4·6·4	5·4·2	5·9·6	5·11·0	5·8·5	5·3·0	4·5·0	3·4·0	2·6·4	1·7·0	0·11·4	
	Diag N	0·3·1	0·11·6	1·7·7	2·9·7	3·9·7	4·6·6	5·0·2	5·1·4	4·9·4	4·0·0	2·10·5	1·5·6	0·8·0			
	Diag O	0·1·4	0·9·3	1·4·0	2·4·1	3·1·7	3·9·4	4·2·3	4·2·7	3·9·7	3·0·4	2·0·4	0·8·2				
	Diag· P		0·3·7	0·8·4	1·5·3	2·0·1	2·6·7	2·10·4	2·10·1	2·6·0	1·6·0	0·6·4					
	Diag· R			0·5·1	1·0·3	1·6·4	1·11·0	2·1·6	2·1·4	1·10·0	1·4·5	0·9·7					

Lines to outside of plank
Buttocks spaced 1·5"
Stations spaced 3·4" except
1·A which is half-way between
1 and 2; and 11·A which is half-
way between 11 and 12.

Waterlines spaced 3·B to 2·B · 12"
2·B to 1·B · 6"
1·B to LWL · 6"
LWL to 1·B · 6"
2·B to 3·B · 12"

Diag L · 3·0" above LWL at ℓ ; 6·8" out on 2·A
Diag M · 2·0"   "   " "   6·8" " " 1·B
Diag N · 1·0"   "   " "   6·8" " " 3·B
Diag O · 0·6"   "   " "   4·3" " " 3·B
Diag P · 0·6" below LWL at ℓ   2·0" out on 3·B
Diag R · 1·0"   "   " "   0·9" " " 3·B

Offsets are in feet, inches and eighths
Deck crown 5" in 12·0"

L.W.L is the base line for heights

PLATE VIII. *A typical Offset Table; showing dimensions sufficiently complete to reproduce the lines of the example without reference to the original lines drawing.*

General Discussion

The details of design of an individual hull have been described so far as the lines are concerned. There are, however, a number of general subjects that are of use in the study and analysis of lines. These are of a disconnected nature, and are intended to point out to the reader the importance of observation rather than to lay down inflexible rules.

The question of amount of forefoot is bitterly argued by designers and yachtsmen. A study of seagoing yachts and "blue water" cruisers indicates that some forefoot is desirable, particularly in broken water. The effect of the lee-surge, produced by the forefoot, on the weatherly qualities of a seagoing yacht seems to be of some importance. In shoal vessels, particularly, some forefoot or "gripe" is needed if the vessel is expected to lie hove-to at all well. For this reason the forefoot is a desirable feature in the design of seagoing centerboard hulls. Without doubt the cutaway forefoot has often been carried to too great an extreme, even in large vessels. The cutaway forefoot may be the cause of uneasy steering in large craft, particularly in rough water.

The question of the engine in an auxiliary cruiser is assumed to have been decided in the preliminary sketch. Before the lines are completed and sent to the builder, the location of the propeller shaft at its angle of pitch and the location of the propeller itself and its aperture should be fixed and dimensioned on the lines. This is a matter that will receive attention when the construction plan and the interior plans are discussed in the next chapter.

The importance of a certain amount of straight, or nearly straight, keel has already been dealt with. The graceful underbody profile of many modern yachts is pleasing to the eye, but there is little or no evidence that there is any particular advantage in such a profile. The underbody profile may be quite angular without harm to the sailing qualities of the hull.

Lateral plane offers a knotty problem, as the center of gravity of its profile is by no means the true center of lateral resistance when under way. It is quite apparent that the entering edge (*i. e.*, the forefoot and the keel, if there is drag) has much to do with the location of the true center of lateral resistance. Lateral resistance is probably more influenced by the distribution of the entering edge and the effect of the lee-surge than by the area of the lateral plane. However, such influences are very difficult to predetermine. The need for experimental work is very marked in regard to this matter. In practice, the drag of the keel is generally employed, since by this means the entering edge of the lateral plane is not only much lengthened, but more evenly distributed fore and aft. The importance of procuring the right lead of the center of effort of the sails, forward of the center of lateral plane, is very great. The impression among experienced designers is that there should be a greater lead in boats that have little or no drag, and which for this reason have the entering edge of the lateral plane well forward, than in boats with a great deal of drag to the keel, and the entering edge well-distributed fore and aft.

In calculating the center of lateral plane in boats that have an aperture in the stern deadwood, it is best to treat the profile as though there were no opening. The drag of the shaft and the propeller more than make up for the reduction of lateral plane caused by the aperture. Without regard to whether or not the rudder is included in calculations for the center of lateral resistance, the eddy formed by the after edge of the rudder has some influence on the location of the true center. However, this cannot be measured and the only resort left to the designer is comparison.

Wetted-surface requires some attention once more. The calculation of this surface is explained in many textbooks of naval architecture, but this is rarely reckoned in general practice because of the time and labor involved. Wetted-surface measurement is best done by developing the space between two stations in the lines by expanding all the curves in both sections and waterlines—from arbitrarily straight bases—say the L.W.L. and a straight perpendicular at the half-station space. This system requires a separate drawing for each station spacing and, though a very close approximation of the area can be obtained, its true expansion as to shape cannot. An instrument known as an "opisometer" can be purchased (this is an inexpensive instrument made for measuring maps) which speeds up wetted-surface measurement. The measurement of wetted-surface is something which is often referred to in naval architecture but which is very rarely done; it is easier to talk about it. While wetted-surface can vary to a very limited degree in a given displacement, and while the amount of wetted-surface is a factor in resistance, no sacrifices in form should be made to obtain theoretical perfection in this element. There are numerous examples of boats having a fairly large amount of wetted-surface that show great speed. The beginner, and the professional too, are often inclined to accentuate some such feature in design at the expense of others equally important. A well-rounded and carefully thought-out design is far more important than theoretical perfection in any one element of design.

Heeled waterlines are often drawn on the half-breadth plan, the projection being the same as that of a waterline or diagonal. Their importance, except in scow forms, is subject to doubt. The curve of areas of the vessel, heeled at different angles that might be met in sailing, shows much more information and are a more reliable guide as to form. Heeled waterlines in the average keel vessel indicate much more distortion than really exists, and show no more than does an ordinary diagonal.

The raking midsection is a very useful feature in the design of short, beamy boats. The catboats have this design to a great extent. Plate VII showing the keel cat illustrates this feature very well, as does the schooner used as an example of design. It will be noticed that a very long run is thus produced, and that the entrance need not be unduly full. It will be found that the use of the raking midsection is somewhat dependent upon the form of the midship section in the body-plan and upon its relation to the underbody profile. Ordinarily, in boats whose body is rather shoal, as in centerboarders, fin keel, and semi-fin keel types, there is more rake in the midsection than in boats of a deep V-section.

The buttock lines in vessels having deep full midsection, as in modern racers, take more curvature than do those in shoal-body vessels. Hence in narrow, deep boats the waterlines aft should be rather sharp and the quarters may be very slack in order to clear the run from the sides rather than from below. The old English six-beam cutters were excellent examples of this. However, even in these it is of great importance that the quarter-beam buttocks show the parabola form.

The location of the center of buoyancy is usually from .015 to .058, or nearly 51% abaft the middle of the load-waterline. Most keel craft have their center of buoyancy about .03 to .04 abaft. However, there are yachts whose center of buoyancy is forward of the middle of the load-waterline. This was also true of some commercial sailing craft; but on the whole such an arrangement of centers indicates that the bow is unduly full forward in proportion to the run, or that there is insufficient drag to the keel. While some examples having the center of buoyancy forward of the middle of the load-waterline sail very fast and are good sea boats, too full an entrance will cause "rooting" or depression of the bow when speed is high, just as an unduly full run will cause a vessel to settle aft under the same condition. Probably the best rule that could be given for the shape of the ends (which will affect the location of the center of buoyancy, of course) would be to state that a fine run should be used in conjunction with a fine entrance, a full run with a full entrance. It must be admitted, however, that it is sometimes very difficult to fix the degree of fullness or fineness that is permissible, and here again the best guide is comparison.

Sheer, in shoal unballasted hulls, particularly, will help a boat to right herself after a knockdown. Even so shoal a type as a sharpie can be made self-righting by the use of this principle, combined, of course, with flaring topsides. This is the method employed to some extent in obtaining self-righting qualities in the design of surf and lifeboats. The buoyancy in the ends must be great enough to support the hull in an unstable position when capsized in order to obtain self-righting tendencies. Straight sheers or nearly straight sheers are rarely attractive in a finished boat.

Another question that is often asked is whether a boat should "roll down" or "roll out." By this, it is meant whether a boat should settle, or whether she should rise, as she heels under sail. Extreme rolling out may be an indication that there is too much buoyancy in the topsides and too much freeboard. On the other hand, rolling down to an extreme usually indicates that the vessel is wave-making to a dangerous extent, and that her run is probably too full. Shoal boats may roll out more than keel boats, without bad effects. The use of very hollow floors and hard bilges tend to produce rolling out, while the more rounding or barrel-shaped midsection tends to produce rolling down. It would be proper, at this point, to call attention to the fact that the initial stability obtained by hollow floors and hard bilges decreases rapidly once the deck is submerged.

In reference to the importance of the location of the centers in the hull, such as the center of buoyancy, lateral plane, or gravity, it should be kept in mind that a well-formed hull will not be unduly sensitive to the small movement of these centers fore and aft, which actually takes place in service. Therefore, do not place excessive importance on extreme accuracy in location of these centers; on the other hand, carelessness must be avoided, and the designer must know in which direction he is moving centers in his design.

The cost of constructing the hull, represented in a given set of lines, must be kept in mind in the process of design. To a great extent this is a matter which is decided in the preliminary sketch. However, there are certain features in the lines which effect the cost of construction. Take, for example, the keel in modern yachts—it is now the fashion to mould the keel into the lines of the hull, to round the corners in the sections and to obtain streamlined forms in the fore-and-aft sections. The latter usually presupposes a keel tapered fore-and-aft. In many hulls, particularly those having all or a very large proportion of their ballast inside, the tapered keel ought to be omitted since it has been estimated that the cost of a moulded keel in a forty-foot hull is from $600 to $800, compared to $150 to $200 for a keel that is parallel-sided. The application of this rule to the example is hardly practical, however, due to the combination of centerboard and outside ballast. Were there no outside ballast, the best procedure would be to place the centerboard alongside the keel so that it passes through the garboard rather than through the keel itself. This would represent a saving in construction and would not harm the sailing qualities of the hull. The only excuse for a tapered keel is to obtain enough area in its sections to give sufficient sectional area in the outside ballast, in order that the proper weight may be obtained; or, as in a case of example, to give enough room for the centerboard. The importance of the width of keel when outside ballast is used has been explained, and it should be remembered that there ought to be enough room to allow sufficient spread to the ballast bolts to prevent the ballast from straining the wooden keel. Obviously, this may lead to a tapered keel, and the whole question, it must be concluded, would revolve around the choice of type used in the preliminary sketch.

Perhaps the best advice that can be given the amateur designer, not only in respect to lines but also in regard to all other features of yacht design, is that he be conservative in adopting "progressive" ideas. Experimental design should be developed slowly and cautiously, for the elements of safety and reliability are of more importance than speed, efficiency to windward, light construction or even labor-saving. There is also the fact to be considered, that a hull-type, rig or fitting may prove successful or fashionable in racers yet be most unsuitable in a cruiser.

The procedure employed in fairing the lines, as described in this chapter, may be varied slightly when the beginner has learned the projections required. Though the description of how the lines are drawn is necessarily involved, the beginner should not become discouraged and throw up the sponge, for a careful reading of the text combined with constant reference to the plates will enable him to understand each projection.

Seaworthiness

With passing years, seaworthiness in yachts seems to have declined. This is due to a number of causes. One is the usual good weather met with in the average yachting season, which puts no great demands upon a small yacht. Another is the fact that few owners make long cruises or runs in open water away from shelter. The third reason is that owners, having no experience with the needs of seaworthiness and safety in heavy weather for the reasons just given, are ready to sacrifice seaworthiness for comfort or convenience. Designers are also to blame in that they comply with owners' demands without emphasizing the dangers incurred. In fact, there is no longer any class of small craft operators who use boats all the year round in all weathers whose opinions are acceptable to yachtsmen as "standards" of seamanship and whose boats are looked upon with respect, for in general seaworthiness has also declined in small commercial boats since motors became available for fishing and other commercial boat use.

The elements of design relating to seaworthiness, particularly in power boats, are important and, considering existing trends, ought to be well understood by students of yacht design. Unfortunately these elements are difficult to measure precisely and to express mathematically. There is little information regarding seaworthiness in small craft obtainable from past model-testing and there has not been a great deal of study of cause and effect in their hull-forms. Therefore comments must be based upon comparisons and limited observations and analysis of known boats of varying types and designs and of their performance in heavy weather.

Seaworthiness is basically the ability of a boat to live in heavy weather without swamping, capsizing, breaking up or being heavily damaged while underway. Obviously, a boat designed to cruise in the open sea should be more seaworthy than one employed in sheltered waters, and a boat that is used in the fall and winter at sea should be more seaworthy than one used only in the summer weather. The distinction between the last two, however, must be somewhat modified by the present cycle of severe summer storms and hurricanes so that any boat making long sea voyages even in summer should be seaworthy to a high degree.

Seaworthiness when the boat is underway in severe weather

requires the most stringent restrictions on form as well as proper strength and working qualities. As a rule a boat seaworthy under such conditions is safe hove-to, drifting or at anchor in an exposed position in heavy weather.

Sea kindliness is the ability of a boat to meet heavy weather and remain reasonably dry, shipping no solid water and relatively little spray. It also is that quality of a boat or ship that permits comfort to the occupants in heavy weather—a slow easy roll with no jerk or sudden stop at the end of each roll, an equally slow and easy pitch. Unfortunately, boats under 40 feet that give an easy roll and pitch can rarely be designed; usually they require such range of stability, through low weights, and such buoyancy, through form and location of weights longitudinally, in order to live in the relatively exaggerated wave heights a small boat meets as compared to a large vessel, that comfort of occupants is very slight indeed. It is generally impossible to stand or walk in the cabin of a small cruiser, power or sail, in heavy weather, if she is a safe design for such conditions. However, this very characteristic of quick motion required in a small boat may prevent her from shipping solid water or much spray if she is properly designed, and is required if she is to live through very severe weather.

It is important for the owner and designer to decide, in the preliminary stage of design, what degree of seaworthiness will be required to meet actual use requirements. As a general rule, very seaworthy yachts are expensive and possible cabin arrangements are very limited indeed; therefore such yachts are generally undesirable and uncomfortable for short alongshore cruisers in good weather, for gunkholing and the like. A yacht, then, must be designed for her intended use, and she is not suited for other uses; this should be thoroughly understood.

The seaworthiness of a boat is determined by her form and, to a very great degree, by the distribution of weight in her. But other elements are far from unimportant—straight, low windage, watertight deck and superstructure openings, ability to free herself of any water shipped, and ease of handling and working in very rough weather. In small craft there is not much leeway in these matters. Weights must be low to give as safe a range of stability as is possible, and well concentrated amidships to give longitudinal buoyancy. The hull must be strongly built and the decks and superstructure as well. Openings to the weather must be small and closed with watertight, strong covers or doors. The effects of such openings on convenience and ventilation are obvious and difficult to treat well in design.

Self-righting is often demanded in seagoing yachts. This may be obtained theoretically and practically, but it is usually of limited value in most yachts, since these require cabins with some provisions for ventilation, convenience and light. Hence, if capsized, a self-righting yacht will usually swamp before she can right herself, as many accidents with deep, heavily ballasted sailing yachts have shown. It is more practical, therefore, to obtain a large safe-angle-of-heel in a seagoing design, whether power or sailing hull, through judicious use of form and ballast or other weights.

Freeboard is also demanded in seagoing boats, and the inexperienced usually insist on relatively high freeboard. While the amount of freeboard is important, usually, in fixing the maximum safe-angle-of-heel, excess freeboard serves no useful purpose. In a small cruiser there cannot be enough to prevent occasional shipping of water, and weight and windage of excessive freeboard are very definitely harmful. Inspection of small craft having reputations for seaworthiness shows that freeboard is rarely very great in proportion to their length, and that they depend upon hull form rather than upon lined dimensions for their good qualities. In power cruisers having the common shoal body employed in such craft, the freeboard is almost invariably excessive and is more of a danger than a help, which trait is augmented by the usual high and massive superstructure and flying bridge. Power cruisers for offshore work are therefore the best of the fishing boat model with deep draft and even with some ballast stowed inside.

Proportions for seaworthiness are only vaguely defined, as seaworthy craft vary a good deal. Following a local practice is often wise, for experience in a certain area may show that boats of certain lengths and widths fit the average seas better than boats of different proportions, but usually the margin for this is great. Excessively wide shoal power boats are, however, commonly poor performers in rough water, and too much should not be expected of the average "roomy" shoal motor cruiser which is only suitable for protected waters.

Windage is a factor of importance. Shoal boats, power and sail, have been known to capsize, at anchor or under way, in summer squalls simply because of the windage. Any boat which is expected to meet heavy weather should have the minimum windage, and this means supression of all high deck structures. It is not practical to give precise rules for allowable windage, for this must vary a great deal with the individual design, but the wise designer is aware of its dangers and resists demands for deck-on-deck superstructures, "flying bridges," and "green-houses." Unnecessary spars and rigging, weather cloths, awnings, large steering shelters and the like should be "designed down" to reduce windage as a principle of good design, often violated today.

The shape of the topsides has much to do with the behavior of a boat in rough water. The topsides must be formed to give the proper increases in buoyancy required to dampen pitching and to suppress spray, or to prevent solid water from boarding the boat while she is moving on her course. As a result, the forward sections are very important. It is usual in motor boats to employ marked hollow flare just abaft the bow for this purpose; it is also considered that extreme hollow flare is attractive and gives additional deck room forward. It is not unusual to see designs in which flare of this kind has been carried to a great extreme.

Flare, in the bow sections, is commonly less helpful than flam. Extremely hollow flare usually allows the bow to plunge deeply, gathering momentum, until suddenly it is brought up by the very quick increase in buoyancy occasioned by extreme flare. This sudden shock, with the usual modern addition of the soft nose bow, brings the full part of the latter deep in the water with a sudden increase in angle of entrance so that the wave being struck by the boat is augmented by an increased bow wave. Flam, however, causes a marked increase in buoyancy as the bow begins its plunge, and the buoyancy increases at a steady, marked rate so that the plunge is quickly braked. Though the size of the bow wave is increased by the increase in angle of entrance, the forebody is not usually immersed to the fore deck. However the flam should not be so great that it will cause the slamming that is seen in sailing hulls having bow overhangs and U-sections under power in a steep head sea. The flam sections then are best formed with a moderate V. Pitching while heeled may often be observed, and one should design flam with this in mind also.

To obtain a deep and narrow V-form it is usually most convenient to employ a deep, marked forefoot; even an angular forefoot in profile is useful. This is not only aid in forming proper sections but also prevents the forefoot from coming out of the water in every small wave and "tramping." Every time the forefoot is thrown out of water there is spray thrown when the forefoot drops in for the next dive, unless the forefoot is exceptionally sharp and the bow waterlines are very hollow or fine. Flare or flam in the topsides can usually be carried the greater part of the whole length of the hull to advantage. This gives additional increase in buoyancy, particularly in low-sided hulls, that is desirable to give dryness in a sea with sea abeam or on the quarter.

Drag to the keel is very important in a seagoing boat; this is a preventive to broaching if the draft is deep enough. In power boats with skegs, the drag need only be in the bottom of the keel and skeg, of course. However, there is no rule for the amount of drag to give safety. If the stern is wide and very buoyant close to or at the load line, as in most fast power cruisers, then great drag is necessary to prevent broaching, particularly in a relatively short, wide hull. In lieu of drag, a skeg formed as a deep fin may serve. Deep rudders are also used in lieu of drag in some designs, but it should be noted that very deep rudders are subject to great strains. In a following sea this gives directional stability. In power boats a skeg is usually employed, giving the same effects as drag to a keel, and the skeg was also employed in shoal-bodied sailing hulls with centerboards or fin keels. Some designers have employed deep rudders either of the balance type or hung on a small skeg. In such designs the rudder and its stock and the skeg must be very substantial; failure of a deep rudder used in place of a deep skeg or keel drag would be very serious in a heavy following sea. If the deep rudder is turned sharply under broaching conditions, it looses its effectiveness and broaching may then develop quickly. Hence the use of deep rudder to prevent broaching can hardly be recommended.

The Stem Profile

The methods of drawing and fairing the lines that have been described apply to both sailing and power hulls without regard to mode of construction or size. Elements in the design of power boats have been mentioned occasionally, where they paralleled those of sailing hulls. There remain, however, a number of subjects that are most commonly considered in designing motor boats.

The stem profile of a motorboat need usually be no more than a straight or nearly straight stem of moderate rake. In planing boats, where a marked forefoot may not be desirable, a curved stem must be used. However, bow overhang has no real advantage in power hulls. Where there is heavy flare in the forward sections it is often most convenient to fair these into a bald clipper or "chicken beak" bow, but care ought to be taken to avoid excessive overhang. In displacement (non-planing) hulls, waterline length is too important to be sacrificed to a "fancy" stem profile.

The "modern soft nose" stem has been very fashionable. This is usually formed with a raking, straight stem profile. In plan view it is sharp at and below the load line, rounding at a rapidly increasing rate as the deck or rail is approached. In many designs, the deck or gunwale in plan approaches an arc of a circle. While such a design fits the modern concept of streamlined appearance and gives additional deck space at the bow, it is a very expensive bow to construct in wood and has no important practical advantage either as to speed or to seaworthiness. In drawing such a stem it is desirable to employ closely spaced waterlines in the topsides and numerous buttocks to obtain fairness and to give sufficient offsets for accurate reproduction in building.

The shape of the topsides immediately abaft the stem is of importance in appearance and seaworthiness. This will be discussed later, but for the present it is sufficient to say that flam is better than flare in obtaining seaworthiness and dryness, but flare is considered the more handsome.

The form of the topsides, as the stern is approached, is also important as to appearance and seaworthiness. It is the general custom to bring the topsides plumb somewhere abaft midlength and to use increasing tumble-home as the transom is approached, in square stern hulls. In double-enders the flare or flam may be carried in some degree to the stern. The effect of optical illusion upon the sheer must never be forgotten, particularly where there is a heavy tumble-home at the transom. In fast motor boats some designers carry flam to the trasom; this is largely a matter of taste perhaps, but as a rule this produces a dry hull in rough water.

Rake in the ends is usually best decided by appearance. Excessive rake is to be avoided, and the relation of rake of bow and stern ought to be considered. Present trends seem to be toward somewhat extreme rake of stem, or toward a "chicken-beak" profile, lately the fashion in liners. This does not seem very attractive when combined with a very raking cruiser or canoe stern or with a flat transom. It would be better, usually, to use much less rake in transom than bow. The tumble-home transom, still sometimes seen in power boats and, sadly enough, in sailing hulls too often, is at best lubberly and even dangerous in a following sea. Heavily streamlined sterns such as the "slipper," where sheer is carried down to the load line at the stern when at rest, have no place in a boat exposed to rough water.

"Streamlining" of motor boats is a present fad that requires commonsense examination. In very fast hydroplanes and run-abouts it has some advantage if done honestly, but this does not justify double stern fins like tail-light hoods of luxury auto-mobiles. The streamlined racing motor boat justifies use of en-closed cockpits, tapered tail and single fin design and rounded gunwales—and the best way to study the scientific streamlining required is in a wind tunnel, since streamlined topsides are en-tirely a matter of wind resistance.

In slow moving craft and cruisers the "streamlining" usually employed is not only unnecessary but harmful. In the first place, wind resistance in these boats is usually not from ahead but from any point of the compass, as wind velocity is usually greater than the speed of the boat. Hence the use of curved profile extensions to breaks in the rail or superstructure is not streamlining and merely adds to broadside or quartering windage. The use of such "streamlining" is hardly adult thinking on the part of the designer, and is not intelligent styling. The develop-ment of sound motorboat design has been retarded by the use of automobile styling, which has no relationship to the require-ments of a boat, either as to comfort or as to safety and speed.

Superstructure is an inherent problem in motorboats. It is usually desirable to show the superstructure in the lines with the necessary height offsets and suitable dimensions. This is important in those designs in particular that, because of the ex-tent of their superstructure, require careful massing and detailed design to avoid awkwardness in appearance. Rake, height, open-ings and "breaking down" of ends of houses should be carefully laid down in the lines plan with necessary dimensions.

The entrance and run of a power boat will be decided by type of hull being used, or by the speed-length ratio sought. The usual process is to decide the cruising speed desired then add the "reserve speed" and power, by use of comparison, to establish this. But the designer usually tries to develop lines that will drive with the least resistance with the given power, or use only part of the power available. The reasoning employed is that owners want an engine to last well and this will not be the case if the full output is continuously used. It is common, therefore, to try to design to the desired speed with about 60% of the horsepower being employed. This, unfortunately, is not a matter than can be done with precision, and experience and judgment are required to achieve the most desired results. In practice the designer therefore strives for a very easily drivn hull, or at least as easily driven as the arrangement and hull proportions permit.

It is usual for the designer of a cruiser to make his load line as fine in the entrance as the length-beam proportion permits, and as the cabin arrangement dictates. Normally the greatest beam at the load line is abaft the midlength in cruisers. The entrance, just abaft the stem rabbet in these craft, is formed with the load line nearly straight; the water lines below become hollow—particularly so if the forefoot is deep. There appears to be some prejudice against hollow in the load line even in displacement boats but there seems to be no harm in it if there are not shoulders formed farther aft as the load line sweeps around the mid-body. The after lines in the topsides will become full as the flare in the forebody dictates Sharp entrances do not imply a lack of seaworthiness. In planing boats of normal types, the entrance is usually rather sharp, as the lift of the forebody is great enough even then. Snubbed waterlines at load and below are undesirable in small motor boats as they create a heavy bow wave that produces a wet boat in a seaway. The "bulbous" forefoot used in large vessels does not seem to work well in small craft as the forefoot of the latter will lift out of water very often, even in a small sea.

The shape of the 'bow lines," or forward portion of the buttocks, in profile is a very useful criterion of entrance-form. Generally speaking, in sail or power hulls, the profile of these lines should show a smooth easy sweep up to the load line or above. Hard turns in the lines, below the load, are to be avoided though with a deep and rather angular forefoot such a form may appear in buttocks close to the hull-centerline without harm. The outer buttocks at quarterbeam and beyond should not have hard spots below the load line. Interestingly enough, this appears to be as true in sailing hulls as in planing boats of round-bottom form.

A little experience with fairing lines will show how necessary buttock and waterline forms are in judging the form of a hull.

The run in motorboats is very important as to speed. It is usual to employ straight-line buttocks to at least some degree, even in low speed hulls. As the speed-length ratio increases, so does the length of the straight-line buttocks in the run, and their angle of intersection with the load line decreases until, in planing hulls, the straight buttocks parallel the load or depart from it as they go aft. The straight-line buttocks are accompanied, in shoal-bodied power boats, by a similar straight-line keel rabbet in the run; the exception being when hollow garboards are used in the after body sections. In non-planing high speed hulls the straight-line buttocks may exceed half the load line length, and likewise the straight-line keel rabbet of the run, bringing the "breast" of the buttocks and rabbet well foreward of mid-length—in the rabbet it is often ⅕ or ⅙ of the load line length abaft the stem.

The immersion of the transom varies with the speed-length ratio, as a rule. In low speed hulls the bottom of the transom is at or above the load line at rest. In fast boats the transom is usually well immersed; however there is apparently some relation between the length of the hull and the depth of the transom that can be immersed; the immersion is greater in the short hulls. No specific rule has apparently been developed for the permissible amount of immersion; it is decided by comparison and the experience of the individual designer with an individual type of boat. Generally, the transoms of planing boats are the most deeply immersed. This is controlled by the run of the straight buttocks and keel rabbet, of course.

V-Bottom Hulls

V-bottom hulls require special consideration here. It is a popular assumption that round-bottom hull forms are more efficient in low speed-length ratios than are V-bottoms and that at some given speed-length ratio, usually 2.5, the V-bottom becomes notably superior. This is a convenient assumption, but it over-simplifies the problem. There are very sound reasons for suspecting that a V-bottom hull may be designed that is equally as efficient at low speed as a round-bottom. Whereas the hull forms for low speed-length ratios are well known in round-bottom forms and are proven by model tank tests, this has not been the case with the V-bottom until recently. Some V-bottoms of low power and comparatively high speed have been produced. From examination of these it appears that the chine profiles of such boats show little or no fore-and-aft camber and are little submerged or not at all. There was one successful launch of this type in which the chine profile and load line coincided for the full length of the hull, the keel rabbet was a straight line, transom to forefoot, and the greatest beam at chine (and L.W.L.) was just forward of the transom. It is possible that a less radical design might be quite efficient and there is need for more model testing and thorough investigation in this field. It is known from experience with auxiliary sailing hulls that low camber chine profiles give efficient hulls at sailing speeds.

In high speed hulls the chine profile has long been a matter of controversy among experienced designers. The most popular profile is high at the stem rabbet, say ⅓ to ⅝ of the bow freeboard above the load at rest, and running downward and aft in a sagging curve, to the bottom of the transom. The chine crosses the load line, at rest, somewhere about ⅓ or more the load line length abaft the stem. However, some designers cross the load line forward of this and some abaft, depending upon the shape of the underbody below the chines. In some designs the chine profile has followed the shape of the powder-horn sheer. There is often a relationship between the chine profile and the running trim of a planing V-bottom, though it cannot be assumed that this is the sole factor; the shape of the bottom below the chine, its deadrise sectional form, the width across the chines as the stern is approached and the whole shape of the planing surface are involved. While many attempts have recently been made to describe the elements of planing boats in mathematical terms and to define the scientific design of the type, there apparently is relatively little scientific data available, and experience and study are required to produce wholly satisfactory results. The amateur interested in such boats would do well to base his theories and designs upon actual boats whose performance he has seen and judged superior, rather than upon published plans or information.

Some designers form the run by employing sections in the body plan having "constant deadrise" or "parallel floors" in all or most of the sections comprising the run, combined with straight-line buttocks of length. This is a very old practice in hull design, going as far back as the early eighteenth century at least. It has been employed by some noted American designers of sailing hulls, and the principle has appeared in many very fast yachts, pilotboats and fishing schooners. In deep draft hulls the parallel floors extended from the hollow garboard to the bilge, in shoal hulls from the keel rabbet. This form of run was also popular in V-bottom sailing hulls, extending from rabbet to chine, and has sometimes been applied to topsides as well. It is occasionally seen in deep-hulled power boats of the dragger type. In rather recent years it has been dignified by the pseudo-scientific name of "monhedron hull form" and applied to planing hulls. The basic theory of constant deadrise is to avoid a warp in the plane of deadrise on the assumption that warping creates undesirable eddies. While there is some historical support for the theory in sailing hulls, as in the case of straight-line buttocks, it has been less studied than the buttock form and therefore can be less rigidly supported. It should be noted, however, that while one warp in the deadrise plane appears in some successful boats, a double-warp should apparently be avoided in both power and sail hulls. The double-warp seems to appear often in deep power boats having canoe sterns, unless the designer takes care.

The effect of stern profile on the run of the buttocks may be an important factor. It is easiest, of course, to obtain a flat run with a transom stern, as required in fast boats. As a result, perhaps, it has become fashionable to speak of the effects of stern profiles in terms of resistance. However, this is not always correct, for most stern profiles can be manipulated in design so as to produce the desirable straightness and angle of buttocks. This can be seen in the "bustle" counter stern once popular in fast steam and power yachts. By forming the canoe or cruiser stern properly, the same desirable buttocks can usually be obtained. The search for desired appearance at the ends of the hull does not justify poor lines. Some stern profiles do have a definite relation to extremes in speed-length ratio, and these are most obvious when designing to high speed requirements.

The width of the after body, in power boats, is an important matter in design. Squatting, or sinking of the stern when the boat is at her running speed, is to be avoided. This can be done by proper choice of buttock form and angle for a given speed, but above the speed-length ratio of 1.5 the width of the stern and of the after body become quite important. Not only does width of stern play an increasingly important part in high speed hulls, but so does deadrise of the floors. In the very high speed hulls, and in planing hulls in particular, the deadrise becomes small and the transom may be as wide as the hull's maximum beam. This may be observed in round-bottom outboard motor boats designed for planing where, for all practical purposes, the hull form resembles the fore body of a much longer boat, with the after body omitted.

Longitudinal steering stability is desirable in power boats and hence some keel outside the rabbet is commonly employed. Even in outboard motor boats of the planing type, a small outside keel is necessary for steering and banking. Such external keels should be flat-sided, for they produce needed lateral plane cheaply and therefore should never be well-rounded athwartships in the mistaken effort to "streamline.". It is undersirable, however, to bring the keel or skeg close to the propeller of an outboard motor, as this produces marked cavitation as the motor is turned in steering, even at low speeds. In cruisers, a skeg is the most practical and cheapest way to give directional stability and drag to the keel line, and to protect shaft, propeller and rudder in grounding. But the after end of any skeg should be well faired off to above and below the stern bearing; this is important in reducing resistance and for propeller efficiency. Also, a wide post or skeg-end will often produce noise and vibration in a power boat. Hollow garboards in the run serve the purpose of a skeg; some designers prefer these to skegs, but in general hull forms with hollow garboards are more expensive to build than those with skegs and it is doubtful if the cost of the hollow garboards is justifed by the small advantage in resistance.

In high speed motor boats the skeg should not be brought close to the propeller for it may produce cavitation. This is very noticeable in outboard motor craft, where a keel or skeg brought close up to the propeller mounting produces marked cavitation when the mounting is turned in steering. It is usual to reduce the depth of an external keel in an outboard motor boat of the planing type some 18 to 24 inches forward of the transom at least, and to taper the keel quite sharply abaft that point.

Dryness in V-bottom hulls does not require a high chine forward, as judicious use of flare or flam in the topsides will suffice. When the chine is high, marked wave formation occurs where the chine crosses the load line, and if the deadrise there is not great the spray thrown may be very troublesome, even at relatively low speeds. Seagoing V-bottom power hulls, such as the Hatteras Boat, have low chines forward, very sharp entrances, and the flaring sides are carried the full length of the hulls and round the wide sterns. Deadrise is rather great. Experience shows that a V-bottom power boat may be designed to be as seaworthy as a round-bottom hull; all V-bottoms do not have the proper form, however.

In planing hulls of the V-bottom type there is sometimes trouble with tripping in a high speed turn; the hull does not bank sufficiently to prevent skidding and then the chine digs in; the boat may capsize or go out of control, "running off on her chine." This is prevented by forming the chine in a narrow flat plane, wider aft than forward and very often warped so that its angle to the L.W.L. is greater forward than aft. No rule can be given for the width of this anti-tripping plane—it is wide in hydroplanes and narrow in runabouts of lower speeds, and its design is determined by experience in a given model and speed.

In very fast boats, round- and V-bottom, it is common to

see a thin sheet of water from the bow wave forced up the side and around the flare, to produce a continual sheet of spray on deck. Spray guards prevent this; they may be narrow, light battens with a surface about parallel the load line at rest athwartships on their underside, and of scantlings of a normal guard. They are useful in round-bottom planing hulls as well as in some V-bottoms, and are usually about half the freeboard height at stern and ¼ or ⅓ at transom. It is not necessary to carry the spray guard clear to the stem, but only far enough to be above the bow wave at running speed, though it is best to carry the guard to the transom astern. In some V-bottoms the spray guard is built into the hull above the chines.

The design of stepped hydroplanes requires special study and is not recommended for amateurs. The angles of the planes in relation to one another are very important. Steps may be of little depth but all must be ventilated. Multi-step hydroplanes are usually four steps, and usually the depth of the steps increases as the stern is approached. As little as ⅛ inch variation in the angle of the after steps will affect performance. Single-step boats are more common and ¾ of the forward plane has less angle than the after ¼; the latter is ½ to 1¼ degrees the greater. The step is usually a little abaft mid-length and the center of gravity is about 5 to 7% of the hull length abaft the step; porpoising is an indication that the center of gravity is too far aft, or the forward plane is too steep. In a fast non-step V-bottom it is a sign of too steep a plane in the forebody. If the stern rises and the bow drops suddenly at planing speed it shows the angle of the after plane is too great or the center of gravity is too far forward. Nowadays the bottom is very narrow (planing surface), the wide anti-skid plane forming the rest of the beam, chine to chine.

The stepped hydroplanes handle poorly at low speed, steer badly and require excessive power. Like sea sleds and hydrofoils, they are effective only at planing speeds.

In all general discussions of design factors, hull form and hull efficiency it is impossible to avoid over-emphasizing and over-simplication. To examine a single factor or element is to take it out of the context of the design and consider it as though it were independent of all other factors and elements, which in fact it is not. This leads to over-simplication of effects and then to over-emphasis of the importance of other factors of the element in the success or failure of a boat. No one element will insure good or poor design and performance. This will only be obtained by a blend of elements and factors, the good in heavy predominance. Even then, the good elements may not be perfect in themselves, for there is contradiction when perfection is sought in all elements. Some elements and factors are, of course, no more than mere theories. It must be remembered that many factors in design are not capable of precise measurement and many are not even of constant value, mathematically, from day to day. Indeed the lines of a boat represent so many assumptions and approximations that it is incorrect to consider them the product of a precise and well explored science. Not even displacement is precisely constant, day-to-day, in a boat. Design calculations are usually near enough for all practical purposes unless the result is expected to apply with a very narrow margin in which to work. Then judgment, experience and common sense apply, rather than calculation alone. The art of using mathematical processes in small craft design rests in knowing how really precise each calculation is, basically, and the comparative importance of the calculated answer.

Beauty in power boat design is difficult to obtain in small craft unless superstructure and headroom in cabins are both restricted.

Plastic and Ferro-Concrete Design

The drafting methods that have been described serve for the design of plastic and ferro-concrete craft, except the construction plans are somewhat simplified. It is not the intent here to set forth construction requirements, for these are still rather fluid as new techniques continue to appear. Only a few general comments can be given here.

Small craft under 40 feet length, of plastic or ferro-concrete construction, are often over-weight when designed by inexperienced amateurs. In sailing craft, this may also affect stability, caused by use of quantities of material to obtain strength while retaining radical forms of hull topsides, deck layouts, cabin trunks, or masting that are now the popular aim of many amateur and professional designers.

The use of plastic and ferro-concrete enables radical hull-forms and "styling" to be employed without producing construction difficulties, such as would result in the use of these characteristics in normal wooden construction. However, radical forms often produce costly construction, therefore these should be limited to areas where such forms would produce some practical and useful result.

In the use of plastic and ferro-concrete construction it is very important that the specifications of a design follow with the utmost precision the instructions given by the manufacturer of the materials. It is well for an amateur designer to realize that these new construction materials do not avoid the need for skill in building—there is no possibility of an unskilled amateur producing a highly finished boat of plastic or ferro-concrete, as is also the case with conventional wooden boat building. New problems arise in the use of these new materials: condensate in cabins, noise transmission, odor, and occasional structural failure. Changes in construction detail, while building, are to be avoided with these new materials. Careful studies of the use of plastic or ferro-concrete are very necessary in amateur design of boats of these materials. The combination of plastic and fiber-glass, or the like, with plank, plywood or steel construction may produce structural failure and maintenance problems due to the different rates of expansion and contraction of the structural materials. For example, moisture may penetrate plank from inboard, lodging between plank and fiber-glass with destructive results to the bond of the two materials.

Multi-Hull Design

The double-hull or "catamaran" has had short periods of popularity since the seventeenth century. Repeated experiments have produced a number of catamaran types. The small racer or day-sailer is light and has two hulls having U-shaped sections combined with very fine ends—the midsections are slightly forward of midlength. The hulls are very narrow and some are reminiscent of the old displacement racing launches of 1900–1910, with slightly immersed transoms. The buttocks are very straight and nearly horizontal. Each hull has a rudder and a centerboard. The overall length-beam ratio is from 1.4 to 2.2 and the beam-draft ratio is about 2.0. The hulls are symmetric with minimum wetted-surface forms. The hull spacings are about one-half the waterline length or greater. These catamarans are sailed heeled, with the lee hull carrying all the weight. Planing is not present, due to varying wind speeds and the poor sailing qualities that a planing hull would produce. Spray steps are usually worked into the forebody below the sheer to increase reserve buoyancy forward as well as to suppress spray. *Weight is critical in the design of these small racers or racing day-sailers.* The connecting beams are usually tubing or light trusses.

The large cruising catamarans are expected to sail on both hulls, upright. The hull forms are therefore of great variety; some are a symmetric V-shape, without centerboard. Some designers have the maximum curvature in the sections inboard, the flat side outboard, but there appears to be no objection to reversing this. It seems possible that the importance of this is slight and that length, displacement and sail area are the important and critical elements. In cruising or ocean racing the catamaran is never intentionally sailed heeled, with the windward hull clear out, as these craft can be readily capsized, like most shallow draft, unballasted boats.

Cabin accommodations are usually skeleton in ocean racers and sometimes awkward in cruisers, except where the vessels are large enough to have deck houses. The construction of a large catamaran requires engineering knowledge far beyond the capacity of most amateur designers. Motor catamarans are sometimes used as houseboats and for this purpose they are very practical.

Trimarans consist of a central hull, which floats the weight of the boat, with outrigged floats on each side. At rest the floats may be clear of the water or in it; their prime service is to give stability under sail. Like the catamarans, they can sail very fast under certain conditions and have great power to carry sail. They are somewhat popular as cruisers, as the central hull can be used for accommodations. They take a small initial heel in sailing, but until the wind becomes strong they sail nearly upright.

The proa is the least popular of the multi-hull types. These are double-ended and have an out-rigged float on one side. The Pacific Island proas kept the float to windward, and the helmsman changed ends instead of tacking. Some "civilized" versions sail with the float alternately to windward and to leeward, but this is probably an inefficient practice.

Multi-hulls share many advantages and disadvantages. They have initial stability to carry sail well. They are very fast reaching and close-hauled, extremely fast when of the racing daysailer type. In large sizes they have great deck room and large accommodations. Powered catamarans have been proposed for research vessels and for fishing craft. Multi-hull sailing craft do not stay well, and are awkward to handle in slips and around piers. They can capsize and must be handled with care in blowing weather. They are very adversely affected in performance by any increase in displacement beyond what they were designed to have. Multi-hull craft above the racing day-sailer in length are expensive craft to build and to *maintain*.

IV. The Construction and Joiner Plans

General Discussion of Construction

THE construction plans are the next drawings to be made. Under this head, the hull structure, deck erections and joiner work are included. In sailing craft there are usually three or four separate drawings under this head: the construction midsection, the construction plans, the joiner sections, and the joiner plans.

Before discussing the drawing of the plans, a general discussion of construction methods and design is necessary. The basic design of the hull structure is the backbone (keel) and the ribs (frames). This is, however, supplemented by the deck beams, and by the skin (planking) and decking. There are a multitude of construction details, some of which are common, others rarely seen, but in the limited space at our disposal only the more common methods can be described.

There are certain maxims of construction which should be kept in view while designing construction details. Mere heavy timbering does not produce strength unless properly fastened and located in the hull structure. Too large, or too many, fastenings weaken rather than strengthen the structure. The simple and easy methods of construction are not only the cheapest, but the least liable to rot. The test of a method of hull construction is not only its strength when new, but also its lasting qualities and cost. There is, usually, no necessity of extremely light and complicated hull construction in cruising craft. However, construction can be quite light and yet be strong, cheap and simple. Observation and commonsense, combined with a little ingenuity, are the best guides in designing hull construction. The methods of construction used in the type, of which one's design is an example, is, ordinarily, the desirable construction for that particular type. The hull strains in modern yachts are not as great as might be supposed, when waterborne (afloat). The greatest strains will appear in grounding or in hauling out. Weight of structure should be heaviest at the keel, lightening as the deck is approached. The method of fastening the various members of the hull structure are of tremendous importance, so far as strength is concerned. Pockets that hold moisture, due to lack of limber, or drain holes, poor ventilation between the planking and inside joiner finish, or ceiling, and inaccessible places in the hull structure, are features that rapidly reduce the strength of a hull as it ages. These conditions encourage rot, the insidious enemy of all wooden construction. Ventilation and drainage are therefore as important in the life of a yacht as is scantling.

Form of hull will govern, to a large extent, the choice of framing and construction methods. The construction methods should be chosen for strength, lasting qualities, cheapness, and yet with due regard to the abilities of the builder. It is bad judgment to expect a builder of common commercial vessels to turn out a highly finished yacht. The machinery and methods of the builder who is expected to build the boat should be studied.

All openings, such as hatches, skylights, etc., in small cruisers, should be kept large enough to be of practical use. There is a tendency to reduce such openings as the size of the boat is diminished. The size of these openings should not be in accordance with the size of the boat, but in accordance with the requirements of their use. The joiner work should be designed with judgment, keeping in mind that it must be refinished oftener than the interior of a house. For this reason complicated mouldings, heavy carving, and deep panels are impractical. The reason is that it is impossible to clean out paint or varnish in deep, heavy mouldings, panels or carving when refinishing. As a result, the crevices are soon filled with paint, dirt and varnish and the lines of the decoration are lost. The lack of crispness and delicacy of

such joiner work is apparent in many of the old yachts that
can be found laid up in storage yards. The cleanliness and sani-
tation of a yacht is often a matter of joiner design. Beaded
tongue-and-groove ceiling, cracks in panels, and deep moulding
and carving, all are dirt catchers and should be avoided. All
lockers should be ventilated to prevent mould and odor. If bulkheads are numerous, openings are indispensable in order to prevent odor and other evidences of poor ventilating from appear-
ing.

Lighting by natural light is of great importance, and the
joiner work should be designed to procure natural light in all
parts of the cabin. All the deck openings must be water-tight
when closed. Sharp corners that will cause bodily injuries must
be avoided, not only in the cabin, but on deck. The strength of
the deck structures should not be overlooked. The proper
method of locking and fastening down skylights and hatches is
a matter for consideration. In designing cabin trunks and other
deck openings, care should be taken that the transverse strength
of the hull is not reduced. The transverse strength of the hull
is equal in importance to the longitudinal strength, and the transverse strength often governs the power to withstand longitudinal
strains. It is not necessary to draw every little detail, but what is
shown should be correct. The feather edge, in timbers or plank,
should be avoided since this edge is impossible to caulk. The
strongest fastening for heavy timbers is the wooden tree-nail
(pronounced "trunnel"); next, the galvanized steel "drift-bolt"
which is merely a steel rod driven through the timbers. The
ordinary bolt with washers and nut is next, the lag screw and
ordinary screws and spikes or nails follow. The type of fastening must be in accordance with the scantling of the timber or
plant, and should not be too large in diameter. Copper and
bronze have the least power to withstand a direct pull. A fastening is to be no stronger than the timber through which it passes.
Where possible, the fastenings should be staggered, so that the
holes for them do not fall in the same line of grain. Washers
should be used on the heads or drift bolts, and on lags and at
both ends of ordinary bolts, when used in timber. Do not use

Fastenings

Nails

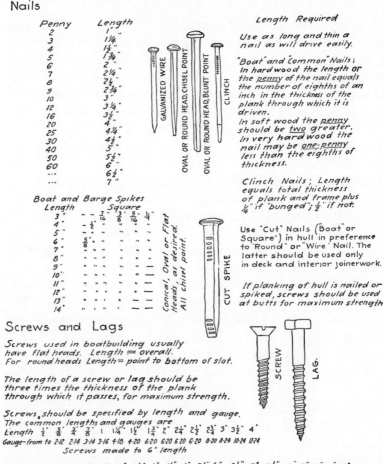

Penny	Length
2	1"
3	1¼"
4	1½"
5	1¾"
6	2"
7	2¼"
8	2½"
9	2¾"
10	3"
12	3¼"
16	3½"
20	4"
25	4¼"
30	4½"
40	5"
50	5½"
60	6"
...	6½"
...	7"

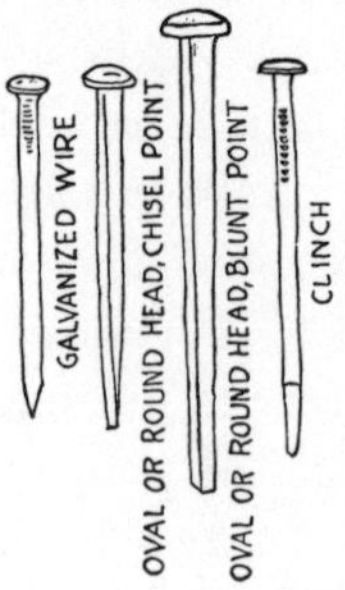

GALVANIZED WIRE
OVAL OR ROUND HEAD, CHISEL POINT
OVAL OR ROUND HEAD, BLUNT POINT
CLINCH

Length Required

Use as long and thin a nail as will drive easily.

"Boat" and "Common" Nails; In hard wood the length or the penny of the nail equals the number of eighths of an inch in the thickness of the plank through which it is driven. In soft wood the penny should be two greater. In very hard wood the nail may be one-penny less than the eighths of thickness.

Clinch Nails; Length equals total thickness of plank and frame plus ¼" if "bunged"; ½" if not.

Boat and Barge Spikes

Length	Square					
3"	–	–	7/16"	3/8"	5/16"	¼"
4"	–	½"	"	"	"	"
5"	–	"	"	"	"	"
6"	5/8"	"	"	"	"	"
7"	"	"	"	"	"	"
8"	"	"	"	"	"	"
9"	"	"	"	"	"	—
10"	"	"	"	"	"	—
11"	"	"	"	"	"	—
12"	"	"	"	"	"	—
13"	"	"	"	"	—	—
14"	"	"	"	"	—	—

Conical, Oval or Flat Heads, as desired. All chisel point.

CUT SPIKE

Use "Cut" Nails ("Boat" or Square") in hull in preference to "Round" or "Wire" Nail. The latter should be used only in deck and interior joinerwork.

If planking of hull is nailed or spiked, screws should be used at butts for maximum strength

Screws and Lags

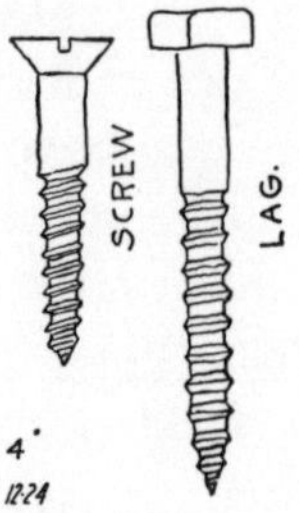

SCREW
LAG.

Screws used in boatbuilding usually have flat heads. Length = overall.
For round heads Length = point to bottom of slot.

The length of a screw or lag should be three times the thickness of the plank through which it passes, for maximum strength.

Screws should be specified by length and gauge. The common lengths and gauges are

Length	½"	5/8"	¾"	7/8"	1	1¼"	1½	1¾"	2"	2¼"	2½"	2¾"	3"	3½"	4"
Gauge-from to	2-12	2-14	3-14	3-16	4-18	4-20	6-20	6-20	6 20	6-20	8-20	8-24	10-24	12-24	

Screws made to 6" length

Lags made to lengths of	3"	3½"	4"	4½"	5"	5½"	6"	6½"	7"	7½"	8"	9"	10"	11"	12"
Dia. from to	5/16-7/8	5/16-1	5/16-1	5/16-1	5/16-1	5/16-1	5/16-1	7/16-1	7/16-1	7/16-1	7/16-1	7/16-1	½-1	½-1	½-1

Bolts

Shearing stress of bolts in a butt, scarph, lap or joint should equal tensile strength of the smallest timber

Tensile Strength, per sq. in. of section; Oak = 1200 lbs., Y. Pine = 1200, Spruce = 800, Fir = 800, W. Pine = 700
Hackmatack = 900, Cedar = 1000

Drift bolts - dia ranges from ¼" to 1"; of wt. iron rod. Treat as bolts in selecting diameters.

Use Common Sense

Fastenings used in construction, with rules for required length and size. The strength of a properly secured fastening is in direct proportion to its tensile strength. The diameter of any edge-fastening should never exceed ⅓ the siding of the smallest timber fastened by it.

fastenings of too great a diameter. This is so common an error that the warning should be repeated. Excess weight in scantling may increase the strains, particularly in certain types of hull, rather than increase strength. The ideal of construction would be a boat that was as strong and sound when twenty years old as when newly launched. However, when designing construction, the life of each kind of material should be kept in mind. Cheap timber, kiln dried, and of coarse texture, will usually show rot within ten years. Therefore, if it is desirable to use cheap material, there is no use in requiring workmanship equal to that required in a yacht that will last twice as long. The cost of the workmanship required in the hull should have a direct relationship to the quality of material used. By proper design, however, cheap lumber might possibly outlast good lumber, even though a cheaper grade of workmanship is used, since ventilation and fastenings are of more importance than finish, so far as lasting qualities of a hull are concerned.

The salting of hulls has been neglected in recent years and few yachts are provided with salt boxes or salt stops. Salting will add many years to the life of a wooden vessel, and there is no reason why salt should not be employed. Reference to the figures showing typical frame details and rudder hanging, show the installation of salt stops or salt boxes. Coarse-grain rock salt, as used in the old ice cream freezers, will do.

Ballast Keel Drawing and Deadwood

The actual drawing of the construction plan may sometimes begin with a pattern drawing for the ballast keel, if the keel is moulded as in the keel catboat, Plate VII. In the example the keel is flat-sided and rectangular in section, so a pattern drawing is not required. The construction drawing will show the timbering of the hull and deck, and the construction details. The keel and deadwood will be first designed. This will include the centerboard case in the example. Timber employed in the keel and deadwood is subject to local conditions, so far as width and length are concerned. The keel piece may usually be found in one piece if the length of the timber does not exceed 40 feet. This applies to Yellow Pine. However, it is very difficult to procure Oak in long lengths in most sections of the country. Splicing or scarphing the keel does not sacrifice strength but it does increase the amount of labor, and therefore the cost. The width of timber employed in the deadwood should not exceed 12 inches; it is cheaper to use a number of small widths rather than a few wide timbers, as wide stuff is often very difficult to procure. Of course, there are occasions when it is absolutely necessary to use wide stock, but it will be found that it is usually possible to work in small stuff instead. The sizes of commercial stock are as follows:—lengths, 10, 12, 14, 15, 18, 20, 22, 24 feet; the widths and thickness, 1″ x 2″, 1″ x 4″, 1″ x 6″, 1″ x 8″, 1″ x 10″, 1″ x 12″, 2″ x 4″, 2″ x 6″, 2″ x 8″, 2″ x 10″, 2″ x 12″, 2″ x 14″, 2″ x 16″, 3″ x 6″, 3″ x 8″, 3″ x 10″, 3″ x 12″, 3″ x 14″, 3″ x 16″, 4″ x 4″, 4″ x 6″, 4″ x 8″, 6″ x 6″, 6″ x 8″, 6″ x 10″, 6″ x 12″, 8″ x 8″, 10″ x 10″, 10″ x 12″, 12″ x 12″, 12″ x 14″. Actually the dimensions are under those given; take a 2″ x 6″, 12 feet long, for example; it would actually be about 1⅞″ x 5⅞″, 12 feet long. The length, however, is often a little short of the commercial dimension, so it is usually well to figure that a piece 12 feet long would only measure 11′-6″ when used in the hull, due to cracks or damage at the ends of the plank. For long lengths a premium must be paid. Oak is difficult to procure in lengths exceeding 24 feet. Yellow Pine and Western Larch can be procured in very long lengths, and in very wide planks. White Elm is sometimes used for keels, but is not usually procurable in lengths over 24 feet. In some localities, cypress and spruce are used. These are procurable in long lengths.

Before going further, the best timber for keels and stem and stern deadwood may be discussed. For keels, Yellow Pine, Western Larch and Oak are undoubtedly the best. For northern waters, Oak is very satisfactory, but if the boat is to be used in Florida waters or in the West Indies, Yellow Pine is the most

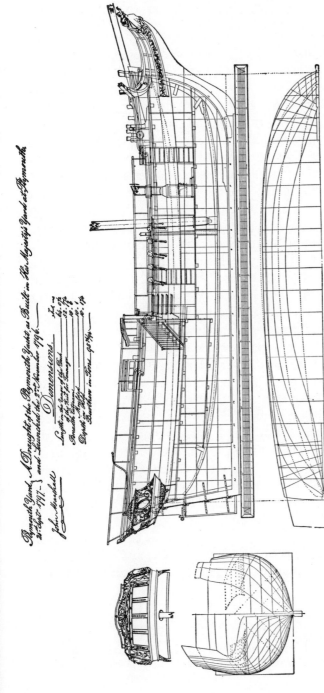

PLATE IX. *Yacht of 1796, showing an example of the traditional excellence of marine draftsmanship. This fine old Admiralty yacht shows the stern, cabin and stern windows, then popular, and the heavy ornate figurehead, bead rails and trail boards. An excellent study of sources of the tradition of sailing hull ornamentation. Reproduction of original draught. The details were drawn in red ink, superimposed on the lines; the latter were in black and blue. Courtesy of the British Admiralty.*

satisfactory. Oak is subject to rot and attack by worms in warm waters and atmosphere of tropical and subtropical climates.

Rock and soft Elm are in the same class as Oak, but are not easily obtainable. Cypress is soft, but it is durable, though hard to work, and soaks up water to a great degree, thus becoming very heavy. Spruce is light, tough and elastic, but decays quickly. It is not extremely durable in keels. Western Larch is strong and durable, and does not split easily, and can be had in very long lengths.* Hard maple is heavy, stiff, strong, wears well, and will serve for keels; other Maples (Sugar and Black are classed as hard) are soft and not so useful (Silver, Red, etc.). Maple has moderate shrinkage, but is said to decay around fastenings. Knees for stem and stern deadwood may be of Oak, Madeira, Western Larch (or Hackmatack).* Oak and Larch knees are most common and are very satisfactory except in the tropics. Madeira or "Horse-flesh" is used in Florida and in the West Indies for knees. Mesquite is used on the Texas coast for knees. It is of the iron-wood family and very hard, heavy and durable. However, it is very expensive. Hackmatack, or Larch, makes excellent knees, and is very durable. Knee timber is either sold for a flat sum or by the inch-thickness. An arm of a knee should not be drawn over 4 feet in length, as long arms are hard to procure and result in the builder paying a premium for them. If very large knees are required, study should be given to the possibility of working in straight-grained stock or built-up knees.

Woods least subject to decay are Cedar, Chestnut, Cypress, Locust, Redwood, Black Walnut, Yew, Douglas Fir, Oak, Pine (Yellow), Gum, Larch, Ash, Beech, Birch, in order. White Pine is doubtful in decay resistance.**

The structure of deadwood and keel, in the example, is shown in Plate XI. The joints or scarphs in the keel and other timbers are shown in the drawing. The length of the scarphs depends

---

* Hackmatack, Tamarack and Larch are all names for the same tree that are used in different localities. Lumbermen usually refer to roots of the Larch (for knees) as "hackmatack."

** For detailed and comparative information on the qualities of American timber see "Wood Handbook" (U. S. Department of Agriculture), Superintendent of Documents, Washington, D. C., price 35 cents.

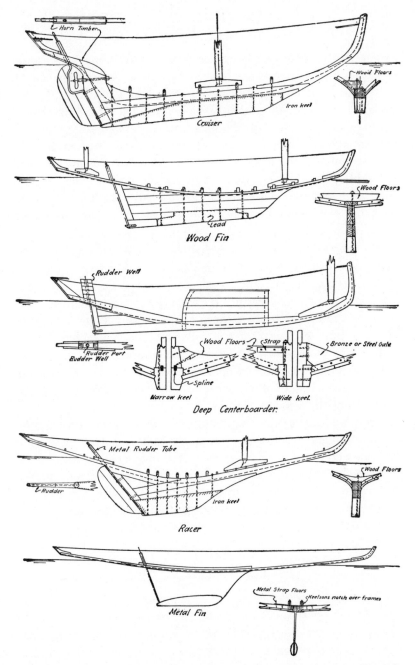

Typical keel construction, showing methods of designing deadwood
and keel.

upon the depth of the keel, or timber, and should make an angle of about 13° with the top or bottom. The common keel scarph is without jogs. If a great load is expected, the scarph can be jogged once or twice, or keys put in to lock the scarph. "Stop-waters" are through plugs of wood, driven into holes bored through lines of the scarphs or seams at the line of rabbet, to prevent leakage. These stopwaters are vitally important and the drawing should show their locations. All seams passing through the rabbet should have two stopwaters if possible; one in any case. The deadwood should be locked together by "jogs," to prevent "working." The Plate will give an idea of the treatment of these details in an actual drawing. Scarphs should end clear of the keel bolts or floor fastenings and are often vertical in the keels of large shoal hulls. The deadwood aft should be very strong in keel vessels with much drag, as the heel of the stern-post is exposed to terrific blows when the vessel grounds. Scarphs should be at least three frame spaces long. The back-bone of the stern overhang is called the horn timber. This is fastened to the top of the sternpost by a mortise and tenon, or, if wide enough, it passes around on both sides of the deadwood. In this last method of construction, the horn timber is often made up of three pieces, laminated.

The sketches in this chapter show various keel construction methods suitable to the usual types of hull. None of these need be followed closely, as the choice of timber and scantling must be left to the designer's judgment. The form of hull should govern, to a great degree, the choice of structure, and the beginner will find comparison of great aid in his choice.

Frame Construction and Spacing

The frames and floors are the next details to be designed. The spacing of the frames, and therefore of the floors which hold the frames to the keel, is difficult to rule upon. Builders and designers vary the spacing in accordance with their judgment and experience. The lighter the frames are, the closer should be the spacing. It follows, then, that steam-bent frames are spaced closer

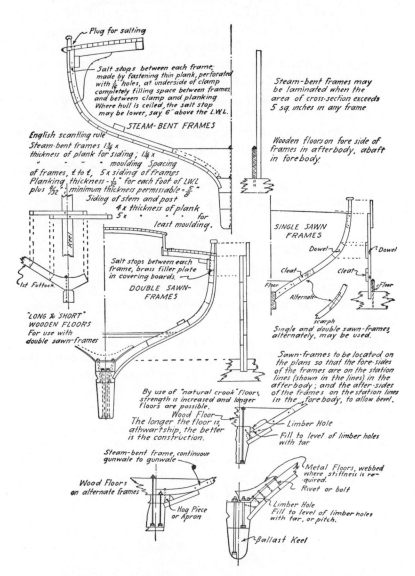

Plug for salting

Salt stops between each frame;
made by fastening thin plank, perforated
with $\frac{1}{16}$" holes, at underside of clamp
completely filling space between frames
and between clamp and planking.
Where hull is ceiled, the salt stop
may be lower, say 6" above the L.W.L.

STEAM-BENT FRAMES

Steam-bent frames may
be laminated when the
area of cross-section exceeds
5 sq. inches in any frame

English scantling rule
Steam-bent frames $1\frac{3}{4}$ x
thickness of plank for siding ; $1\frac{1}{2}$ x
" -   " - moulding Spacing
of frames, ℓ to ℓ, 5x siding of frames
Planking thickness $-\frac{1}{32}$" for each foot of LWL
plus $\frac{9}{32}$" ; minimum thickness permissable $= \frac{5}{8}$"
Siding of stem and post
4 x thickness of plank
5 x " - " - for
least moulding.

Wooden floors on fore side of
frames in afterbody, abaft
in forebody.

SINGLE SAWN
FRAMES

Dowel   Dowel

Cleat   Cleat

1st Futtock

Salt stops between each
frame, brass filler plate
in covering boards.

DOUBLE SAWN-
FRAMES

Floor   Floor
Alternate

scarph

"LONG & SHORT"
WOODEN FLOORS
For use with
double sawn-frames

Single and double sawn-frames,
alternately, may be used.

Sawn-frames to be located on
the plans so that the fore-sides
of the frames are on the station
lines (shown in the lines) in the
afterbody ; and the after-sides
of the frames on the station lines
in the forebody, to allow bevel.

By use of "natural crook" floors,
strength is increased and longer
floors are possible.
                    Wood Floor
The longer the floor is,
athwartship, the better
is the construction.

Limber Hole

Fill to level of limber holes
with tar

Steam-bent frame, continuous
gunwale to gunwale

Wood Floors
on alternate frames

Metal Floors, webbed
where stiffness is re-
quired.
Rivet or bolt

Hog Piece
or Apron

Limber Hole
Fill to level of limber holes
with tar, or pitch.

Ballast Keel

Notes and Details: Frame, Floor and Keel Construction, Salt Stops,
location of Floors in relation to Frames, etc.

than are sawn frames. The choice between sawn frames and steam-bent frames is also a matter of opinion. As a practical consideration, however, it is very difficult to retain the designed lines in a steam-bent frame yacht if there is much S-shape in the section. If building is done with care, steam-bent frames should hold their shape (properly seasoned, bent and secured with floors, stringers and clamps). A combination of steam-bent frames with sawn frames would undoubtedly be very satisfactory in this respect, but both this construction and sawn frames are heavier than steam-bent frames. There is not much difference in strength if the workmanship is good. In some localities, steam bending is rarely done as the native timbers are not suitable. In the South and in the West Indies, sawn frames are used as a result of this condition.

There is no regular proportion in spacing swan frames. The use of double and single frames further complicates the difficulty. A double frame is made up of overlapping the "butts" (joints). The single frame is made up of the butts in the frames being offset, or by the use of butt-blocks.

Large sailing craft, having heavy outside ballast, should always be built with sawn-frames, or on composite construction, or have very wide and strong wooden floors fastened to plank and preferably placed on top of frames or between and free of them, if frames are bent. About $\frac{1}{30}$ of the waterline length is a reasonable spacing for sawn frames in boats up to 40 feet waterline. Above this the spacing is often arbitrary. In fishing schooners, the spacing varied from 17" to 24" in boats of 40 feet to 90 feet waterline. In very large schooners the spacing was about 24 inches. The spacing of steam-bent frames ranges from 8 to 14 inches. The following are good proportions.

L.W.L. Length	FRAMES Moulded	Sided	SPACING Center to center
15'	¾"	× 1"	8"
20'	⅞"	× 1¼"	10"
25'	1"	× 1½"	12"
30'	1¼"	× 2"	12"

35'	1⅜"	×	2½"	12"	Bent on the flat
40'	1¾"	×	2½"	12"	Bent on the flat
50'	2"	×	3"	12"	Difficult to bend
60'	2¾"	×	3½"	12"	Difficult to bend

Bent frames are sometimes tapered from heel to head. The modern practice is to employ wide frames, thin enough to bend without fracturing or producing "run-outs." Floors are best placed on top of such frames. These frames are very strong if not cramped in bending.

These proportions may be increased somewhat; for example, a 25-foot load-waterline yacht could have the scantlings of the 30-foot, in the table, without being unduly heavy. Another suggestion for deciding the spacing of the frames is to use the thickness of the hull planking as a factor; for steam-bent frames, thickness of plank multiplied by 9; for sawn frames multiply by 15 (for double frames) or by 12 (for single frames). The thicker the planking, the greater may be the frame spacing as indicated by this method. The floors are spaced the same as the frames, and usually side as much as the frames. Wrought iron floors, galvanized, are rather popular, but in the writer's experience they do not withstand the effects of time as well as the wooden floors of Oak, Larch, or Yellow Pine. The fastenings of steel or iron to wood tend to develop rot very often. If metal floors are desirable for reasons of arrangement, they should not be carried into the ends unless they have vertical webs either cast or welded.

Bent Frames

Today, tapered bent frames are rarely employed as they are expensive. It may be assumed that bent frames exceeding 2" thickness and 4" sided are very difficult to bend and thus cause expense out of proportion to the value. It is not common practice to laminate steam-bent frames when they exceed 2" depth, but such frames should be wide—2" × 3" or 2" × 4", for example. It is usual to specify the frames that are to be glued together. This is also expensive, and it is probable that frames bent in two courses or laminated need only be tacked together, for the plank fastenings should secure the laminae sufficiently well. It is considered good practice with unglued, laminated frames to use planking nails long enough to go through all and to be clenched on the inside of the frames. With glued laminae this is not often done but would be desirable where great strength is required.

With laminated frames the practice of fastening the floors to the sides of the frames should be dispensed with. It is obvious that any secure fastening of the floors to the sides of the frames will cut laminae unduly and tend to cause delamination in glued frames. It is better, therefore, to place floors on top of the frames and to nail, spike or bolt the frames to these vertically.

Floors need not be attached to the frames at all. By using rather long floor timbers extending two or three plank strakes outboard the keel, the planking, when well fastened to both the frames and to the floor arms, will be sufficient to tie frames and floors together. This practice has proved satisfactory in boats requiring beaching, which places heavy strains on the keel, floors and garboards, so it will serve in boats not exposed to such strains.

When the floors are placed on top of the frames, their strength may be increased by the use of a built-up floor design. The writer has employed such floors in large bent-frame hulls for some years, and though the hulls had heavy diesel engines, and two went heavily ashore, no sign of weakness has been reported in any of them after ten or more years. The floors are formed of two long arms on top of the laminated (unglued) bent frames; the arms butt on the keel centerline and mould to floor depth there. They are carried well outboard nearly to the bilge amidships, and taper in moulding to the thickness of the bilge clamp if one is used. The long arms are of the siding of the floor timber but are less thick than the siding of the frames, as a rule.

The frames are nailed, spiked or bolted to these long arms. At the keel, the long arms are joined by a floor timber edge bolted to the keel and bolted to the long arms with carriage bolts or fastened with boat nails in small hulls. The floor timber is thus alongside the frame but not fastened directly to it. Such built-up floors need not be employed on every frame. It is usually sufficient to place the long-arm floors on every third frame. In cases where great strength is required short floors on top of the frames might be placed on the frames between those having built-up floors. In sailing hulls the long-arm floors could be placed to allow keel bolts to pass through the floor member.

In sailing hulls it is sometimes desirable to employ rather heavy floors, carried well outboard, and located between and clear of the frames to take the ballast-keel bolts. Such floors spread the loading well outboard without having the floors cut up by numerous fastenings.

The strength required in a frame is a debatable matter. It is probable that less strength is required in any given frame than is generally supposed. What is needed in a frame, apparently, is a cleating effect to tie the planking together and stiffness to hold the hull form in shape. There is no mode of calculation that gives us a precise estimate of required frame strength, though often calculations are made based upon assumed loadings and treating the frame as though it were a unit of construction not joined to the rest of the hull structure. Hence, though assigned strength requirements may be met there is no proof that the assigned strength is actually necessary.

Metal floors of this description are often very expensive. Wooden floors are generally used in the extreme bow and stern, as they are cheaper than webbed floors. The common metal floor so often used in modern yachts is a mere strap without sufficient stiffness for use at bow and stern. The depth of the wooden floor over the keel should be somewhat greater than the moulding of the frame at its heel. It is understood that the siding of a frame is its width viewed from inside the boat as seen in the profile plan. The moulding is the measurement of the frame along the face, seen in a section through the hull (viewed from forward or abaft the frame).

The frames in the example are steam-bent. These steam-bent frames will be somewhat heavier than the table indicates, say 3″, but the moulding of the frame will be reduced to, say, 1⅞″. If the size of the frames is increased, the spacing may be greater. On the other hand, if the scantling is reduced, the spacing should be reduced also. For the example, the frame spacing of 12 inches on centers was chosen arbitrarily. Steam-bent frames are made of Oak or Rock Elm while sawn frames may be of Oak, Western Larch, Madeira, or Yellow Pine. Wooden floors are usually of the same material as the frames. The frame-spacing should be laid off on the "frame base line" in the lines. In this operation care should be used so that no frame falls on a station line (unless sawn frames are being used) since the station lines represent the moulds used to shape the hull during construction. The moulds should not be removed from the hull until the planking is on, unless frames are carefully battened, braced and secured to prevent change of shape.

Construction Section—Ballast Bolts

The next step in the actual drawing of the construction plan should be to draw the midsection which may be traced or lifted from the lines. In this, the cross-sections of all the longitudinal members, the moulding of the frames and the depth of the floor, crown or deck, etc., will be shown. Plate X shows a typical construction midsection. If there is ballast outside, the method of bolting it to the keel should be shown. If the ballast keel is very heavy and very deep, as in the keel catboat, some of the ballast bolts should pass through the floors of the frames that are over the ballast. The ballast bolts should be staggered where the ballast keel is widest. However, in small boats this is not so important. If the bolts are not staggered, they should be of larger diameter than when they are. The spacing of the bolts is governed by the spacing of the floor, as a rule. In boats of deep heavy ballast keels, a bolt should pass through every other floor, with at least one bolt through the keel between, as the minimum requirement. If the keel is comparatively light, the bolts are brought through the keel only. The diameter of the bolts will depend upon the weight and shape of the ballast keel. Wrought iron or steel bolts, galvanized, are used with iron ballast, since copper cannot be used in conjunction with iron and steel in saltwater. Composition or tobin bronze bolts are used with lead ballast. The diameter of ballast bolts ranges from $\frac{1}{4}''$ to $1\frac{1}{2}''$. Examples are:—ballast weight 2000 lbs., bolts $\frac{3}{8}''$; ballast weight 5000 lbs., bolts $\frac{7}{8}''$; ballast weight 10,000 lbs., bolts $1\frac{1}{8}''$; 20,000

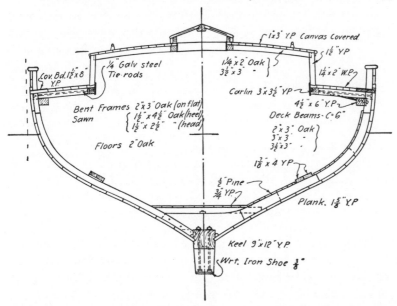

PLATE X. *Construction section, showing hull having both steam-bent and sawn frames. There are usually two steam-bent frames between each pair of sawn frames. This construction is excellent in hulls having markedly S-shaped sections, or very hollow garboards. Note method of indicating scantlings.*

lbs., bolts 1½″. These diameters are not unalterable, as spacing should be considered. The keel ballast bolts should have grommets fitted between the metal and wood keels, and should be set up on washers. The grommets are made of heavy canvas or lampwicking, set in white lead or old paint. The heads of the bolts are countersunk into the bottom of the keel, but in lead keels the bolts are often cast into the ballast.

The fastenings of the deadwood and floors may be shown and specified, but the location and size of fastenings must be left to the judgment of the designer, or builder, as scantling and form of construction will control the choice. The deadwood is usually fastened with galvanized steel drift bolts, the floors are fastened with bronze or galvanized steel bolts, set up with grommets and with nuts and washers, the heads being countersunk into the bottom of the keel. It is extremely important that all bolts be a drive fit; it is best to specify that bolts shall "follow a —— size auger." In specifying any fastening, whether nail or bolt, it is very wise to specify the size hole that shall be bored to take it, to avoid over-boring.

Keelson

The use of a keelson, or inside keel, over the top of the floors is relegated to large craft of over 75 feet overall, as a rule. Keelsons are usually of the same timber as the keel.

Stringers

Stringers in the bilge should be employed with steam-bent frames, but are not usually required with sawn frames in vessels of less than 50 feet overall length. The stringers prevent sagging of the ends only if they are run from the stempost to the transom. They help to hold the shape of the steam-bent frames at the bilge if properly located. Care should be taken that they do not run through the berth tops. It is best to bolt the stringer to a knee at the stem (breast hook) and to another knee at the transom to lock it firmly into place. The stringers are fastened to the frames with lags, bolts, screws, spikes or nails, according to scantlings. Stringers are usually of Yellow Pine or Western Larch in long lengths.

Clamps and Shelves; Scantlings

Clamps and shelves are longitudinal, usually of Yellow Pine or Larch, that follow the sheer in the profile. In some hulls both are used, while in others either one is considered sufficient. These members increase longitudinal strength and stiffness, and help prevent "panting," that is, the tendency of the sides to move in and out as the vessel sags and hogs. Clamps are on edge while shelves are on the flat, and both run from stempost to transom, and are firmly bolted thereto. They are fastened in the same manner as the stringers. The shelves lie flat under the deck beams and are edge-bolted to the clamp, as a rule, as well as fastened to the deck beams. If clamps are omitted, the shelves are edge-bolted to the frames, before the planking is put on, as well as fastened to the deck beams. Engine beds are of Oak or Yellow Pine. They are firmly bolted to the floors and may have chocks to prevent side sway. They are usually notched down over the floors to lock them in place, and are shaped to fit the engine and the hull. The scantlings of these members can be decided by comparison, or by the following rules:

Stringers:—thickness; 1¼ multiplied by the thickness of the planking; width,—(tapered to bow and stern) 3 to 6 times the thickness, depending upon the amount of sheer given the stringers.

Clamps:—thickness; 1½ multiplied by the thickness of the planking; width,—(tapered to bow and stern) 4 to 6 times the thickness.

Shelves:—thickness; 2 to 2½ times the thickness of the planking; width,—(tapered to bow and stern) 1 to 3 times the thickness.

Engine beds:—scantling is fixed by the engine lugs and hold-down bolts.

These proportions are not absolute, as many boats vary widely in scantlings of these members.

Planking

Planking is usually of White Cedar, Port Orford Cedar, Mahogany, Teak, Yellow Pine, Oregon Pine, Oak, Western Larch or Cypress. White Cedar, Port Orford Cedar, Teak, Yellow Pine and Mahogany are considered the best in about the order named. White Cedar and Port Orford Cedar are light, tough, and easily worked. Teak is hard, strong, and very durable. Yellow Pine is strong and durable; it is much used for commercial vessels. Mahogany is strong, takes a high finish and is durable. All of these can be procured in long lengths. Cypress becomes watersoaked, does not finish well, but is durable. Oak is hard to work and sometimes checks badly. Oregon Pine is cheap, but not as durable as Yellow Pine. Long Leaf Yellow Pine is the best of the pines for boat building purposes.

The use for which the boat is built should determine the kind of planking to use. Cedar is best for small craft; larger craft might have Mahogany, Teak, Yellow Pine or Oak. Fir is now used on medium sized boats, but Cedar is probably superior. Ash has a tendency to rot at waterline unless properly seasoned. Good Pine (Yellow) is now difficult to obtain. Alaskan Yellow Cedar, Southern Juniper and Western Larch are still available in some areas.

Caravel planking is generally used in yachts. By this is meant smooth planked, as opposed to lap planking commonly seen in light dinghies. This lap planking is known variously as clinch or lap strake planking. The thickness of caravel planking is wholly a matter of judgment. In many cruising boats, the planking is finished to 1″ when the displacement is between 2 and 12 long-tons. When the displacement is between 12 and 30 tons, the planking is usually about 1¼″ to 1½″ in thickness. Modern practice is to use somewhat thicker planking than these proportions, however. The rules of the insurance societies, such as Lloyd's or the American Bureau, may be used. Comparison is undoubtedly the best guide. Clinch. or lap strake-built craft, however, have much thinner planking, usually about ½ or ¾ of that required in the caravel planked hull. The garboard, and sometimes the sheer strake, are often a little thicker than the rest of the planking, in heavy displacement craft. In some localities it has been customary to use what is known as a "wale," that is, a belt of thick planking around the hull above the waterline. The depth of this wale should be ⅛ of the depth of the hull amidships and the thickness about 1½ the thickness of the rest of the planking at the topsides. The wale is very rarely used in modern yachts, however.

Bulwarks

Bulwarks may be merely a plank on edge, or may have stanchions, depending upon the required height, of course. Very low bulwarks may be made of a square strip of timber. These are called "log rails." If the bulwarks are over 8″ high, stanchions

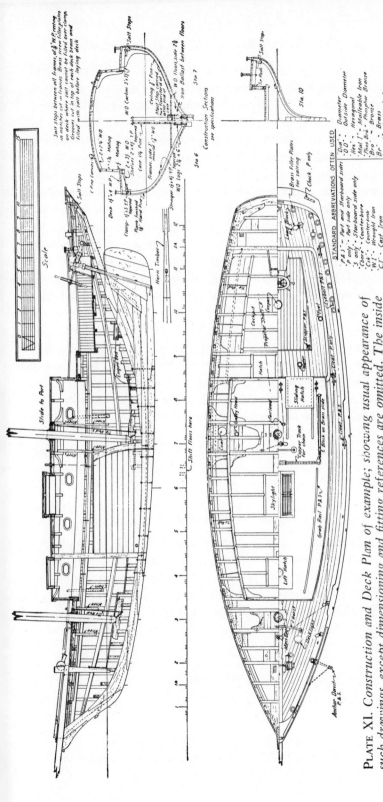

PLATE XI. Construction and Deck Plan of example; showing usual appearance of such drawings, except dimensioning and fitting references are omitted. The inside dimensions of all deck openings, and distance from centerline, should be given. The location and rake of masts, referenced to nearest stations, should be dimensioned, as should the chain-plates also. Dimension, likewise, for location of propeller shaft, length of horses, and position of trunk (width, length, etc.). Give name, size, maker's name and catalogue number of all fittings. Note details shown in special plans or sketches; specify all important fastenings.

should be used. These are fastened to the side of the frames and come up through the covering board or deck to the underside of the rail-cap, or are placed between the frames and fastened to the clamp and ceiling on the inside. In the way of the shrouds, the stanchions are often made somewhat heavier than elsewhere. It is not desirable to bring steam-bent frames up through the deck to the rail-cap, as bulwarks are liable to damage and such construction is expensive to repair when injured. Rot often attacks the stanchions, so they should be capable of being replaced without great expense. It is better to insert stanchions between frames and clear of them, fastening stanchions through planking and clamps only. This simplifies repairs, though it adds to the initial cost of building and makes errors in the shape of the topsides probable. Oak or Yellow Pine or Locust make good stanchions. The rail-cap should be wide enough to cover the thickness of the planking and the heads of the stanchions, with a little to spare. In section, the top of the rail-cap is usually parallel to the waterline. In the way of shrouds, the rail-cap should be wider, and there should be enough width to allow belaying pins to be located on the inboard side, if the bulwark is high enough to permit their use. The rail-cap should finish off at the quarters, and usually at the stem, over the bowsprit, with knees. In reference to the example, Plate XI will enable the reader to follow the construction. Stanchions are of the same timber as the frames, as a rule.

Deck Beams and Scantlings

Deck beams are very important members. They should be sawn to shape in small craft and bent over hold stanchions in large, and should be firmly fastened to the sides at either the frames or at the shelves, as their location permits. If a piece of paper is folded lengthwise, in the shape of a boat, and the ends then forced upward and together, the sides are seen to spread and flatten. This is just what happens to a boat when she grounds heavily. It is evident that transverse of strength is required to overcome this tendency called "panting." The deck beam is the solution, but it is extremely important that the outboard ends be firmly fastened to the sides. The trunk and hatches will cut through these beams, however, so "carlins" or fore-and-aft timbers must be worked in at such openings, to lock the short beams to the full beams running all the way across the hull. Usually the short beams are dovetailed into the carlin, which in turn is dovetailed into the full beams forward and abaft the opening at the deck, whose margin is formed by the carlins and the full beams. In the way of the masts, heavy deck beams are worked in; these are called the "mast partners," and are located fore and aft of the mast. These are also firmly fastened to the sides at the frames and clamps with knees, as will be explained later. Carlins should be used in the way of all openings, whether for cockpit, hatches, trunk, or for similar structures. A few tie-rods of galvanized steel should be employed, running from inside the carlins to outside the shelves and clamps, or to the outside face of the frames if the opening is long, as in the case of a cabin trunk. These are set up with nuts and washers; the heads are countersunk into the inside faces of the carlins. The decking is laid overall. At the bulwarks, and sometimes at the trunk or deck-house, a covering board, a little wider or thicker than the deck planking, is often used. This covering board in large vessels is replaced by a waterway of greater thickness and a nibbing piece is employed, into which the deck planks are notched. Figure 11 shows a typical deck construction plan, and Plate XI shows details of the deck construction used in the example of design.

Carlins

In the design of the deck framing the designer should consider the probable direction of strains. This is particularly true in designing the carlins at long deck openings having trunks or coamings. It is usual to make the carlins as deep in moulding as the deck beams and to side the carlins as the beams, apparently under the assumption that the direction of strain will be vertical and that the carlins, therefore, will deflect downward. This is rarely true, for in practice the vertical deflection is more than supported by the depth of coaming or trunk-side and by the

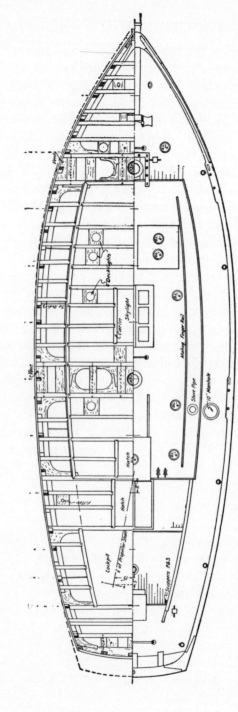

FIGURE 11. *Example of a deck-plan used in a keel cruising schooner, showing partners, tierods, knees, blocking, etc. Note how partners are fitted.*

fastenings thereof. In a long opening, however, hull-panting often loads the carlin athwartships. Therefore the deepest moulding of such carlins should be athwartships and the depth of the carlins vertically can be relatively small, say 50% to 65% of the depth or moulding of the deck beams.

The thickness and depth of the sheer clamp may also be considered in this light. If there is to be a shelf there is no need for a thick sheer clamp, as it only supports the deck beam ends for vertical loading and so should be rather deep and thin. The shelf should be deep athwartships but shallow vertically. In considering weight saving in structure it is more important to analyze direction of the strains imposed upon members than to examine the quantity of the loadings since there is no way to accurately determine the quantities of loadings except by impractical comparison methods. Deck beams, particularly the beams forward and abaft deck openings, should be half again the scantling of the short beams. Short beams should have a cross-section whose area is equal to the frame at the head. The deck, in general, should be about as strong as the sides of the hull, but should not be as heavy if it is possible to avoid it. Thickness of the deck planking is fixed by the construction of the deck. Canvas-covered decks are usually lightest. "Bright" decking should be built of narrow stock, and the butts should shift as in planking. The thickness in a small boat should not be less than 1¼" more, if the deck is to be caulked. The spacing of the deck beams should not exceed two frame spaces, and is usually much less, being more or less fixed by the deck openings. White Pine is much used for decking; deck beams and carlins are of the same timber as the frames. Canvas for decks usually ranges from #12 to #8, #10 or #8 for working decks. Plastics and glasscloth have replaced canvas to a very great extent.

Caulking

Though it is customary to caulk with cotton, oakum is better and lasts longer. Oakum must be driven lightly when only a few strands are required, as hard driving breaks up the fibre.

Butts and Scarphs

The butts in planking, decking and clamps, as well as all scarphs, should shift at least three frame spaces. Butts in planking and decking may be in the same frame space, but must be separated by at least six strakes. A strake, it is understood, is a plank. The covering board, and sometimes the sheer strake, should be scarphed, instead of using butt-blocks, particularly in long, lightly built hulls having comparatively little depth amidships. Clamps are usually scarphed, but may have large butt-blocks. Scarphs are stronger than butts, as well as lighter.

Transom Construction

The transom should be heavily framed, and knees should be employed to lock it to the horn timber and to the clamps or shelves. The transom, above the deck, is sometimes open, that is, without planking, showing the stanchions, and finished off at the top with the rail-cap. Usually the transom is made by planking it up athwartship in the usual manner, but if finished bright it is generally made laminated. The planking method is the most lasting. The transom planking should be somewhat thicker than the rest of the hull planking; the ends are mitered.

Knees and Blocking

Knees are the braces that stiffen the hull structure. Those that lie flat under the deck are "lodging knees," while those that are upright are "hanging knees." Those that lock the clamps, stringers or shelves to the stem timber are "breast hooks." Those that lock the transom to these members are "quarter knees." Those that hold the stem and stern transom to the keel are the "knees of the deadwood." Knees should be worked in at the partners and at all places where "working" is to be expected. Knees that are set raking are called "dagger knees" and are commonly used to give bracing in a diagonal direction at the mast-partners, bitts, or elsewhere. Floors and knees, more than any other members, fix the life of the hull, and decide whether or not the hull will "work." Hence their position and number should be carefully considered. If knees cannot be had, straight-grained stock must be employed for the same purpose, but must be employed with care.

Blocking, in the way of ports, deck lights, filling caps, and other small openings should be used to give a firm fastening for the fittings, and to stiffen the decking or planking in the way of such openings. Blocking will also serve the purpose of lodging knees, if used with judgment, and is much less expensive.

Centerboard Case

So far, we have touched only the items of construction met in keel boats of the cruising type. The construction of centerboard cases cannot be overlooked. There are two excellent methods of construction—the choice depending upon the depth of the keel. Figure 12 shows these methods. The frames may be fastened to the keel in the ways indicated. Unless the boat is large, the fastening of the frames to the keel is not difficult. The centerboard should be of good thickness. In cruising centerboard yachts, of about 20 feet waterline, the board should be 1⅛" thick. A boat whose waterline is over 20 and under 40 feet should have a board 1⅛" to 3" thick. Metal boards are not satisfactory in anything but small light racing boats, as they are more liable to warp and jam, than are the wooden boards. The pivot of the centerboard should be well up above the bottom of the keel, to prevent the board from swinging out of the case, should the lanyard break. The board should be so installed that the lanyard and the inside of the case can be easily inspected. This means that the top of the case should be easily removed. The building of a bulkhead on top of the case is very undesirable. The enclosing of the lanyard is often done to help the appearance of the interior, yet it must be remembered that the lanyard should be open to inspection, and should be capable of being easily replaced. The practical method would be to leave the top of the case open and the lanyard fully exposed, but some do

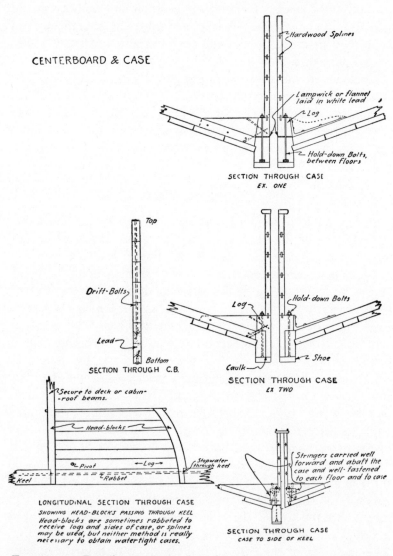

CENTERBOARD & CASE

Hardwood Splines

Lampwick or flannel
laid in white lead

Log

Hold-down Bolts,
between floors

SECTION THROUGH CASE
EX. ONE

Top

Drift-Bolts

Lead

Bottom

SECTION THROUGH C.B.

Log

Hold-down Bolts

Shoe

Caulk

SECTION THROUGH CASE
EX TWO

Secure to deck or cabin-
-roof beams.

Head-blocks

Pivot   Log

Keel   Rabbet

Stopwater
through keel

LONGITUDINAL SECTION THROUGH CASE
SHOWING HEAD-BLOCKS PASSING THROUGH KEEL
Head-blocks are sometimes rabbeted to
receive logs and sides of case, or splines
may be used, but neither method is really
necessary to obtain watertight cases.

Stringers carried well
forward and abaft the
case and well-fastened
to each floor and to case

SECTION THROUGH CASE
CASE TO SIDE OF KEEL

FIGURE 12. *Details of Centerboard and Case construction, and design of floors in way of case. If pin passes through case above log, the strake through which it passes should be thicker than indicated in the sketches.*

not like the appearance of this, just as some consider the presence of the mast in the cabin unsightly. When possible a chain lanyard should be used on the centerboard.

A centerboard under the floor of the cabin is often shown in designs and is called for in some racing rules. Yet this form of construction is very unsatisfactory since these cases rot out quickly and harbor worms. L-shaped boards with the lanyard forward are popular abroad, but are not in favor with Americans. Boards of this description usually are subject to wringing strains, which tend to make them jam in the case. The centerboard, in large vessels, is often off center, usually to starboard of the keel, the opening being in the garboard, and the board passing down along the side of the keel. The advantage of this is that it enables an inexpensive narrow keel to be used, and this construction has no visible effect on the sailing of the vessel. Some small open fishing boats were also fitted this way. The board in very large vessels such as four-masted schooners is often 6 inches thick. The construction of board and case should not be made complicated, under the impression that great strains are thus overcome. The construction of the C.B. case is shown in Figure 12, and it will be noticed that the end-timbers or "end-blocks" run through the keel. One of these, usually the forward one, should run to the cabin roof, or deck. This prevents side sway. The carrying of the log through the keel enables the caulking to be done from the outside. The use of splines and rabbeted case-logs will increase the strength and life of the case and tend to prevent leakage. The centerboard should be of Oak, Larch or Yellow Pine, edge bolted, and counter weighted with lead. The ballasting of the board will insure its sinking when lowered. The bolting should be done with galvanized steel or bronze bolts. The pivot-bolt or pin should be so fitted that it can be replaced, and should be of large diameter, to take care of the wear; or it may be bushed, for this purpose. Chain lanyards have been recommended. This chain may be galvanized wrought iron, or steel. Bronze flexible wire is sometimes used, but chain is preferable.

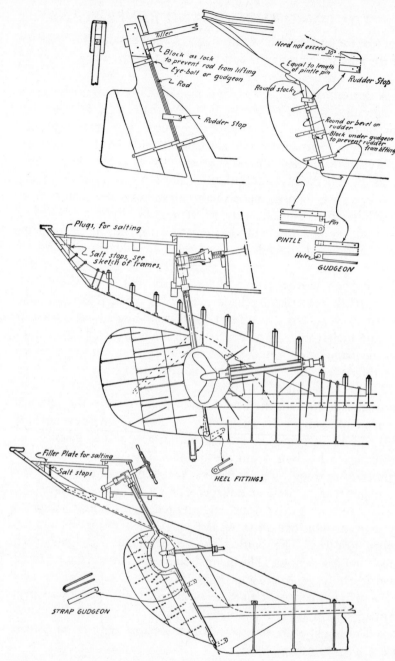

Tiller

Block as lock to prevent rod from lifting

Eye-bolt or gudgeon

Rod

Rudder Stop

Need not exceed 30°

Equal to length of pintle pin

Round stock

Rudder Stop

Round or bevel on rudder

Block under gudgeon to prevent rudder from lifting

Pin

PINTLE

Hole

GUDGEON

Plugs, for salting

Salt stops, see sketch of frames.

Filler Plate for salting

Salt stops

HEEL FITTINGS

STRAP GUDGEON

FIGURE 13. *Rudder details and after deadwood construction.*

Rudder Stock

The diameter of the rudder stock may be decided by comparison, or by rules of the classification societies. A cast bronze rudder bracket is usually employed, if the rudder is cut away

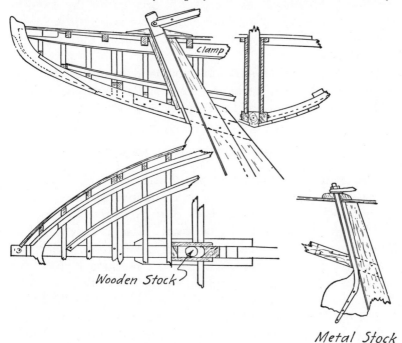

Construction of Canoe Stern and rudder-wells.

in the wake of the propeller aperture. Bronze straps, or pintles and gudgeons, support the rudder, while a heel casting supports the rudder-post at the bottom of the keel. Figure 13 shows the methods of fitting the rudder. The rudder-post passes through the stern overhang in some boats. In such cases, there is a rudder-port, or well, made of bronze, brass, or galvanized iron pipe of sufficient diameter to take the rudder-post. The bottom of this pipe is usually threaded into the wooden horn timber, or is threaded into a flange screw fastened to the top of the horn timber or to the bottom of the plank. The top of this pipe, if a steering wheel is employed, is braced with a partner plank, and a pipe flange is often worked on, to lock this timber to the rudder pipe-well. If the rudder-post passes through the deck, the top of the pipe is usually carried through the deck, to a casting, or a wooden chock. With this arrangement, a tiller is usually employed. The length of the tiller is decided by the room in the cockpit; usually $\frac{1}{10}$ of the load-waterline length is an approximation of the common practice in fixing the length of tillers in large craft.

Wooden rudder-ports are sometimes used in large craft. These should be built up in the same manner as the centerboard cases. The fitting of outside rudders requires no description.

Comparison of Planking Methods

The methods of planking are described in all books on amateur boat building and need little attention here. Sometimes the seams of the planking are backed up by battens running the full length of the boat on the inside. This is called "Seam-Batten Construction," and is used most in V-bottom, high-speed power craft. Light craft often have the planking lapped, like clapboarding on a house, which, as has been said, is called "clench-built" or "lap strake." This is often used for lifeboats, and is the strongest method of planking when weight is considered. It is, however, hard to repair. Properly speaking "clench" means to turn over the point of the nail or to rivet; as this is the usual practice in lap-strake construction the term "clench-built" is used in some localities in lieu of "lap-strake." Caravel-built is the smooth-surfaced planking seen in most yachts, having caulked seams, but no seam battens. Strip-built is a popular method of planking. In this case, the planking is composed of narrow strips, each strip fastened to the frame, and also edge-fastened to its neighbor. For a guide to choice of method, the following advantages and disadvantages are given, but local methods of building are the best guide:

Seam-Batten Construction:—1. Great longitudinal strength and resistance to vibration. 2. Freedom from leakage. 3. Allows the use of very thin planking. 4. Costly. 5. Requires first-class workmanship. 6. Requires special framing, since the battens must be notched through the frames. 7. Hard to repair.

Clench-built:—1. Great longitudinal strength and resistance to vibration. 2. Allows the use of very thin planking. 3. Requires good workmanship and practical knowledge of this type of construction. 4. Permits the use of very light framing. 5. Hard to repair. 5. Can shrink or swell without leaking.

No caulking is required in the above types.

Caravel-built:—1. Cheapest, and very common. 2. Generally preferred by all builders. 3. Requires thicker planking than either of the foregoing methods. 4. Requires caulking. 5. Requires heavy framing compared to the two former methods. 6. Very easy to repair.

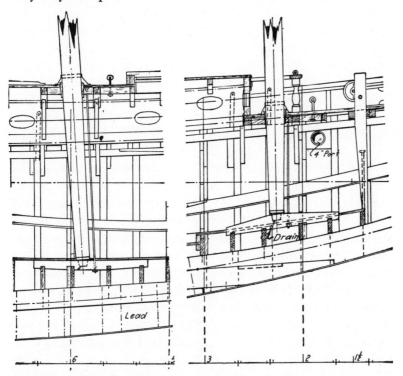

Partners, mast steps, tierods, and surrounding construction in a keel schooner, ceiling omitted.

Strip-built:—1. Local method only, requiring little skill. 2. Cheap. 3. Very strong. 4. Very few or no frames required. 5. No caulking required. 6. Very hard to repair. 7. Very heavy, requires thicker planking than other methods.

General Construction Methods

A few other points of construction remain to be taken up. Rabbeted chine logs, such as are used in high-speed V-bottom power craft, are very expensive. Metal knees, usually cast bronze or wrought iron, galvanized, are sometimes used to replace large wooden hanging knees or heavy lodging knees. In very long craft, a steel-plate sheer-strake is often worked in, inside of the usual plank-sheer strake, to increase longitudinal strength. This usually permits the omission of the clamps. Diagonal bracing, between planking and frames, is used in large craft, particularly in the way of the mast partners and amidships, to strengthen the hull. Diagonal bracing may be of galvanized wrought iron or bronze straps. These straps must be fastened to all the frames they cross, as well as to each other, and are notched into the frames or let into the inside of the planking.

The practice of placing the chain-plates, for shrouds and backstays, inside the planking is very common in yachts. This is done to avoid ugly stains on the outside of the hull, as such fittings are usually made of galvanized wrought iron or steel, and so are subject to rust. However, when so located, a change in position of the mast would be very expensive. For strength and lasting qualities it is probable that the chain-plates should be on the outside of the planking. Chain-plates should be located on frames or on false frames so that a strong fastening may be obtained. In light boats, they often pass completely around the boat inside. In fastening the chain-plates to the hull, the fastenings usually pass through the frames, or if outside, through all. Usually the bolt employed when the chain-plates are outside the planking is secured on the inside of the vessel by wedges, so that the chain-plates are easily removed The size of the chain-plates and their fastenings may be decided by comparison or by calculation of strength. Galvanized steel, wrought iron, or bronze are the common materials used in making chain-plates and their fastenings.

Ceiling

The ceiling is the inside planking of the frames, in other words, the inside cabin walls below deck. The ceiling should have numerous ventilating holes bored in it, and should not be carried up to the underside of the clamps; rather, an opening of a few inches should be left. Square edge tongue-and-groove stock should be used, in preference to beaded tongue-and-groove. The ceiling is merely for finish purposes and is very thin; ¼″ to ½″ in thickness is the usual range in yachts from 20 to 200 ft. load-waterline length. The ceiling should be omitted wherever possible, as it encourages rot. In single-handers and other small craft, it may be entirely omitted.

Cockpits and Coaming Scuppers

Cockpits are usually self-bailing. In yachts, where the cockpit floor does not rest on the frames, it is usually hung from the deck beams with galvanized steel tierods. The sides of the cockpit, under the deck, are usually vertically staved with nar-

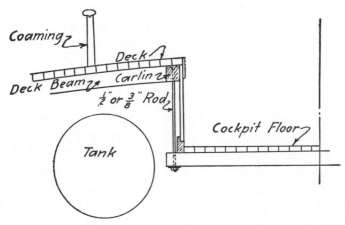

Method of supporting cockpit in way of tanks [small craft].

row tongue-and-groove stock. The coaming is made of wide planks in most yachts. A cap or moulding is sometimes placed on top of the coaming. The scuppers are of lead or copper pipe. Hose, in place of lead or copper pipe, makes the most practical scupper installation in yachts up to 60′ overall, at least. Pipe diameter is usually from 1″ to 2½″, depending upon the size of the cockpit. The cockpit floor should be as strong as the deck; the whole structure should be water-tight. In laying out the cockpit consideration should be given to the effect of heeling on the drainage of the cockpit well. Many boats have a tendency to flood their cockpits through the scuppers, when under sail, and require to have the scuppers plugged. It may be possible to overcome this by crossing the pipes so that the pipe leading from the port side of the cockpit discharges on the starboard side of the hull, well below the waterline.

Mast-step

The mast-step should be firmly bolted to the top of the floors, and should usually be three frame spaces long. In the event that metal floors are used, the mast-step is bolted to the keel, of course. The mast-step should be drained by holes drilled into the side or bottom of the step. The position on top of the floors is best, as the heel of the mast is not so exposed to moisture and rot. The step should be of Oak, Larch or Yellow Pine, and can be as wide as the shape of the hull will permit. It must be thoroughly bolted into place, and may be notched over the floors, to lock it in position.

Bowsprit

The bowsprit, if employed, should be kept off the deck to avoid rot in all but very small craft. Making the bowsprit rectangular in section, where it passes through the bulwarks at the bow, is both cheaper and stronger than making it round or elliptical. The plank bowsprit is the most practical type in small hulls; if it rests on deck it should be laid in white lead or thick paint. It is better to keep bowsprits off the deck.

The bitts, particularly riding bitts, should be firmly built into the hull. Usually the riding bitts are carried to the keel, or floors. If the arrangement is such that this is undesirable, the bitts are cut short, and hanging knees, to the underside of the deck beams, are employed. One of the greatest faults in many modern yachts is that bitts of too light a scantling are employed. Care should be taken that the bitts are of practical size, not only in scantling but also in height.

The amateur designer will do well to study the actual construction details of yachts, as seen in the builders' yards in his vicinity. A great range in methods of construction exists, and scantling, timber and fastening details vary widely in the different yards along the coast.

Hawse Pipes

Hawse pipes usually have tremendous attraction for the amateur designer. Ordinarily, it is best to avoid this fitting, but sometimes they are necessary. If stockless anchors and hawse pipes are to be employed, the hawse pipe should rake at least 45° to the load-waterline; as if less the anchor will not come home in the hawse with a low-powered windlass. It is usually necessary to experiment with a model.

Amount of Detail

The drawings of the construction of a yacht may show the amount of detail illustrated in Plate XI. In all types it is not necessary to give as much detail as this, however. Some designers do not attempt to show a picture of the construction of the hull, depending largely upon the specifications to show their requirements. Unless otherwise directed, the builder is permitted to make minor changes in the construction to suit material at hand, or to make work easier.

The construction plan, or the "lines," should show the position of the center-line of the propeller shaft. In regard to the propeller aperture, when a center-line installation is desired, it has been found best to cut the aperture in both deadwood and rudder, in sailing craft, to avoid eddies harmful to steering. This, however, requires careful planning to avoid weakness in the rudder, and the rudder should be strengthened by carrying the metal stock around the opening of the aperture.

Engine-beds

The engine-beds should be located by use of sketch sections, to make certain that they can go in where indicated on the plans. Nothing will cause more trouble than finding that the engine will have to be moved, after the hull is constructed. The engine-beds, therefore, should be carefully projected, and there should be enough timber at their after ends to insure a firm hold for the hold-down bolts. Sections must be projected from the lines, where required.

Construction Drawing Procedure

The construction should be drawn while the sheer elevation is being worked out, as the location of various members may be projected from one to the other. If a ballast keel pattern plan is to be drawn, this should show the finished ballast keel, with both locations and sizes of the ballast bolts. The latter ought to be repeated on the construction drawing, in the profile.

Fastenings

The question of kind of fastening, whether galvanized steel, or bronze and brass, is a matter of location and cost. In northern waters galvanized fastenings will serve, but in tropical and sub-tropical waters, bronze or copper is desirable. Good galvanized steel and wrought iron will last a reasonably long time and are cheaper than brass or bronze, and also have the greatest holding power. Bronze screws are excellent fastenings for planking. Screws and lags can be used for fastening members that are liable of requiring replacing. Large wooden craft are commonly fastened with locust treenails. The most common fastening employed in some commercial craft is the cut nail, rectangular in section, and having a rather thick head and with a chisel point. This type of nail is known as the "boat nail," and may be had in either galvanized steel, wrought iron, or copper and bronze. The galvanized boat nail is undoubtedly a very good fastening, and is suitable to most forms of construction, though it must be admitted it is little favored in yacht construction at present. It is the least expensive of all fastenings.

Diagonal Planking and General Construction

A few more general notes that may be of interest. Diagonal planking methods offer advantages that may be noted. Double planking and diagonal planking have two disadvantages: difficulty of repairs and liability of rot. The use of three layers of planking, the two inside layers diagonally laid, with seams running in opposite directions, and the outside layer put on fore and aft offer the advantages of great strength, and, since frames may be omitted, of comparative lightness. Such construction, however, is very expensive and is not common in cruising yachts. Knees may be made up by use of steam-bent timber, particularly for hanging knees. Light shallow hulls require some kind of fore-and-aft trussing, or a plank-on-edge keel. Partner-beams, particularly in heavy displacement hulls, should be carefully designed. Vessels that carry a heavy press of sail are subject to a great strain in the neighborhood of partners and chain-plates. Catboats and other craft that have no stays or shrouds should have carefully designed mast-steps and partners. The use of many lodging and hanging knees, as well as heavy beams and blocking, will counteract such strains, if properly used. The locking of timbers by notching, scarphing or tenoning will prevent "working" or movement of the hull structure. As far as possible, strains should not be carried by the fastenings alone. There is less objection to the metal knees and straps in the topsides than there is in the bilges, as the latter members are exposed to dampness. Ventilation of the bilges may be carried out by means of pipes inside the bulwark, the tops of which are reversed, and a metal, wood or rubber float placed at the exhaust end to prevent the entrance of water. When such ventilation is used, however, it is highly important that cut-off valves be placed inside the hull so that the vents may be closed, when their outlets are submerged in heavy weather. If the float fails to close the vents, and no cut-off valve has been installed, a most disastrous leak will result. In heavily rigged craft when the chain-plates are sometimes carried clear around the hull inside, the chain-plates are commonly outside of the frame, and pass over the keel, or pass outside of the clamps and under the mast-step, being fastened to these members. Such construction gives great strength, but is very expensive and hard to repair. It is rarely used in cruising boats, of course.

The beginner should not blindly follow any particular method of construction; rather, he should work out his own method, based on what he would do if he were building the boat with his own hands. Any construction that requires special work, or that would not be easily understood by the builder, is certain to be expensive and should be avoided if possible.

General Construction

The search for lightweight but very strong construction is part of the necessary considerations entering in the design of a boat intended to be fast under power or sail. However, this everlasting demand for lighter weight in structure can lead a designer to confusion and lack of common sense. The most common failure in "lightweight" construction is to "small piece" a structure to the point where no reduction in weight takes place in comparison to a simple, single-unit member of reasonable scantling. When one is considering weight-saving design the only guide is calculation and precise weight measurements, not mere guesswork and the "it-looks-lighter-this-way" approach. An example of mistaken estimate of weight saving is in masts. In a number of cases the use of thin walls in hollow masts was found to make a marked saving in weight of the bare mast; but the rigging and fitting necessary to hold the mast added more weight than was saved, and the resulting total weight was far in excess of what it would have been with normal walls in the hollow masts.

Cost in construction is something no designer today can afford to neglect. In the study of cost, the designer must estimate the amount of labor required to do a given operation against the inherent value of the operation. For example, how long does it take a carpenter to make and fit a half-dovetail beam end into a carlin and how necessary is this to strength and lasting qualities in the completed hull? No quick, easy answer can be given to such questions. The designer can cut costs of construction, without real loss in strength, life or good appearance, only by departure from the old and accepted "yachting standards." This calls for ruthless examination of every item in the accepted standards and prolonged study of boat construction, old and new, with particular regard to life and strength.

There is a tendency, nowadays, to accept any claim for a material being "long-lived," "maintenance-free," etc., but the careful boat designer will verify such claims if he can, or have no faith in them if he cannot—and so inform his client. It is all right to experiment if the man paying for the work knows that he is experimenting and is willing to take the risk. But to experiment without informing the man who must pay the bill is not "progressive yacht design" but simple dishonesty. A boat designer cannot guarantee a boat but he can avoid taking chances unnecessarily while leading his client to think everything done is based on "good practice" and known qualities. It must be recognized that every new design has many elements of an experiment at best, and to crowd too many experiments into one new design is not evidence of good judgment even when an owner is agreeable. It is well to remember that there have been some very disastrous failures of "new materials" and "new methods" in spite of a lot of publicity about their alleged good qualities. Therefore a boat designer must be cautious in using materials that have not been proven by observed usage, or methods that have not been extensively used in boatbuilding.

The quality of material used is obviously an important matter in cost. When, therefore, the cost of a boat is a matter of great importance, the question that faces the designer in making a selection is this—"Is the cost worth the advantage gained?" The use of non-ferrous metals and alloys in boats is a case in point. These will cost about six times what galvanized iron fastenings cost, in a given boat. Non-ferrous metal will outlast galvanized iron in fastenings; boats with the latter will rarely have fastening trouble in less than 10 to 14 years. Will the timber used in the new boat last that long? It is well to remember, in selecting metals and alloy, that galvanized rolled steel is much stronger than cast bronze or many alloys, and it may be strength rather than beauty that should guide the selection. Look with superstition upon "pride of ownership" as an argument for use of costly materials. If there is no practical advantage in using a costly material the rule is simple—don't! This is as true of timber as it is of metal, and as true for fittings and equipment as well.

Cabin Trunk and Coaming Construction

The cabin trunk sides and ends rest on top of the deck, and are edge-bolted through the decking and the carlins. An inside coaming covers the exposed construction members on the inside of the trunk. Usually a rabbet is cut into the top of the decking, and the trunk sides and ends are fitted to this rabbet. The caulking of this seam brings the strains onto the edge-bolts, but leakage is largely avoided. Do not put the trunk inside of the carlin, as caulking will tend to separate the trunk from the carlin, whereupon leaks will be the result. This last construction is sometimes seen, but it will not stand the effects of time. Hatch and skylight coamings should be fitted as the trunk sides. All such fittings should have the coamings of sufficient thickness to take the edge-bolting required.

Dimensions on Construction Plan

The construction plan usually shows some dimensions, such as location of masts, rake of same, bitts, bulkheads, length of cabin trunk, etc. However, this is not done in Plate XI as required reduction would make the plan difficult to read.

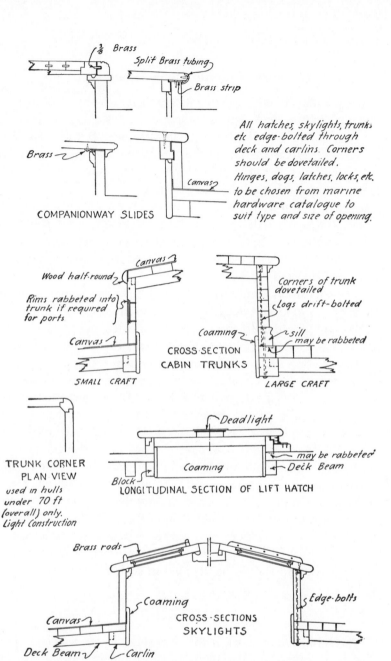

COMPANIONWAY SLIDES

All hatches, skylights, trunks etc edge-bolted through deck and carlins. Corners should be dovetailed. Hinges, dogs, latches, locks, etc. to be chosen from marine hardware catalogue to suit type and size of opening.

CROSS-SECTION CABIN TRUNKS

SMALL CRAFT

LARGE CRAFT

TRUNK CORNER PLAN VIEW
used in hulls under 70 ft (overall) only. Light Construction

LONGITUDINAL SECTION OF LIFT HATCH

CROSS-SECTIONS SKYLIGHTS

Typical Details of Deck Joiner Work.

Deck Construction Details

Ring-bolts should be through bolted under the decking, and fastened to the deck beams, where such fastening is required. Pinrails should be bolted in the same manner. If there are lead-blocks on the cabin roof, tierods from the mast-partners to the mast-step must be employed to prevent the strain on these blocks from lifting and working the cabin roof. This is particularly important if the lead-blocks on the cabin roof are for halyards. When the mast is carried through the cabin roof, care should be taken in the design of the partners to prevent "working" of the structure. Weakness at the partners is so common that it deserves repeated reference.

Deck-houses in large craft should rest on a sill, which is bolted through decking and deck beams. Care should be taken to procure as much strength as is consistent with lightness in these structures. Doors should swing forward, in the sides of deck-houses. Drop-windows of the automobile type are generally employed, though commercial craft usually use windows that slide outside of the house. Overhang of the deck-house roof should be slight, to reduce windage, except at the fore-end of pilot houses where a visor of metal or canvas is employed to shade the for'd windows. Sunken deck-houses must be designed with care, and should combine the features of the trunk cabin with those of the ordinary deck-house in construction. Let it be kept in mind that deck-houses are not desirable in sailing craft where ease of handling is at all important. While deck-houses increase accommodation, and make desirable living quarters, they are more or less of a danger in both large and small sea-going craft, and should be avoided in such types as far as possible.

Joiner Work

The cabin joiner work is the next thing to be designed. Two plans are required, a cabin plan and elevation, and a joiner section plan showing sections through the vessel in the way of the cabin furniture. In large vessels, two elevations, one to port and one

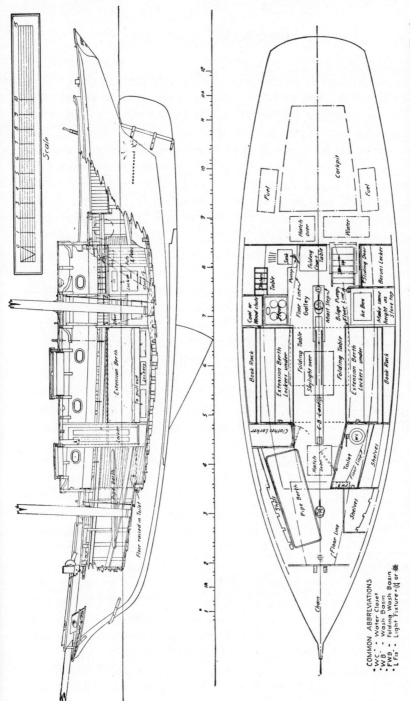

COMMON ABBREVIATIONS
W.C. - Water Closet
W.B. - Wash Basin
F.W.B. - Folding Wash Basin
L.Fix. - Light Fixture ⌘ or ✹

PLATE XII. *Inboard Profile and Arrangement Plan of Example; showing method of indicating layout and Joiner Work. Dimensions omitted; locations and lengths should be referenced. Drawn and Projected in company with "Joiner Sections" drawing, employing "Construction Plan" and "Lines" as guides. Note maker's name, catalogue number, etc. of all fittings.*

to starboard, are required. In small craft this is rarely necessary, unless the two sides are quite unlike each other in design. It is well to work the plan, elevation and the sections together, as it is necessary to project from one view to another. In drawing these two plans, the beginner will soon discover whether or not he made proper allowances in his sketch plan and whether or not his sketch arrangement can be worked into his hull as designed. He will discover just how little of the space enclosed in the deck outline in his sketch is available for cabin fittings and living space. It is possible that he will have to make minor changes in his layout even if he has used great care in the sketch. Enough sections should be taken to find out how the arrangement will fit. Sketch sections, in addition to complete sections on the joiner section plan, may be required. It is not unusual to find that the cabin joiner work, if located in the hull as proposed in the preliminary sketch, would not be inside the hull, but would extend through the sides. Therefore, great care in checking the projection in the sections is necessary.

The desirable features of joiner work have been discussed in the drawing of the sketch, and little is left that requires explanation. Reference to Plates XII and XIII will show the drawing and projections required better than can be explained with words; the projections required are of a simple nature, as can be seen, and are similar to those used in the lines. Finish and color are matters of artistic sense rather than of practical construction. It is only possible to make suggestions, such as the following: The use of too much natural-wood finish makes a dark cabin. Avoid too much carving, moulding, paneling or decoration. A quantity of small panels makes a cabin space look crowded and small. Mirrors increase the appearance of room and space, if the mirrors are large. Bulkheads or other joiner partitions may be made of plywood, and thus avoid seams and crevices. Design of joiner details gives chance for use of ingenuity and good judgment. Ventilation of lockers and similar spaces may be carried out by means of Venetian blinds or metal grilles. Book cases, cabinets, small lockers and shelves are subjects for tasteful design. A working knowledge of cabinet work

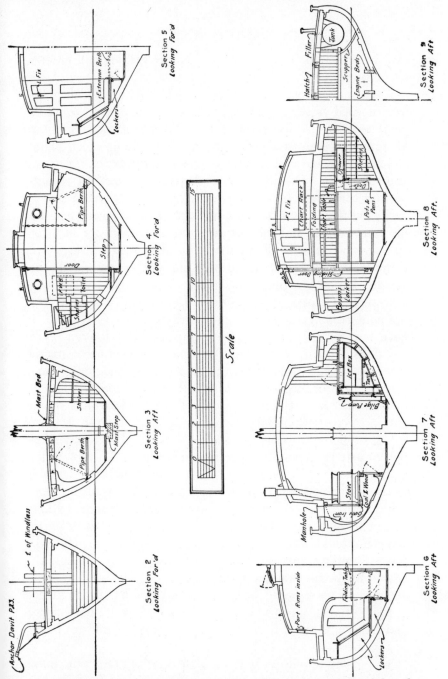

PLATE XIII. *Joiner Sections of Example. Dimensions omitted. In giving these, refer to centerline and top of floor in cabin. Give height of floor from L.W.L. on this or some of the other drawings. Notes as on "Inboard Profile and Arrangement Plan."*

may be procured from books on furniture making and interior decoration.

As to practical questions, the transom berths are difficult problems if used as seats. Cushions that are hard enough to make good seats are usually too hard for sleeping purposes. The use of springs of the box type is common, but take up much room, and are expensive as they must be fitted to the vessel. They are also subject to depreciation through rust. The method of supporting the upper berths, folding tables and extension berths vary, and there is no standard practice. The designer must use his inventiveness and judgment. Screw fastenings are best for all joiner work as it allows the removal of cabin fittings and furniture without damage to the finish. Drawers should be avoided if possible, but, if necessary, some method of locking is required. Carpets are undesirable. Linoleum is best as it does not hold dampness and odor, and is easily cleaned. Grating floors have been tried, but they make a damp and bleak interior. With any floor covering there should be a mode of ventilation for the space below the cabin floor, or "sole," small grids or gratings may be used for this purpose. Lighting fixtures should be located so that they are of real service, and overhead fixtures should not interfere with headroom. Natural light, by use of deck lights, skylights or ports, should be required. Too much attention cannot be given to ventilation and lighting. Heating is also too little considered. Stoves, fireplaces or oil heaters are desirable features in the average cruising yacht. In tropical waters a deck-galley, range, or oil stove is a most practical fitting. In long passageways in the cabin, some form of hand-rail is required, along the bulkheads, to give something to hold onto when the vessel is rolling heavily. The use of handrails underneath the cabin roof beams is also a useful feature.

Chain lockers should have floors and not be wedge-shaped at the bottom as chain will jamb. These lockers are best square, and rather deep than wide. Wide chain lockers permit capsizing of the chain pile and resultant fouling.

The galley should be laid out with care, as much time must be spent there when cruising. Everything should be as handy and as compact as possible. In small craft, lack of floor space is not a serious objection if there is room to work. Ventilation is of utmost importance. If headroom is lacking, a good seat is necessary. Plenty of table space in the galley is a good feature, as it gives the cook some place to open cans, carve meat or prepare food. Suitable dish and pan racks should be laid out. The toilet should be laid out to procure satisfactory plumbing. The practical questions in regard to this space were discussed in Chapter II. The galley range and the coal or wood box should be designed so that fuel can be loaded from outside the boat, unless there are serious structural objections. If possible, the icebox should be under or near a hatch, so that ice will not have to be carried through the cabin. The use of period furniture and decoration has been little considered, unfortunately. While there are many types of decorations for yachts, the colonial farmhouse and Norman-English period furniture and decoration might serve. The severity of line of certain decoration is desirable for marine work generally. Rococo and highly ornamental fittings should pass out of fashion in yachts. There is little doubt that a great deal of money is spent on such joiner work, due to precedent, but the progressive designer should find a more modern and handsomer style. At all times, simplicity and usefulness are synonymous with good taste in decoration.

Joiner Material and Details

The timber used in joiner work is of endless variety. To name a few, Teak, Mahogany, White and Oregon Pine, Rosewood, Oak, Butternut, Red and White Cedar, Porcupine, Bamboo, Cocobolo, Spanish Cedar, Redwood, Birch and Walnut. Table tops, dresser tops, and similar items should be thick and substantial looking. The use of thick, wide stock will prevent the flimsy appearance so often seen. Door trim, panel stiles, and other moulding should be wide, for the same reason, but not so wide as to look clumsy. Elm is excellent for a bright-finish interior.

While plywood bulkheads are usually satisfactory, thin veneer is not, in marine joiner work. Generally speaking, good wide plank for table tops, dresser and buffet tops and for bulkheads is the most pleasing.

The joiner work should be designed for practical comfort, beauty and strength. It is impossible to give anything but general directions, as there are hardly two yachts exactly alike in cabin details. All drawing projections should be made with care, to make sure that there is sufficient room for the proposed furniture and the scale of the drawing should be reasonably accurate. If special dimensions are required, they should be given on the plan. If special details are desired, a small sketch should be given the builder. Details of skylights, hatches, doors, lockers, tables, or other items, may be furnished as required. However, it is not necessary for the designer to detail every item, as consultation with the builder, while the vessel is under construction, will give satisfactory results. The drawings in this chapter are suggestions, and may be used for reference. In all construction drawings, the fastenings of each piece of lumber in the structure should be carefully considered. The best approach is to imagine that you are doing it yourself. This is a commonsense method that will prevent any ridiculous mistakes.

These drawings complete the construction plans. The sketch showing the idea of the design. the lines showing the shape of the hull, and the construction plans showing how the hull and cabin fittings and other structural details are to be built, have been described. The next step is the drawing of the rig. In power craft, this plan would be replaced by an outboard profile which shows the appearance of the completed yacht. In sailing craft, the sail plan usually serves the purpose of an outboard profile as well as for the design of the sails and rigging.

V. The Sail Plan

Sail Plan Drawing, General Discussion

THE details of the "sail plan" of the design were fixed when the sketch was drawn. The "sail plan" is therefore a detail plan, and shows the outboard profile of the finished design. The leads of running rigging and the arrangement of standing rigging should be shown. The location of blocks, tackles and similar fittings ought to be indicated. Usually, the rigging sizes are indicated too, but the practice is not wholly standard. Some designers give very complete plans, some do not. The type of rig will undoubtedly govern the amount of detail required.

In this chapter, a discussion of various types of rig and sail plan, in detail, is in order. The first step, in the design of rig, is to consider the initial and upkeep costs. The cheapest rigs of all are those that require little or no staying. It would seem that even large rigs could be designed that would not require as much staying as do many modern rigs. It is not proven, as yet, that it is best to rely to a great extent upon shrouds and stays to keep the rig aloft, though many rig designs do. In the past, the American builders were of the opinion that rigging should be omitted wherever possible. Their famous schooners were known the world over for speed, power to carry sail, and for their small quantity of standing rigging. Fashion has changed, but whether the change is an improvement or not is open to question. The greater the importance of standing rigging, the more the necessity of constant watchfulness to prevent the loss of the rig through failure of some part by corrosion. When a large amount of rigging is required, the work of taking care of a vessel is usually increased, and the cost, both first cost and upkeep, greatly increased. Windage, an important factor of resistance in rigging, is greatly increased by shrouds and stays; excessive windage is harmful to speed, to windward, or close hauled. In general, it would seem better, for cruising yachts, at least, to design spars that are capable of standing without excessive staying. The search for lightness is much overdone in cruising designs as even the very best of light materials are subject to failure, due to rot and corrosion; certainly a large factor of safety is highly desirable.

The next subject is the number of sails. Though this was referred to in Chapter I, further investigation is possible. In cruising yachts, particularly those that are of small size, a large number of light sails is an undesirable feature. With proper design, tackles, and intelligent handling, it is possible for one man to handle a fairly large sail.

Sacrifices to gain excessive weatherliness are not in good practice, particularly if the sacrifices are those of good behavior on other points of sailing or of safety at sea. It is becoming increasingly apparent that the extremely high sail plans of modern cruisers are unsafe at sea, no matter how efficient they are as propelling agents. This lack of safety is illustrated by the difficulties, or impossibility, of making repairs aloft at sea. When a shroud or stay parts on one of these modern high, light rigs, it is generally impossible to send a man aloft if there is any sea running because of the whipping of the mast. For this reason, if no other, experienced ocean racers and cruisers are beginning to look with suspicion upon many rig designs of the ultramodern types.

Returning to the matter of the number of sails, small yachts should carry a large area of sails in their working rig and should omit, as far as possible, all light sails. Staysail rigs of varying designs have become popular in recent years; however, it has been observed that most of these rigs require constant attention to halyards and continual use of winches to keep the sails properly set. Many staysail rigs suffer from having the working area cut up into too many small sails as well.

The choice of rig can receive only a general discussion here. Such a discussion is more of an index of rigs than it is a guide to choice. Local conditions, personal opinions, and cost are the guides the designer will follow in drawing rigs.

Catboat

One-masted rigs are the most common. The catboat is taken as the first for discussion. There is unfortunately much prejudice against this rig, due to the bad features developed in

CAT

racing cats of extreme proportions. Yet, with proper design, this rig is quite satisfactory for small cruising boats. Modern leg-of-mutton, or jib-headed mainsails. are not suitable for cat-boats, due to marked changes in position of the true center of effort of the sail that take place as it is reefed. But this objection might be overcome by raking the mast sharply aft. The gaff, in the usual cat rig, should be well peaked, particularly in large

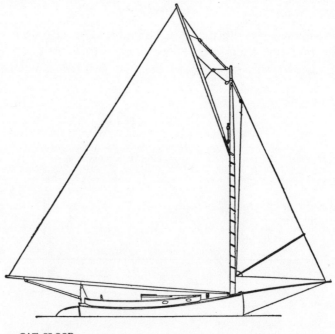

CAT-SLOOP

craft. The boom should not be long, the cruising cat should not have a large spread of sail. Small catboats could have sprit sails instead of gaff or leg-of-mutton mainsails. A portable bowsprit can be fitted, to carry a light jib, set flying. If shrouds are de-sired, horns or outriggers should be fitted on each bow to give enough spread to the rigging to make its use worthwhile. Most experienced catboat sailors are of the opinion that a heavier press of canvas can be carried with an unstayed mast, than with one that has shrouds and stays. This is apparently true of some other rigs, as the bending of the mast spills some of the wind and prevents the vessel from being overpressed. A catboat's mainsail should be capable of being reefed to a small area, and the boom should be fitted to be topped up, if required. The long boom shown here was developed from shorter, racing booms and should be used in cruisers or day sailers.

Sloops and Cutters

Sloops and cutters are now difficult to differentiate. Originally a cutter had a housing bowsprit, and had the mast nearly

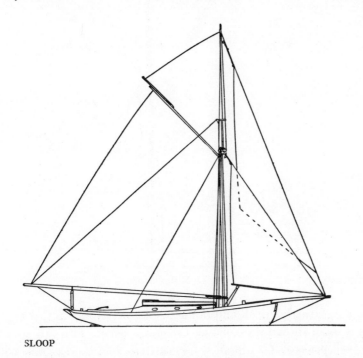

SLOOP

amidships. These cutters sometimes had a square topsail and course. The sloop had her mast nearer the bow, and a fixed bowsprit. Later, the sloop had a single headsail, a jib, and had her mast well forward while the cutter had double headsails, forestaysail and jib, and had her mast farther aft; some cutters retained the housing, or reefing, bowsprit. Modern examples of these rigs show even less difference; "cutter" and "sloop" are loosely applied rig names. The popular idea of the definitions of these rigs appear to be: when the mast is well aft, the vessel is a cutter, while if the mast is well forward, she is a sloop. In

CUTTER

these rigs, the boom should not be excessively long, nor, if a gaff rig is used, should the hoist be extremely great. The gaff should be well peaked, if a topsail is not carried. The forestaysail, with the double head sail rigs, should be of good size, and the jib smallest. If a jib-headed mainsail is used, extremely long masts should be avoided, as they are unsuitable for cruising craft, as has already been pointed out.

In the double headsail rig, the forestay should come down on the stern head or deck, or else be carried around the bowsprit, and then down to the stem, to form the upper bobstay, so to speak. These rigs are usually well stayed, with two or more shrouds, particularly if topsails are carried. The strain on the mast

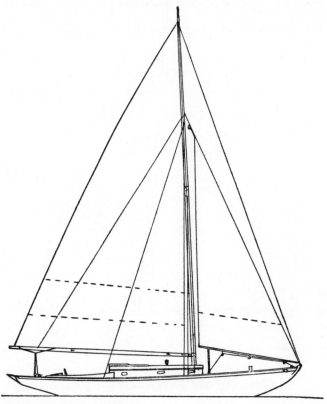

SLOOP, *Jib-headed Rig.*

head is very great, with these rigs, yet it is well to avoid too many shrouds. Permanent backstays, backstays and runners, and similar items of rig are often required, depending upon the design of the rig. In very small sloops, particularly those under 22 feet overall, it is perhaps better to omit the shrouds, and depend upon a large mast diameter to give strength enough to carry the rig. Backstays are a nuisance in small cruising craft and should be omitted if possible.

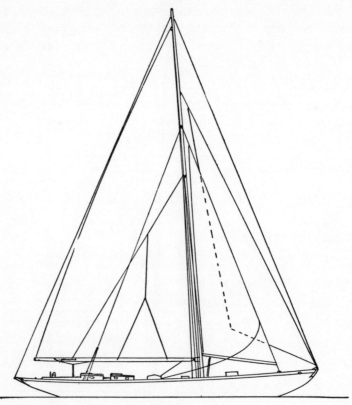

CUTTER, *Jib-headed Rig.*

Odd Rigs and Experimental Types

Lateen sails, sliding-gunter sails and lugsails are used in one-masted rigs, mostly in foreign types. These rigs are so rarely employed in this country, in yachts, that no attention can be given them here, yet it shall be remembered that these sails are effective, and may be used, if desired. The gunter rig is rather expensive because of the necessity of special spar ironwork.

There are numerous experimental rigs, entailing the use of tripod mast, shear-masts, and jackstays, but none of these has developed enough to be trustworthy for cruising yachts. Most of the ideas in these rigs have been tried before, without much success. A cruiser has no business carrying a rig that is so delicate that it needs constant attention or that is liable to failure in rough going.

Two-masted rigs are very common in this country, and have numerous combinations of sail plans.

Yawl

The yawl is primarily a sloop, or cutter, with a small mizzen set on the transom. This rig has had periods of popularity in this country, but the fashion does not last. While having numerous advantages (shared, however, by other rigs) for small seagoing craft, the yawl rig appears to have serious objections. The worst of these is attributed to poor design, and can be overcome. A yawl should balance and steer well under mizzen

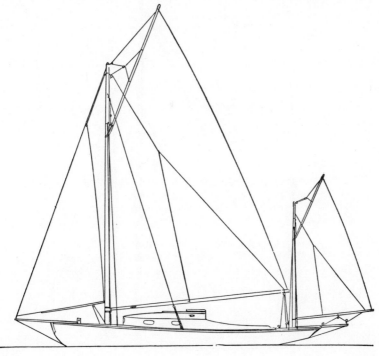

YAWL

and jib (a fore staysail if the double head sail rig is used) and also should balance under mainsail alone. This entails quite a shift of centers, and it is presumably correct to use this rig on yachts having long keels and a well-distributed displacement. But some designers do not agree with this and believe that the yawl rig can be designed to work well with centerboard or short keel; boats having these characteristics have worked out well in practice. In small yawls, or open boats, the mizzen may be set on either quarter, rather than on the centerline. This does not harm the sailing qualities of the rig, and permits the use of the tiller. In small open boats, the cat-yawl rig is sometimes used. This is a yawl, without jib or fore staysail, and, of course, no bowsprit. The sails, in the yawl rig, may be jib-headed, gaff, sprit, lugger, or sliding-gunter. The mizzen is usually sheeted to

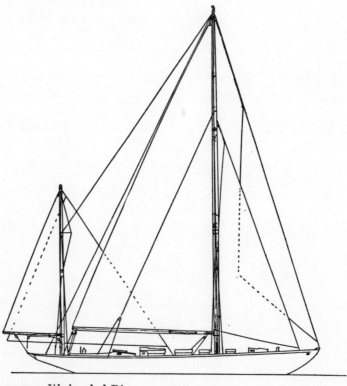

YAWL, *Jib-headed Rig.*

a boomkin, or outrigger, which should be nearly as strong as a bowsprit. The structural difficulty of the yawl rig, in most yachts, is to get a deep enough housing or "bury" in the hull for the mizzen or jigger mast, to give it the ability to carry sail with-

CAT-YAWL

out having to depend wholly upon the shrouds which usually have insufficient spread at the deck because of the narrowness of the stern or counter.

There is another important feature in the design of a yawl: that is, the center of effort of the mizzen and jib alone should be located a little abaft of effort of the whole rig, as the windage of the mast, when the mainsail is off, and the vessel under jib and mizzen only, is great, and will otherwise affect the steering qualities of the yawl.

Ketch

The ketch has become rather popular during late years. Generally speaking, the rig has few advantages not possessed by schooners or yawls, and has, in small craft, some rather serious objections. The ketch is much used abroad, in fishing vessels,

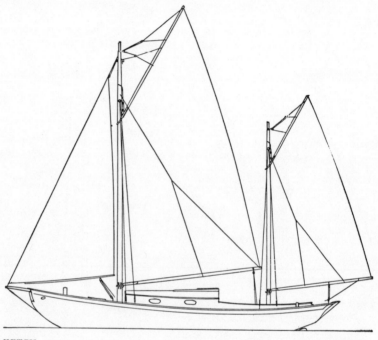

KETCH

but has never been popular on this side, except in the modifications that may be classed as "cat-ketches." When the sail-area is small, the rig is undoubtedly very handy in heavy weather, but its advantages are usually lost when the sail-area becomes large. The most common objection to the rig is that, in small auxiliary yachts, the mizzen mast must be located in the cockpit, and the heel of the mast must come directly over the engine or propeller shaft, which necessitates careful construction, and often extra expense. The ketch rig, at its best, is basically a

schooner with the mainsail about ⅔ of the area of the foresail. Ketches may be fitted to carry square courses and topsails satisfactorily. The gaff rig is preferable in this type of

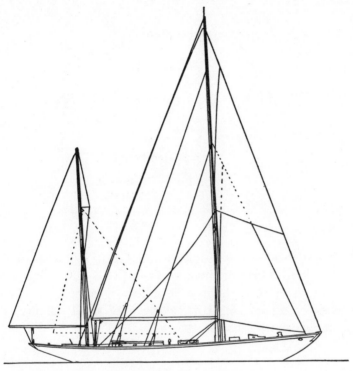

KETCH, *Jib-headed Rig*.

masting, unless the hull is of light displacement, when the
jib-headed sails should be used. The same conditions are to be
met in locating the center of effort of the rig as in the yawl.

Cat-ketch or Periagur Rig

Cat-ketches, however, have been long popular in the smaller
fishing craft in this country. These boats were variously rigged,
some with gaff sails, some with leg-of-mutton sails and others
with spritsails. The sharpie, Block Island boats, Isle of Shoal

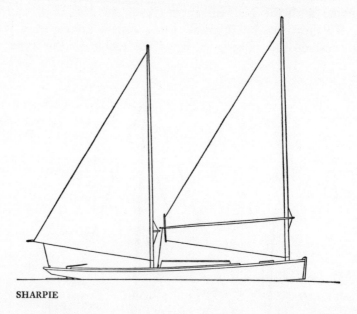

SHARPIE

boats, and many New England and Great Lakes small craft were so fitted. None of these types carried a bowsprit, nor did many of them carry light sails, unless "yachting," or racing. With easily driven hull, particularly if of small stability, such rigs are eminently satisfactory.

Schooner

The national rig is the schooner, and, except in small craft, it is deservedly popular. No nation has ever equaled us in speed, beauty and size of our schooners, though many excellent schooners have been built abroad. The rig varies, somewhat, in different localities. The Gloucester, or Essex, schooner rig is the most popular, though this rig was not intended for a small crew when originally conceived. The old sailing, coasting schooner-rig, and the Chesapeake "pungy," as well as the pilot schooner-rig, are more easily adapted to yachts. The objection to the "Fishing Schooner" rig is the long boom and large topsails usually designed for it. The pilot schooners, and other commercial schooners, carried a large proportion of their sail-area in their lower canvas and had few light sails. They had shorter, lighter spars and booms, and were designed to handle easily with small crews. Schooners with square topsails on the foremasts, or on both masts, were popular years ago, and have great advantages,

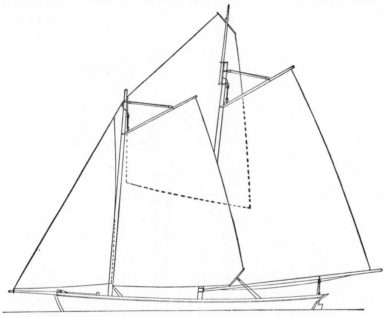

PILOT-BOAT SCHOONER *with "lug-fores'l"*.

but such a rig is suitable only for large vessels with fair-sized crews. Many schooner yachts set a square course on the fore-mast, and invariably the square sail is cut widest at the yard, and narrowing to the foot, under the impression that the area most desirable is aloft. The theory is that when the vessel is in the hollow between two large waves, the sail, being well aloft, will hold the wind and not be becalmed by the wave to windward. The basis for this theory is that square-rigged vessels generally sail under reefed-topsails when in such a position. However, it should be observed that the area of these reefed-topsails, when compared with the total sail-area of the ship, is very small, and, as a result, the vessel bears them easily, and also because of rig, and number of the crew, the reefed-topsails are easily handled. In small yachts, however, the square sail is larger in proportion to the total sail-area, and usually the vessel cannot carry it in winds of such strength as to build up seas that would becalm the lower sails. There is also the objection that it is difficult or impossible

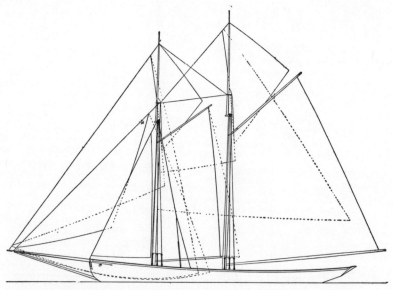

SCHOONER, *showing ordinary and "boomed overlapping" fores'l.*

to go aloft to furl or reef the square sail in a small vessel. Another objection is that this shape of sail slats badly, as there is no support obtained from the narrow foot. This condition is exaggerated when the narrow foot and wide head are combined with great hoist. In general, the wide footed squaresail, with boom, overcomes these objections. Many ingenious rigs have been designed to overcome this difficulty, but most of them require too much rigging to be handy. The easiest and most practical method of designing the square sail is to have the yard very short, and the foot very wide, say twice the beam at the foremast, and the yard equal the beam. The sail, instead of being fitted with reef points, should have two or more "bonnets" (sections of the sail that can be unlaced and removed) at the foot. It is easy to boom this sail out from the deck with a spare boom, and it can be controlled better with the sheets rather than by the braces, which, due to their length, do not have as much control over the sail as is desirable.

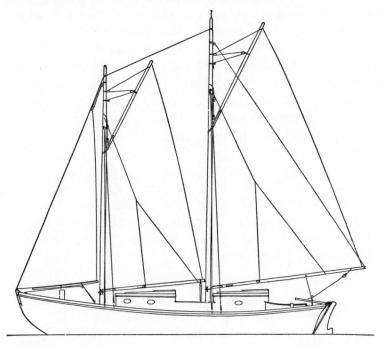

KNOCKABOUT SCHOONER

The designer should be warned against hoisting square sails on jackstays, on the foreside of the mast. Few realize how much chafe there is, at sea, in such rigging, and this method has proven generally unsuccessful. Chafing is present in all rigging that touches a spar, shroud, or other object, and is doubly noticeable if there is a strain on the rigging that is chafing. The only way a square sail can be set, and be made to stand day in and day out, is to employ parrels, after the manner of the old square-topsail schooners and sloops.

In very small schooners it is necessary to have a large area of sail in the foresail, and therefore it will be found that the loose-footed foresail, without a boom and with a good overlap, is most productive of speed. It is best to cut the foot of this sail high at the tack and lower at the clew. This gives a better stand to the sheets. The clew can be very low. The club, at 45° across the clew angle, should be of the plank type to give stiffness. Some schooners, years ago, set a regular lugsail on the foremast, for reaching in light or moderate winds. With this in use, the gaff forsail was furled. The fore and main sail, in the schooner rig, can be gaff or jib-headed. Some yachts have jib-headed mainsails and gaff foresails; this rig has become more and more popular. The staysail schooner had a passing vogue, but was not suitable for ocean cruising with a small crew. The combinations of sail shapes in the schooner rig are endless. Cat-schooners are rarely seen now, but these were popular years ago, and have good features for small craft. Knockabout schooners, having no bowsprit and the headsails inboard, are deservedly popular in the larger vessels but the hull must be carefully designed to suit this rig. The knockabout schooner rig, *i.e.*, without bowsprit, requires a rather lofty rig in order that its working area may be sufficient to obtain speed.

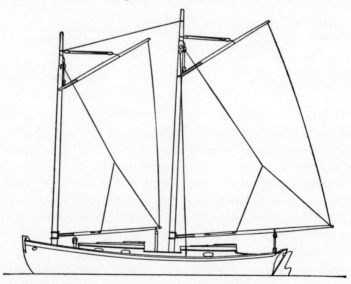

CAT-SCHOONER

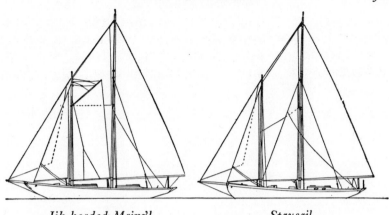

Jib-headed Mains'l   *Staysail*

SCHOONER RIGS

Square and Three-masted Rigs

The brig and brigantine rigs are suitable for yachts, but should not be used in craft of less than 70 feet overall, nor over 120 feet. The best sizes for this rig are between 70 and 100 feet overall. Either of these rigs, in vessels of this length, would not require an unduly large crew. It should be stated that *all* vessels having square sails, either topsail, or double topsail, schooners, or brigs and brigantines, should have their displacement well-distributed, and *should not be cut away very much, in the underbody profile.* This is because there is much shifting of the center of effort of the rigs as sails are furled or reefed; hence the vessel must not be sensitive to rather marked variations in the relative position of the centers of effort to lateral plane. This lack of sensitiveness can only be had in a vessel having a long keel and a deep forefoot, combined with a well-distributed displacement. These rigs are very heavy, when compared to a schooner, and brigs and brigantines require more ballast and stability than do fore-and-aft rigs.

Three-masted rigs, in yachts, are those of the schooner, bark and barkentine. There are few square-rigged three-masted yachts in existence, due to their heavy operating cost. Three-masted schooners are often seen, however. Most of these are designed with the rig of the three-masted commercial schooner, and it

must be admitted that this rig is rather ugly. As was suggested in
Chapter I, a three-masted schooner rig, with masts of varying
height, would be an improvement, not only in looks, but in handling. However, it is admitted that the proposed rig produces

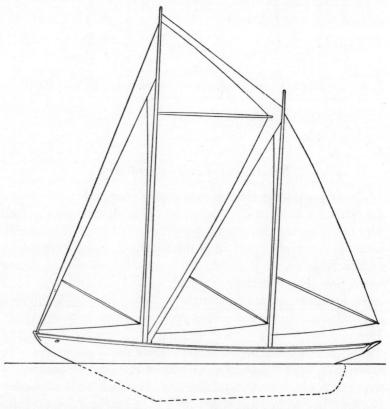

*"Fenger," "Main-Trysail," or "Kite-sail" Rig showing "Pattamar"
underbody profile most suitable for this type of rig.*

problems in staying which will require ingenuity to solve. There
is an opportunity to develop three-masted rigs for small craft,
of small beam and little stability such as sharpies, canoes, and
other long, narrow boats, that would not only be efficient but
graceful and useful as well.

Suggestions

So much for the general remarks on types of rigs. The sketches in this chapter show many rigs and some details. In regard to details, each designer usually has his own idea of what is best, and rarely do two agree. For that matter, few designers can agree upon what is the most desirable rig for a given size and service. Hence the following remarks are merely at random. The masts of two or three-masted rigs should not rake the same. The foremast is usually the most upright, and the mainmast rakes more. The mizzen mast rakes the most. The booms of the fore-and-aft sails should be as high as possible above the deck; nothing is more annoying than unnecessarily low booms. On the other hand, booms should not be so high as to make reefing and stowing difficult. The halyard blocks on gaff or head of sail should be in reach of the deck when sail is stowed. The amount and location of rigging and blocks should be carefully studied to give the best results. Since location of masts has been discussed in Chapter I, no further remarks are necessary in relation to this.

Laying Out Spars, Diameters

The most difficult feature of designing rig is the choice of dimensions of spars and diameter of rigging.* Presumably, this should be calculated, but it is extremely difficult to analyse the loads, and many strains cannot be accurately estimated. The loads on the masts, spars and rigging vary widely and shift rapidly in actual sailing. Hence, most designers refer to previous designs, and by comparison, fix the size of these items to suit the type of design at hand. In racing craft, calculation is often used, with reasonable success, but the occasional loss of spars in this class, even in moderate weather, clearly indicates that much

---

* For rough method of calculating rigging diameters, see Appendix. Spar timbers: Black Spruce—strong, stands bending well; White Pine—stiff, strong; Pine—very stiff, strong; Fir—stiff, strong; Yellow Pine—heavy, very stiff and strong.

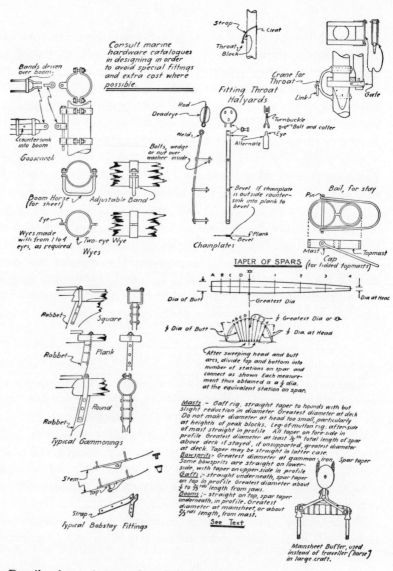

Details of spar ironwork and design of spar taper.

judgment is required to make these calculations accurately. Hollow spars, for example, are almost impossible to rule upon for proper diameter, as the workmanship and design of such spars govern their stiffness and strength far more than does diameter alone.

The sail plan is started by redrawing the hull of the yacht in the same manner as in the sketch. However, the finished hull can now be referred to, in the lines and construction plans, and any alterations made in these drawings should appear on the sail plan. The position of the center of lateral plane should now be found, using the lines, and balancing the underbody profile as described in Chapter II. This center should be plotted on the sail plan, and by finding it on the lines, an accurate check is to be had.

The rake of the spars in the construction plans should check that in the sketch. Using this rake and position lay off the centerlines of the masts, taking the lengths from the sketch. Now, we must consider the diameters of solid masts. For catboats the mast diameter at the deck should be about .02 the total length of the mast, heel to truck (overall) for gaff rigs, and about .025 for jib-headed rigs. This is for unstayed masts in centerboard cats; keel cats should have diameters ranging from .022 the total length of the mast, to .028 in the order above. The diameter at the halyard eye should be about .65 the diameter at deck for gaff-rigged boats, and .42 for jib-headed rigs. If a track is used on the mainsail, the mast should be a straight line on the after side, from boom to halyard eye, the taper being in the forward side. Usually the taper is a long gentle curve from deck to halyard eye. The masts, where mast hoops are used, usually taper very slightly to the gaff jaws and then more quickly to the truck. The diameter at the jaws is usually about .90 the diameter at deck.

Masts in sloops and cutters without topmasts have a diameter at deck of about .02 the total length of the mast, with a diameter at the halyard eye of about .70 the diameter at the deck (for gaff rig). For jib-headed rigs, the diameter at deck is around .023, and about .52 of the diameter at the deck, at the halyard eye. The remarks as to taper in catboats' masts apply to sloops and cutters. If extensive staying is used, the diameter of the mast is reduced about 10%. Where topmasts are used, the mast diameter at deck is about .022 to .025 the length from *deck* to *hounds* (lower cap) and the diameter at the lower cap or hounds is about .90 the diameter at deck, the diameter at the masthead, or upper cap, being about .65 or .70 the diameter at deck. The diameter of the topmasts is usually about .02 the length of heel to truck, at the upper cap, and the diameter at the heel is about .6 the diameter at the upper cap, while the diameter at the topsail halyard is about the same as at the heel. In some sloops and cutters there is no taper from deck to hounds, in the mast. In some heavily rigged cutters, the diameter of the mast at deck was as great as .03 the length, deck to hounds, and the diameter at hounds was .9 that at deck, while at the masthead it was .8 of the diameter at the hounds. The bowsprit was usually designed by eye, but it should have a diameter, or its equivalent area of cross-section, of from .028 to .04 of the length of the bowsprit outside, at the gammoning. The diameter at the outer end is about .72 of the diameter at the gammoning.

The masts of schooners have diameters as follows: diameter at deck, .023 to .029 the length, deck to hounds. The diameter at the hounds is about .85 the diameter at deck, and the diameter at the masthead is about .8 the diameter at the hounds. Bowsprit diameter fixed as in cutters. In most schooners the foremast has a slightly greater diameter than the mainmast, particularly if topsails are carried. If the leg-of-mutton mainsail is carried, the diameters of the mainmast at deck and halyard eye should be the same as those of a jib-headed rig on a sloop or cutter. In large schooners, without many shrouds, the mast diameter at deck is .02 the total length, heel to masthead. This is for hard pine masts; 10% should be added for weaker woods. Unstayed masts, for schooners, should be about .021 or .025 at deck.

Masts in yawls and ketches should follow the proportions of the schooner; the shorter mizzen will cause it to have a very small diameter.

These diameters are for cruising boats, and are greater than the proportions usually used in racing craft. The diameters are of sufficient size to enable the masts to stand without excessive staying; none at all in small craft, if the stock is reasonably clear and sound.

The diameters of solid gaffs are from .015 to .018 of the length, the diameter at the jaws is .9 the greatest diameter, and the diameter at the head is .72 the greatest diameter.

The diameter of main booms, for laced sails, is .015 the length at the mainsheet block, and at the jaws it is .8 the greatest diameter, while at the after end it is about .7 the greatest diameter. With loose-footed sails, the greatest diameter is between .016 and .02 the length. The diameter at the jaws is about .7 the greatest diameter, and the diameter at the outhauls is about .75 of the greatest diameter. The boom tapers slightly from the sheet toward the jaws, until about one-seventh its length, from the mast, when it tapers a great deal, and the same for the outer end. The yawl's main boom has a diameter of .016 its length, ketches .018. The schooner's fore boom has diameters as follows: greatest near sheet .022 to .026 of its length, jaws .9 of the greatest diameter, outer end .8. Forestaysail boom: .02 of its length for greatest diameter at the sheet, .7 to .8 the diameter at the stay, and .6 to .7 at the outer end. Sprits of the "wishbone" type must be designed with great care. "Aeroplane Spruce" is commonly employed in the construction of this spar and the sectional area of the arms should be obtained by calculation.* The spread of the "wishbone" sprit is commonly 17% to 18% of the length, measured from bolt-rope (luff) to clew (depth of sail at sprit). Both arms of the "wishbone" sprit should come from the same stick in order that there may be the same number of annual rings per inch in section; this indicates that the strength and stiffness will be the same in each arm.

Jib club: diameter, .02 to .023 of the total length, for'd end, diameter, .6 the greatest diameter, outer end .75.

Gunter topsail, lug topsail, and similar topsail yards have diameters of .015 the whole length: diameter at ends, .73 the greatest diameter.

* See Appendix for this.

The diameter of the spinnaker boom is from .012 to .014 of its length, and the diameters at the ends, .85 of its greatest diameter.

The length of the lower masthead, when fidded topmasts are used, should be .125 to .2 of the total length of the mast, heel to hounds, for schooners, while cutters, sloops, ketches and yawls have mastheads .2 to .24 the hounded length (heel to hounds, or lower cap). If a topmast is carried on the mizzen of a ketch, the lower masthead should be .12 to .125 the hounded length.

The eye of the throat halyard bolt comes about .04 the height, deck to hounds, above the underside of the yoke. The jaws of the gaff are about .062 below the yoke. This allows enough drift between the blocks to prevent an unfair strain as the gaff swings to leeward.

The design of hollow spars requires much experience; the amateur should consult a spar builder specializing in the construction of such spars. The design of hollow spars, and spars having special sections, has made rapid strides in recent years. Because the variation in design is so great it is impractical to give rules for sectional-area or the thickness of shell since these matters are wholly dependent upon the length, strains and form of section of the spar. As a general rule, however, the greater the number of pieces glued up in a cross-section of the mast, the stiffer it will be. Square, rectangular and round sections are now employed in the design of hollow masts, while booms are round, T-shaped or a mere plank on edge. Obviously, the design of such spars is not for the beginner and has no place in the design of any but extreme racing cruisers or out-and-out racing craft; calculation and experimentation are the only guides in the design of spars having special sections.

Rake of Masts

In regard to the rake of masts, it is thought desirable to rake the masts somewhat in nearly all types of rig. The rake may be very great, without harm. The extreme rake, in Bugeyes' masts, is a present-day example. Rake increases the efficiency of the jib-headed or leg-of-mutton sail in windward sailing, it is claimed, due to the increase in leading edge that is possible without an increase in the total height of the rig. Excess rake, however, creates a tendency for the booms to swing inboard when running in light weather, which many consider undesirable.

With these proportions and notes as a general guide, lay off the spars on the sail plan, getting the spars to accurate scale. The designer should use judgment in employing the proportions given, remembering that light displacement boats, of small stability, require masts of less diameter than do powerful boats.

Sails

When the spars are drawn in, from reference to the preliminary sketch, the sails may be drawn. Some designers show only straight leaches, some show the roach. For the sake of appearance the roach should be shown in all sails, but the roach should not be included in the calculation for area and center of effort, a straight line being used in its place. The sailmaker should be permitted to fix the roach, or "round," when making the sails, as he knows what allowances for stretch are required for a given make of canvas. The improved windward ability of modern yachts over old craft is largely due to the efforts of the progressive and intelligent sailmaker, rather than to any advance in knowledge of hull-form on the part of builders or yacht designers alone.

The recent fad for carrying the heads of the jib or jib and forestaysail close up to the masthead has grown out of an attempt to obtain all the area of sail measured for under racing rules; this fad is another that has been adopted from the racer by the cruiser. Though this method of cutting the headsails is fashionable, it has no great advantage in a cruiser and if the foot of the sail is narrow the high-headed sail will not stand well. Often the blame for the failure of such headsails to draw well is placed on the sailmaker whereas it should be placed on the designer instead. It would be wise to consult a good sailmaker now and then, when designing ultra-modern rigs, in order that impossible demands will not be made of the man who must cut the sails.

Cheek Block

Eye and eye-plate

Upset Front Shackle and Swivel

Long Side Hook

Fiddle Block (with Upset Front Shackle)

Screw-eye

Front Backstay Hook

Backstay Heart

Flat Sheet Bridle (for boom bridles)

Rope Strop

Solid eye

Self-locking Snap-block

Loose Swivel Hook

Side Sister Hook

Swivel-eye Shackle

Swivel-eye

Lashing-eye

Side Shackle

Eye and Thimble

One Band Gooseneck

Front Shackle
and eyeplate

Bronzeblock
(with bronze
shackle)

Bolt

Front Shackle
with becket

Front
Snap
Shackle

Upset Side
Shackle

Ring

Round jib sheet
Blocks

Swivel deck plate

Upset Front
Shackle with
link

Front
Hook

Front
Shackle

Side
Hook

Front Sister
Hook

Upset Front
Shackle

Blocks may be ordered with nearly all fittings, either "front" or "side" as required to locate properly. "Front" indicates eye of shackle, ring or hook faces sides or "cheeks" of block. "Side" indicates eye of shackle, ring or hook faces lead or "arse" of block. Specify number of sheaves (single, double, treble, etc.), material of cheeks (bronze, galv. iron, wood, etc.), and fitting ("front" or "side") such as ring, shackle, hook, etc. Beckets must be fitted to the block to which standing part of tackle is secured.

After the sails are drawn in (and this drawing should represent the sails fully stretched), the center of effort should again
be calculated, as directed in Chapter I. If an error is found, it
should be corrected by further alterations in the rig. When the
balance of center of effort and center of lateral plane has been
checked, the rigging may be drawn in. In the space allotted,
there can be no complete description of rigging methods, as this
alone would fill a book. The designer should study actual boats

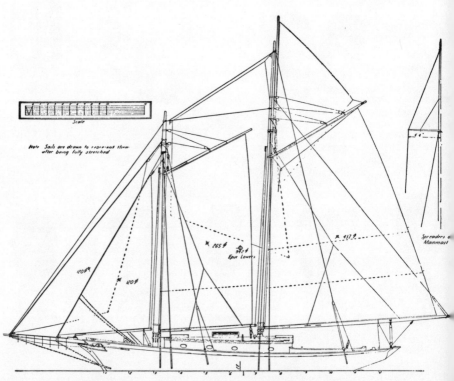

PLATE XIV. *Sail Plan of example; dimensions omitted. Give dimensions of sa*
lengths and diameters of spars; note fittings. Give circumference of all wire riggi
and turnbuckle diameters. Specify blocks and fairleads. Give rake, bury, deck
hounds length, stick length and diameters of masts. Give one diagonal measureme
on four-sided sails.

and published drawings, particularly of the type of boat that he is designing.

Blocks

The sail plan is often supplemented by a block list, and by diameters of standing rigging required; the latter are sometimes marked on the plan. Be certain that the blocks are of sufficient size. Very small blocks make the rig hard to handle. In ordering blocks, the catalogue of a block-maker should be used. These show the size of block required for a given size of rope, but it is well to order the size next above the maker's suggestion. Wooden shells are most popular among experienced cruisers, and cost less than bronze-shell blocks.

Blocks are made with single, double and triple sheaves, for yachts. The shackle is at the top of the block, to hang it by, and is fixed to the block in four different ways, front, upset front, side, and upset side shackles. Blocks are also fitted with hooks, sister hooks, snatch hooks, lashing eyes, eye and thimble, punched eye, ring, loose bolt and swivel, in the same manner. If it is necessary to splice one end of the rope to a block, a becket is required, at the bottom of the block. There are many special blocks, such as swivel deck leaders, fiddle blocks, snatch blocks, cheek blocks, bullet blocks, splice blocks, centerboard blocks, etc. The illustrations show the various common blocks, and the reason for the various types of shackle and block is obvious. The catalogues of Merriman Bros., 185 Amory St., Jamaica Plain, Boston, Mass., U.S.A. give much information as to blocks and rigging fittings, such as jib snap hooks, turnbuckles, cleats, small winches, sail slides and tracks, gaff saddles, goosenecks, clew outhaul slide blocks, traveler, etc. Others manufacture similar lines.

Turnbuckles, Shrouds, Stays, etc.

Turnbuckles are required on shrouds and stays and should be at least twice the size of the stay, in diameter. Shrouds and stays are usually of flexible steel wire or iron wire (galvanized); in small boats aircraft wire is used. The sizes range from $\frac{1}{8}''$ to $\frac{1}{4}''$ diameter. Plow steel wire ranges from ¼″ to 1¼″ diameter. The use of chain for bobstays, centerboard pennants, and for other rigging subject to chafe or corrosion, is suggested.

In place of turnbuckles, deadeyes and lanyards are sometimes used. Both systems have advantages, but the choice is subject to local conditions, type of hull and rig, and also to personal opinion. In rough water and strong winds there is little doubt that some flexibility is desirable, in all rigs, and this is an argument for deadeye and lanyards. However, they require more attention than do turnbuckles and need overhauling more often. A study of the rigs shown in this book will give an idea of the various methods, but the designer should work out a rigging most suitable for his design from comparison, and with the advice of a rigger, if it can be had.

The manufacturers of canvas should be asked to furnish the designer samples of sail canvas; these samples are to be used when ordering canvas for decks or sails. Don't use very thin and light canvas for cruising boats.

General Rigging Details

Methods of rigging, types of fittings, cut of sails and the general makeup of rig vary widely along the coast and the amateur has opportunities of designing original rigging, by combining the various methods, to suit the work at hand.

Methods of stowing and handling the boats should receive attention. If the boat requires davits they should be located and by use of cardboard outlines made to represent the plan-view of a boat; the stowing and hoisting out should be studied to make certain there is no interference. Anchor davits, or anchor stowing gear, should be specified. The use of masthead tackles for hoisting purposes should receive consideration.

There are numerous purchases and tackles; the most common are as follows: Single Whip, Whip upon Whip, Single Burton, Luff Tackle Double Spanish Burton, and Gun Tackle Purchase. There are also Twofold, Threefold, etc., purchases. The principle of the block and tackle is the distribution of weight in various points of support, the mechanical advantage derived depending

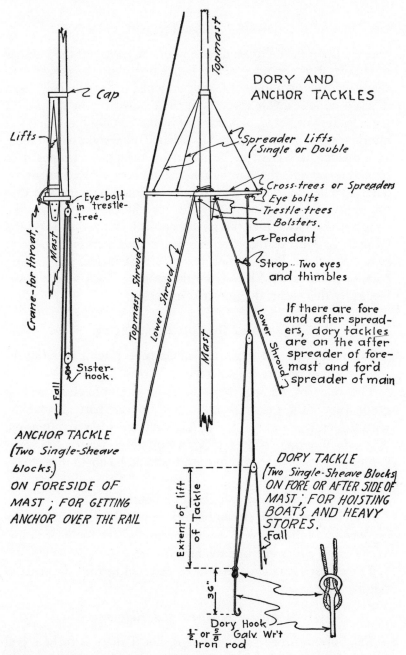

DORY AND ANCHOR TACKLES

Cap

Lifts

Topmast

Spreader Lifts
(Single or Double

Cross-trees or Spreaders
Eye bolts
Trestle-trees
Bolsters.
Pendant

Strop - Two eyes
and thimbles

Eye-bolt
in trestle-
-tree.

Crane - for throat,

Mast

Sister-
hook.

Fall

Topmast Shroud

Lower Shroud

Mast

Lower Shroud

If there are fore
and after spread-
ers, dory tackles
are on the after
spreader of fore-
mast and for'd
spreader of main

ANCHOR TACKLE
(Two Single-Sheave
blocks.)
ON FORESIDE OF
MAST ; FOR GETTING
ANCHOR OVER THE RAIL

Extent of lift
of Tackle

DORY TACKLE
(Two Single-Sheave Blocks)
ON FORE OR AFTER SIDE OF
MAST ; FOR HOISTING
BOATS AND HEAVY
STORES.
Fall

36"

Dory Hook
½ or ⅝ Galv. Wr't
Iron rod

*Boat and Anchor Tackles. Fisherman Type. The spinnaker tackle
is often used in yachts for an anchor tackle.*

entirely upon flexibility and tension of the rope and the number of sheaves in the *moving* block; hence in tackles the power is to the weight as the number of parts attached to the moving block. Therefore, (A) divide the weight to be raised by the number of parts leading *to, from,* or *made fast* to the *moving* block and the quotient is the power required to balance the weight to be raised; (B) divide the weight to be raised by the power proposed to be employed and the quotient is the number of sheaves in, or parts attached to, the moving block. It should be remarked that the upper block of a tackle (or the fixed block) has to bear the weight to be raised plus the power applied. No power is gained by increasing the diameter of the sheaves, but increased diameter reduces friction. In arranging the blocks of tackle, the hauling part, or "fall," should lead from the *moving* block where possible, as by this means the power is increased.

Safe Loads for Running Rigging

The maximum safe strain of Manila rope (factor of safety of $4\frac{1}{2}$) is $\sqrt{\text{tension}} \times 10 = \text{diameter}$.

The rule for finding the equivalent circumference of first grade Manila for a given load, in tons, on one part of a tackle, with a factor of safety of 3 is, Circumference $= \sqrt{10 \times \text{tension}}$. The safe working load of a given circumference of Manila is $\dfrac{\text{Circumference}^2}{10} = \text{safe load in tons}$. It should be noted that blocks are fitted for wire, rope and chain, as desired.

For Hemp rope the circumference required by a given working load is as follows: $\sqrt{7 \times \text{load}} = \text{circumference for white rope.}$ $\sqrt{9 \times \text{load}} = \text{circumference for tarred rope.}$

The maker's catalogue should be referred to for safe loads of rigging wire.

Ironwork in Spars and Rigging

The bobstay-irons vary in design, but if there is to be a real strain on the bobstay, the bobstay-iron should have long straps, and should be bolted athwartships, through the stem. There are castings that are fastened to the fore side of the stem, but these are weak, as the load is brought to bear directly on the heads of the fastenings subject to shape of stem and casting.

Shrouds and stays are eye spliced around the mast aloft, generally, and are supported by bolsters. With the jib-headed mainsail and track, the shrouds are sometimes spliced into an eye bolt, or tang, or to a mast-wye (band with eyes) so as not to interfere with the track. Thimbles are required at these eyes.

Gammoning irons should follow the rake of the rabbet, in profile. To do this, it is usually best to make the iron in two or three pieces, bolted at the top, or to put a weld in, so that the top will lie flat on the top of the bowsprit. The use of an eye and link on each side is sometimes seen. The gammoning iron must be firmly bolted through the stem head. Galvanized irons, made of a single piece of iron, fastened to the face of the stem and passing through the bowsprit, are sometimes used on small boats, but are suitable for use with the plank-bowsprit only.

It is impossible to galvanize spring steel, as all of the methods used destroy the temper.

The size of all rigging ironwork should be carefully considered. However, their dimensions are subject to design and to the exact requirements of the rig, so that it is impossible to give any fixed rules.

The use of gaff jaws or gaff saddles is a matter of cost and appearance; the saddle, however, is less liable to breakage if the peak halyard should part. It is impractical to use sail slides and track with gaffs fitted with jaws or saddles since the latter will twist the track off the mast. Gaff track-slides, in place of jaws, are impractical in all but very small craft, and are not in great favor even there.

Boom-jaws or goosenecks are chosen to suit the pocket-book and to procure the required appearance; jaws are cheaper, and give a greater range of hoist, but the gooseneck is neater in appearance, does not wear, and is very strong. Except on small boats, the gooseneck should have two mast bands, well spread

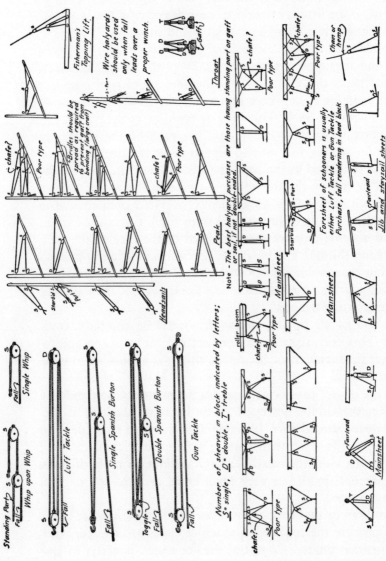

Common tackles, sheets and halyards. Notice that those showing danger of chafing are marked poor. Mast lacing starts at the throat or where the mast hoops stop and works downwards; the lacing is passed around the forward side of the mast through the eyelet and back to the same side between the luff and the mast around the forward side of the

apart, so that the boom can be hoisted or lowered a little. On small boats, one mast band can be used, but it will have to be shifted as the sail stretches and so should be of the clamp type.

The use of track, lacing or mast-rings, to hold the sails to the mast, is a matter that must be left to the designer's judgment and to his choice of rig. There is one point that might be made in respect to this choice, however, and that is the method of getting aloft. If mast-rings are used, the rings ought to be close enough together to be used in climbing·aloft, say 16″ to 24″. If lacing or the track is used, however, it is necessary to rattle-down the shrouds in order that a man may be able to go aloft.

Spreaders can be of wood or metal; here again neatness aloft and cost are the chief guides to choice. Spreaders of bronze or galvanized steel, solid or hollow, may be purchased, as standard equipment.

Travelers, for deck, house top, or bowsprit, may also be purchased ready-made, or to suit requirements. Some kind of a stop, at each end of the traveler, is desirable to prevent block from catching. This stop may be of rubber or metal. Marine hardware catalogues can be consulted for these items of ironwork.

Jib-club fittings may be purchased, ready-made, or to suit requirements.

Clew out-haul slides and blocks, as well as cheek blocks, can be purchased, designed for this special use.

In regard to mast bands, such as wyes, spider irons and straps, it should be remembered that these are liable to encourage rot in the spar. Spider irons are bands around the mast to take belaying pins; also the wye that the topmast futtock shrouds are spliced into is also called a "spider iron" or "futtock wye."

The use of bands on the boom is open to the same objections, but in this case, it is less serious. In small craft, the main sheet block is usually hung on a boom band that has either an eye or a traveler, and usually the topping lift is seized into an eye band. The lazy jacks usually pass through a wooden cleat on the underside of the boom. The outhaul leads through a cheek block on one side of the boom to a cleat well forward on the boom, and if the sail is large a whip or gun tackle purchase is seized into the hauling part. If the boom has much overhang beyond the transom, and cannot be easily reached, a reefing tackle (gun tackle purchase usually) should be fitted. This has the upper block hooked into the lower reef cringle and the lower block is a cheek block, on the opposite side from the outhaul cheek block. This tackle should be fitted to unship, as it chafes the sail. The topping lift of the fore boom of a schooner is a single whip, with the block at the *mainmast* cross trees, or at the spreaders. In large schooners, a footrope on the mainboom is necessary, where the boom overhangs the stern.

The lazy jacks are bridles, with a bullet-block and a pendant. The pendant usually leads through cheek blocks on the masthead, and belay on deck.

If the mainboom is long and light, the main sheet block, or blocks, should be hung on bridles, not on bands. If a topsail is carried, a belaying pin rack on the jaws or gooseneck is required to belay the topsail tack rope to, and also to belay the topsail sheet. The belaying pins at the foot of the mast and at the chainplates can be used for halyards, topping lift and lazy jacks as required. Cleats are used in small boats for this purpose.

Sprit yards and booms, in small craft, have a figure-eight, made of rope, at their heels, with one eye around the mast, to act as a support. In sharpies and larger craft with sprit-booms, an outhaul tackle is used at the mast, to force the boom aft, when required. The figure-eight is called a "snotter," and is only to be used in open boats under 20 feet, as no adjustment is possible other than raising the "snotter" on the mast, thus forcing the sprit upward and its head aft.

Leads of Rigging; General Remarks

The leads for the sheets are of great variety as can be seen in the sketches. There is no standard, though the gun tackle purchase is probably the most common in small craft. The use of complicated sheet leads is common in racing craft, but is a great nuisance in a cruiser. If quarter blocks are employed, multiple sheave blocks are usually undesirable on the boom, as the spread of the leads from the sheaves causes dangerous chafing of the sheet.

The danger of foul leads to running rigging should never be overlooked. Wherever a fall rubs against a block, stay, shroud, spar or other object, iron thimbles or lignum vitae fair leads on short penants should be employed to pull the fall away from the object it fouls.

The blocks of the jib and staysail halyards are usually at the sides of the masthead. The main and fore throat halyards have their blocks fitted with upset side shackles, as the fall will not jamb if so fitted. The peak halyards block is usually fitted with an upset front shackle. The blocks on the gaff are fixed as follows: The throat halyard block, upset side shackle, shackled to link-and-eye in the jaws or saddle. The peak halyard block is fitted with bridle fitting (and a wire bridle holds it to the gaff) in most craft as is done if there are two or more peak halyard blocks. The halyard block, in a jib-headed mainsail, is usually replaced by a sheave in the masthead, or by cheek blocks. In some craft there is a special sheave in the head board of the sail as well.

Jib sheet and mainsheet blocks require thicker shells than ordinary blocks. Lead blocks usually have extra thick sheaves. All beckets are to be fitted with thimbles unless chain is used.

The use of marine hardware catalogues will be of great value to the amateur, as he will find many useful and clever suggestions for fittings above and below deck and for rigging details. The numerous types of cleats, chocks, winches, bitts, thimbles, shackles, hooks, blocks, fairleaders, eye-plates, deck and crotch hooks offer fittings for practically every type of rig.

The location of cleats and chocks, on the edge of deck, top of house, or top of bulwarks, should be laid out so that there is no danger of their interfering with sheets or other running rigging.

Fidded topmasts are out of place in small craft, but are used in schooners and large sloops and cutters rigged with gaffsails. Masthead shrouds, passing over or by the spreaders to the cap of the lower-mast, should not be used as the strains on the masthead are increased by this rigging. It is possible, by using long mastheads, to set topsails on pole-masted rigs, without the use of the fidded topmasts. Also, topsails can be set over the leg-of-mutton mainsails, if desired, as was done with the old Bermuda sloop rig.

The reefing, or housing, bowsprit of the old cutters, now obsolete in yachts, was operated by winches, and a heel rope or chain was used to force it outboard. The rigging of this bowsprit requires special fittings not required by fixed bowsprits. This type of headgear was used in schooners, occasionally. Like the fidded topmast, it was struck in heavy weather.

Methods of setting up or tightening all standing rigging should be included, as all wire or Manila rope stretches with use. Turnbuckles, lanyards, or tackles should be fitted for this purpose, where required.

When large sails are necessary, the halyards are double ended, one fall leading to deck, and the other seized into a gun tackle purchase, or single Spanish Burton, which is used to sway up the halyards after the sail is hoisted. These tackles, for this particular use, are called "jigs."

Some rigs require special rigging, and in these the beginner must study an available example, either actual boat or drawing, to reproduce it in his design. However, in the common rigs, the foregoing remarks will usually apply.

In general, it is better to lash blocks to masts and spars, rather than use wyes or bands. The lead of all standing rigging should be in the direction of the strain, where possible. Throat halyard blocks at the mastheads should hang clear of the mast. Care should be taken to lead running rigging aloft so that there will be as little chafe as possible. If there is unavoidable chafe, padding with rope, canvas, or leather should be used to reduce it. If jaws, on the gaff or boom, are used, the mast should be protected from chafe by use of sheet copper, galvanized sheet steel, or rawhide. The shrouds, at deadeyes or turnbuckles, should have "sheer poles," of metal or wood, lashed to the eye splice to prevent them from twisting. These are required most, when deadeyes are used. The higher the lead of a piece of running rigging is, on the mast, the further from the mast it should belay at deck.

Downhauls should be fitted on all large sails, to enable the sail to be got down when full of wind. The downhaul blocks should be small and located so as not to jam when the sail is being hoisted.

In reference to distribution of sail, in strong winds, there is a curious feature that is often overlooked. When the vessel is well heeled, in heavy weather, a sail well forward, say a jib topsail, for example, will not usually swing her bow to leeward, but rather tend to force the vessel head to the wind. This is particularly true of staysails of all kinds, even though they be well forward of the center lateral plane. The reason for this action is the forward component created by the driving force of the sail forward, as opposed by the resistance of the hull, the lever being created by the angle of the mast. Hence, with the hull as a pivot, the driving force of the sail as a force, and the horizontal length of the mast when heeled as a lever, a strong turning effect is produced. This is the cause of some vessels carrying weather helm excessively, when heeled. All boats are not thus affected, but it is sometimes marked in vessels that have much forefoot. It is not noticeable if the boomed sails are set, instead of staysails, however. This point is mentioned to explain why apparent difficulties often appear in the actual rig, and the importance of proper handling of an individual type.

The shrouds, in large vessels such as fishermen, are put over the masthead in pairs, the two after shrouds are cut in one piece and seized together in a loop over the masthead; the for'd shroud is single and is usually shackled to a short pennant looped around the masthead and seized. Ratlines on the shrouds may be spaced from 12 to 14 inches apart, and when three shrouds to a side are employed, it is customary to rattle all three up about 8 to 10 feet above the rail, and two all the way up.

When the sail plan is completed to the satisfaction of the designer, the drawings are complete. There remain only the specifications and choice of fittings not shown in the plans to be considered.

VI. Specifications

THE "specifications" should not only minutely describe the items of construction, finish or fittings shown in the plans, but also those not shown. The "specifications" should be written with care, as it is the final reference, also as it has preference over the plans and is a legal paper recognized by the courts. It is customary to include the builder's contract in the specifications.

In order to enable the reader to write his specifications easily, all items to be described are listed; the designer will omit those not applicable to his design, of course.

The preamble to the specifications is usually a standard form, thus:

SPECIFICATIONS FOR DESIGN No. ——
Designer's name
Address

1. All drawings and specifications are the property of the naval architect and are instruments of service for fulfilling this particular contract. They are not to be used for any other purpose without permission of the naval architect (or owner). All blueprints are to be destroyed, or returned to the owner (or designer) on completion of the vessel.

2. In General

(This paragraph describes in general terms the quality of workmanship and material.) Example: "In carrying out these specifications it is understood that all workmanship shall be of the highest standard, that the timber employed shall be reasonably clear and free from defects and that all materials shall be of good quality, to the entire satisfaction of the owner."

"The specifications and drawings are intended to supplement one another, so that any work shown in one and not in the other is to be executed without extra charge. It is understood that the vessel is to be completely built and fitted; if no mention is made as to who will furnish or install an article, it is understood that it will be furnished and installed by the builder."

3. Inspection

Example: "The vessel and all material intended for it must be open to inspection of the owner and naval architect or their representatives, at all reasonable times. Any defective material or workmanship must be removed whenever discovered, the cost to be borne by the builder."

4. Dimensions

"It is intended that the plans and specifications are to produce a vessel of the following dimensions:"

> Length overall ——
> Length on the waterline ——
> Beam extreme ——
> Draft extreme ——

(The following items may now be described)

1. *Owner to supply* (crockery, china, bed linen, galley and pantry utensils and hangings).

2. *Builders to supply* [lifesaving and firefighting equipment, U.S. government equipment, *i. e.*, life preservers, fire extinguishers, notices, rules, fog horn, etc.; all anchors, cables, ways, bells, binnacles, compasses and certain other navigating equipment, canvas outfit, galley and pantry outfit (except utensils), upholstery and furniture].

3. *General description* of vessel (rig, etc.).

4. *Plans*, to be supplied by the designer and by builder (list).

5. *Loft work* (laydown and approval) Instructions for.

6. *Certificates* (U.S. government, etc., Classification Societies).

7. *Trials* (duration, speed required, consumption of fuel, etc.).

8. *Delivery* [where and when (date)].

Hull and Scantlings, Joiner Work

1. *Construction* (type of framing, planking or shell in general)

2. *Stem, Knight-heads, Hawse Timbers and knees* [(including fastenings) kind of lumber, stopwaters, caulking]*

3. *Stern frame, transom and knees, horn timber.* [(including fastenings) kind of lumber]

4. *Shaft log, etc.* [stopwaters]

5. *Keel shoe and keelson* [mast-steps, fastenings, caulking, ballast and its fastenings, kind of lumber]

6. *Rudder* (fastenings, hanging and construction)

7. *Centerboard case, fish well*, etc. (fastenings and construction, kind of lumber, stopwaters)

8. *Floors* (construction and fastening)

9. *Frames* ("   "   "   , kind of lumber.) *Salting or Preservation*

10. *Web frames* (construction and fastening)

11. *Knees* (location, length of arms and thickness, fastenings, kind of lumber)

12. *Stringers*, clamps and shelves (fastenings and location, kind of lumber)

13. *Planking or plating* [(fastenings, bungs, caulking, butts, no. of strakes, shift of butts, planing, sanding) kind of lumber]

14. *Mouldings, guards*, etc.

15. *Deck waterways, planksheer and deck framings* (partner-beams, knees, carlins, bitts, blocks, cockpit and coamings, kind of lumber)

16. *Bulkheads* (construction, kind of lumber)

17. *Tanks and tank beds* (fastenings)

18. *Engine beds* (fastenings, construction)

19. *Chain lockers* (fore and after-peak)

20. *Hatches* (companionways)

21. *Cabin trunk and roof or deck-houses* (construction)

22. *Miscellaneous foundations* (lighting, pumping, etc., machinery beds)

---

* Rule for width of caulking seams: ⅛" wide at ½ the thickness of the deck. In heavy flat decks the seam width is ½" in 10" of thickness. Broken level in hardwood decks, straight level in soft.

23. *Bulwarks* (construction, etc.)

24. *Mast-step and partner bracing* (knees, blocks and beams, tierods and fastenings)

25. *Skylights* (operating gear, construction and screens)

26. *Hawse pipes or chocks* (anchors and cables or chain)

27. *Name and hail* (stem and stern scrolls and carving)

28. *Bitts, fairleads and chocks* (deck ironwork)

29. *Flag staffs,* etc.

30. *Airports, fixed lights, screens and windscoops*

31. *Scuppers and drains*

32. *Ceiling and insulation*

33. *Mast and spars* (size and material, mast and spar ironwork and boom crotches, mast coats)*

34. *Awnings and canvas outfit*

35. *Painting* (outboard and deck)

36. *Joiner work and decoration* (general, material, workmanship, bulkheads, cabin floor, doors, sash, stairways, hardware, floor covering, drapes, curtains, etc., furniture, and upholstery, galley lockers, drawers, springs, finish, glazing and panels)

37. *Galley fittings* (range, sink, icebox, insulation of chimney, coal or wood box, floor covering, plumbing, pumps and lockers)

38. *Standing rigging and fittings, chain-plates*

39. *Running rigging and fittings*

40. *Sails and fittings* (itemized descriptions)

41. *Blocks, cleats,* etc. (" ")

42. *Steering gear, Miscellaneous ironwork and castings*

43. *Marking of designed L W L on completed hull, propelling machinery and engineering.*

44. *Inside Ballast* (material, stowing)

MACHINERY, ETC.

1. *Engines* [(propelling) starting equipment]

2. *Air compressors,* etc.

3. *Bearings*

4. *Stuffing boxes*

5. *Pumps*

6. *Controls*

---

* It is better to lash mast coats to a mast than to tack them.

7. *Mechanical counters*
8. *Couplings*
9. *Drains*
10. *Engine tools and workbench*
11. *Exhaust pipe and muffler*
12. *Fuel line*
13. *Oil line*
14. *Fire control*
15. *Engine room floor covering, pans, etc.*
16. *Gauges, instruments*
17. *Gratings*
18. *Hoists*
19. *Shaft*
20. *Beds*
21. *Piping* (valves, fittings, hangers, sizes)
22. *Pumps* (type, size, location)
23. *Ventilation*
24. *Tanks* (fillers, hanger, beds, plates, gauges, etc.)
25. *Spares*
26. *Thrust bearing*
27. *Auxiliary motors*
28. *Storage batteries*
29. *Bells*
30. *Capstan, winches, windlass, chain stoppers, anchor davit*
31. *Water coolers*
32. *Clocks*
33. *Drainage system, drain and plumbing*
34. *Electric lights* (wiring, generator, batteries, etc.)
35. *Fans*
36. *Lighting fixtures*
37. *Fresh water system* (tanks and plumbing)
38. *Fuel oil system*
39. *Steering gear*
40. *Navigating light* (running and anchor lights)
41. *Motor controls and instruments*
42. *Whistle and horn*
43. *Radio*

44. *Searchlight*
45. *Sounding gear*
46. *Switchboard*
47. *Spares and stores, boarding steps*
48. *Boats and davits* (winches, etc.)
49. *Compass* (adjusting)
50. *Cleaning of hull,* etc.

In describing each item, material, dimensions and other classifications must be given. The name and address of the makers of the required fittings should be given, as well as the catalogue number and description. The wording of the specifications should be easily understood, and each description should be concise. Nothing should be left unspecified, as delayed decisions invariably result in a long list of "extras," hence expense. The block list is usually a part of the specifications.

Appendix

USEFUL TABLES AND PROPORTIONS
Weight of a Cubic Foot of Materials

NAME	POUNDS PER CUBIC FOOT	NAME	POUNDS PER CUBIC FOOT
Alcohol	50.	Iron, cast	450.
Aluminum	165.	Iron, wrought	480.
Asbestos (sheet ⅛″ thick)	65.	Ironwood	71.
Babbitt, white brass	456.	Larch (Tamarack, Hackmatack)	35.4
Beech wood	43.8		
Birch wood	40.	Lead, cast	708.5
Brass, common	533.	Lead, sheet	711.5
Brick, common	120.	Mahogany, Honduran	53.
Bronze	544.	Mahogany, Spanish	35.
Cedar, American Red	30.8	Maple wood	49.
Cedar, white	23.	Muntz, metal	511.
Cement and sand (3 to 1)	130.	Nickel, cast	516.
Cement, stone and sand	144.	Oak, American, Red, Black, Yellow	45.
Cherry wood	42.		
Chestnut wood	30.	Oak, American "pasture" white	50.
Coal, hard	47.		
Copper	554.	Oil, diesel fuel	53.
Cork	15.7	Oil, lube	58.2
Cypress wood	34.	Oregon Pine or Douglas Spruce	35.
Elm wood (Canada)	45.		
Fir (Douglas) wood	32. to 34.	Pine, Long Leaf Georgia Yellow Pine	40 to 47.
Gasoline	42.		
Glass, plate	172.	Pitch	69.
Greenheart wood	62.5	Pitch Pine, U. S. Yellow Pine	41.
Gum wood	37.		
Hemlock wood	32.	Poplar wood	32.
Hickory wood	47.4	Punchings, Boiler	350.
Ice	57.5		

341

NAME	POUNDS PER CUBIC FOOT	NAME	POUNDS PER CUBIC FOOT
Redwood (California)	26.2	Tin	462.
Spruce, northern	26.	Walnut, black	38.
Spruce, southern	30.	Water, fresh 63. pure 62⅓	
Steel, rolled	490.	Water, salt	64.
Steel, cast	493.	White Pine, northern	28.
Sycamore wood	36.8	White Pine, western	27.
Teak	46.	Zinc, rolled	449.

NOTE: Commercial timber usually weighs from 5 to 10 per cent more than the weights given.

Tank Contents

(To convert Imp. gallons to Am. multiply by 1.2; to convert Am. gallons to Brn. divide by 1.2).

One cubic foot equals 7.48 gallons Am.

One Am. gallon equals 231 cubic inches or .134 cubic feet.

One Imp. gallon equals 277.27 inches or .160 cubic feet.

Weight (approximate) of Sail Canvas or Duck

It is standard practice, in specifying sail canvas, to give weight per linear yard. Sail canvas is usually 22″ wide; No. 8, of this width, would weigh 11 oz. per linear yd. (width divided by 2). For each number below No. 8, add one oz. (No. 7 = 12 oz., No. 6 = 13 oz., No. 5 = 14 oz., etc.). For each number above No. 8, deduct one oz. (No. 9 = 10 oz., No. 10 = 9 oz., No. 11 = 8 oz., No. 12 = 7 oz., etc.). 24″ canvas:—No. 8 weighs 12 oz.; the variation between each number above and below this is 1.09 oz.

Weight, Close Link Common Chain (Approximate)

DIAMETER IN INCHES	WEIGHT IN POUNDS, PER 100 FT.
3/16	40.
1/4	70.
5/16	105.
3/8	158.

DIAMETER IN INCHES	WEIGHT IN POUNDS, PER 100 FT.
½	275.
⅝	410.
¾	580.
⅞	780.
1	1000.

Weight of Chain Cable (Approximate)

DIAMETER IN INCHES	WEIGHT IN POUNDS, PER FATHOM	
½	14.	For steel link Anchor chain
⅝	24.	
¾	32.	
⅞	43.	
1	56.	

(diameter ^{2}) $\times$ 54 = weight per fathom of chain cable.

Weight of Rope, per Fathom (Approximate)

CIRCUMFERENCE	DIA.	LBS. OZ.	CIRCUMFERENCE	DIA.	LBS. OZ.
1 in.	5/16 in.	0–3–¾	3 in.	1 in.	2–¼
1¼ in.	7/16 in.	0–5–¾	3¼ in.	1 1/16 in.	2–7
1½ in.	½ in.	0–8–¼	3½ in.	1⅛ in.	2–13
1¾ in.	9/16 in.	0–11–¼	3¾ in.	1¼ in.	3–2⅜
2 in.	⅝ in.	0–14–¾	4 in.	1 5/16 in.	3–11
2¼ in.	¾ in.	1–2–½	4¼ in.	1⅜ in.	4–1
2½ in.	13/16 in.	1–7	4½ in.	1½ in.	4–11
2¾ in.	⅞ in.	1–11–⅞	5 in.	1⅝ in.	5–12

Weights, Measurements and Areas

2000 lbs. equals 1 short ton
2240 " " 1 long ton (marine)
112 " " 1 hundredweight (marine) abbreviation "cwt."
20 hundredweight equals 1 long ton
6 ft. equals 1 fathom
120 fathoms equals 1 cable length
1 cable length equals 120 fathoms equals 960 spans equals 720 feet

Circles Circumference equals diameter x 3.14159
Side of equal square equals diameter x .88623
Area equals diameter 2 x .7854
Area equals radius 2 x 3.14159
Diameter of a circle of the same area as a square equals side x 1.12838

Size of Blocks

Diameter of sheave should be not less than 8 times diameter of rope.

DIA. OF ROPE	DIA. OF SHEAVE
3⁄16″	1½″
¼″	2″
5⁄16″	2½″
3⁄8″	3″
7⁄16″	3½″
½″	4″
5⁄8″	5″
3⁄4″	6″
7⁄8″	7″
1″	8″
1⅛″	9″
1¼″	10″

Use 4-strand rope if sheave must be smaller than above.

Capacity of Round Tanks

Tank capacity = sq. dia. × length × .0034 = (Am.) gals.

DIA.	GALS. PER INCH
4″	.0543
5″	.085
6″	.122
7″	.165
8″	.217
9″	.275
10″	.340
12″	.486
14″	.666
16″	.87
18″	1.1
20″	1.36
22″	1.645
24″	1.962

Numbers of Sail Cloth in Cruisers

L.W.L. LENGTH	MAINSAILS (Main & fore or mizzens in schooners & ketches)	JIBS (and jiggers in yawls)	STORMSAILS
20 feet } 24 "	#15	#14	
30 "	#11	#12	#7-#8
35 "	# 9 to #10	#11	#5-#7
40 "	# 8 to # 9	#10	#4-#6
45 "	# 8	# 8 to #9	#3-#5
50 "	# 6	# 9	#2-#4
55 "	# 5	# 8 to #7	#1-#4
60 "	# 4	# 8 to #7	#0-#3

NOTE:—For weights of numbers, see formulae on page 290.

Timbers Used in Yachts Built in Nova Scotia and New Brunswick

Keel & Frames—Yellow Birch, White Oak or Rock Elm
Bottom Plank—Yellow Birch
Topside Plank—Spruce, White Oak (Yellow Pine and White Cedar
  are imported for plank)
Decking—Spruce (Yellow Pine is imported for decking)
Mast and Spars—Black Spruce
Deadwood Timbers—Yellow Birch, White Oak, or Rock Elm

Chain and Anchors

L.W.L. LENGTH	DIAMETER CHAIN IN INCHES	CIRCUM. OF HAWSERS	ANCHOR Heavy in lbs.	ANCHOR Light in lbs.	ANCHOR Kedge in lbs.
25 feet	$\frac{1}{4}$"-$\frac{5}{16}$	$1\frac{1}{2}$"-2	50	40	
30 "	$\frac{5}{16}$"-$\frac{3}{8}$	2"-$2\frac{1}{2}$	75	60	
35 "	$\frac{3}{8}$"-$\frac{7}{16}$	2'-3'	100	75	50
40 "	$\frac{7}{16}$"-$\frac{1}{2}$	$2\frac{1}{2}$"-3	150	100	50
45 "	$\frac{3}{8}$"-$\frac{1}{2}$	$2\frac{1}{2}$"-$3\frac{1}{2}$	175	110	75
50 "	$\frac{3}{8}$"-$\frac{1}{2}$	$2\frac{1}{2}$"-$3\frac{1}{2}$	200	150	75
55 "	$\frac{1}{2}$"-$\frac{9}{16}$	$3\frac{1}{2}$"-4"	225	175	100
60 "	$\frac{1}{2}$"-$\frac{9}{16}$	$3\frac{1}{2}$"-4"	275	200	100
65 "	$\frac{9}{16}$"-$\frac{3}{4}$	$3\frac{1}{2}$"-$4\frac{1}{2}$	300	225	125
70 "	$\frac{3}{4}$'	$3\frac{1}{2}$"-$4\frac{1}{2}$	350	250	125

Weights are for Herreshoff pattern anchors.
NOTE:—For stockless anchors, add 40% to weight.
    For Fisherman pattern anchors, add 15% to weight.

Deck Beams, Heavy Hulls

BEAM AMIDSHIPS	SIDED AND MOULDED	MOULDED AT ENDS
10'	$3\frac{1}{2}-4\frac{1}{2}$	$3-3\frac{3}{4}$
11'	$4\frac{1}{2}-5$	$3\frac{1}{2}-4$
12'	$4\frac{3}{4}-5\frac{1}{4}$	$4-4\frac{1}{4}$
13'	$5-5\frac{1}{2}$	$4\frac{1}{4}-4\frac{1}{2}$
14'	$5\frac{3}{4}$	$4\frac{3}{4}$
15'	$6\frac{1}{4}$	$5\frac{1}{4}$
16'	$6\frac{1}{2}$	$5\frac{1}{2}$
17'	$6\frac{3}{4}$	$5\frac{1}{2}$
18'	7	$5\frac{3}{4}$
19'	$7\frac{1}{4}$	6
20'	$7\frac{1}{2}$	$6\frac{1}{4}$

When windlass has a "wildcat" for handling chain the wildcat should fit the size of chain used. In this case BBB chain quality is required. The BBB chain is more uniform in size and stronger than standard chain. A Gypsey windlass having two barrels is the most practical for cruisers.

Some designers estimate the anchor weight required on "per foot of overall length"—for light anchors $1\frac{1}{2}$ to $1\frac{3}{4}$ lbs. per foot of overall length; for heavy anchors, $2\frac{1}{4}$ to 3 lbs. per foot of overall length. For mushroom anchors (permanent mooring), 5 to 8 lbs. per foot of overall length will serve as a guide. The heavier the displacement of the hull, the heavier the anchor required, as a rule, though a light displacement hull having deck-houses will require a proportionately heavier anchor than one without deck-houses, due to the effects of windage.

Windlasses should be chosen with regard to the sizes of chain or hawser they must handle; this information may be obtained from maker's or marine hardware dealer's catalogues.

Length of Anchor Rodes in Feet

L.W.L. LENGTH	LIGHT ANCHOR	HEAVY ANCHOR
15–20	100'	100' ∓
20–25	125	200
25–30	150	200
30–35	150	250
35–40	200	300
40–45	200	350
45–50	300	450
50–60	400	550
60–70	500	650

The above lengths are approximate only, but may be taken as practical minimums for general conditions.

Steering Wheels for Sailing Craft

Diameter measured from outside of handles

L.W.L. LENGTH	DIAMETER OF WHEEL	NO. OF SPOKES	FOR SHAFT DIA.
18–22	22″	6	$^{15}\!/_{16}$″
22–26	25″–28″	6	1″–1⅛″
26–32	28″	6	1⅛″
32–40	30″	8	1¼″
above 40	36″	8	1⅜″

Standard Belaying Pin Lengths

ENTIRE LENGTH	LENGTH OF HEAD	DIA. OF SHANK
8″	3⅛″	⅜″
9½″	3⅝″	½″
10″	3⅝″	⅝″
11½″	4⅝″	¾″
15″	6½″	1″
17″	7″	1⅛″
19″	7¾″	1¼″

Belaying pins are made of galv. malleable iron, bronze and brass up to the 11½″ size; the larger sizes are of malleable iron. Hardwood belaying pins 15″, 17″ and 19″ are usually obtainable, if desired, but are rarely used on yachts (though preferred by seamen).

Calculation for Strength of Rigging

FOR CRUISERS ONLY

1. First the area of the sail whose luff is attached to the mast is multiplied by 1.5, to obtain the estimated pressure of wind in the sail. To this is added the strain of the sheet. This may be considered as ⅘ the area of the sail, converted to pounds (one square foot = 1 lb. pressure).

2. Now, lay off the height of the mast above deck and the half-breadth of the hull, at the chain-plates, to scale (distance chain to centerline of mast). Draw a rectangle, on one side of the mast, whose area equals the total of the two loads just obtained. The length of the rectangle is from the gooseneck of the boom to the halyard block or shoulder for the uppermost shrouds. Draw, on the opposite side of the mast, the proposed arrangement of shrouds.

3. Divide the rectangle into two or more parts, each point of division being located at the point where shrouds are attached to the mast. Each of the panels thus formed represents a load on a portion of the mast. Commonly, only the upper half of each panel is considered as the load of each set of shrouds. Perhaps the best way to express the load is to assume the load A (see Sketch A) as ½ (cdef) + ½ (abcd) and the load B as ½ (abcd).

4. In most cases, stays carrying the headsails or staysails are brought to the mast at points close to those of the shrouds. So, for the lower shrouds, it is necessary to add the strains set up by one or more headsails or staysails. For these, the area of each is multiplied by 1.5, and ⅘ the area is added to the result, to obtain the total

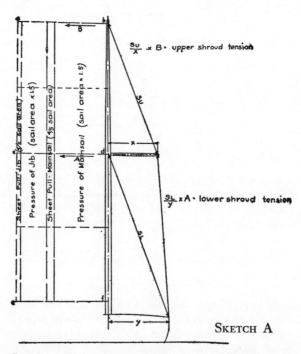

$$\frac{su}{x} \times B = \text{upper shroud tension}$$

$$\frac{sL}{y} \times A = \text{lower shroud tension}$$

SKETCH A

Load panels must be laid out according to rig design; the load of a fisherman staysail or balloon topsail should be placed against the upper portion of the mast (or against the topmast) only, for example.

load. Half of this is considered to be the load on the lower shrouds.

5. Therefore, the load on the lower shrouds is half the upper and lower panels plus half the load of the lower staysails or headsails (panels added in sketch).

A = calculated load
y = half-breadth of hull, chain-plate to c of mast
SL = length of lower shroud

Then $\dfrac{SL \times A}{y}$ = tension on lower shrouds.

There must be an excess in the tensile strength of the wire chosen for the lower shroud, over the calculated tension. This excess may be expressed by the "factor of safety" 2 to 3 being the common factors in this calculation, though many designers use 5. As an example, suppose the calculated tension on a lower shroud is 1200 lbs. The "factor of safety" is to be 2, then the tensile strength of the wire to be chosen is 1200 × 2 = 2400 lbs. or 1.2 tons.

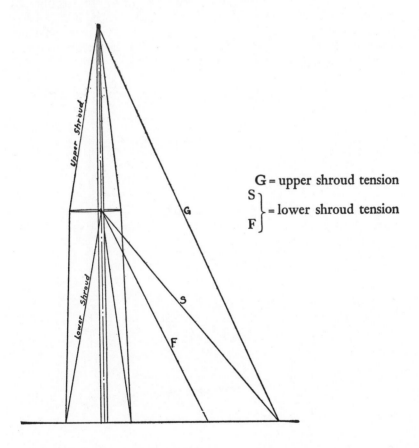

G = upper shroud tension

$\left.\begin{array}{l} S \\ \\ F \end{array}\right\}$ = lower shroud tension

The upper shrouds are calculated in the same manner. In most cases the load of the upper shrouds include half of the upper panel plus half the total load of an upper staysail or headsail and its sheet.

B = calculated load

x = half-breadth of spreaders

SU = length of upper shroud

Then $\dfrac{SU}{x} \times B$ = tension on upper shrouds.

The tension on the stays corresponds with the shrouds, thus the upper stays would have the same diameter as the upper shrouds, the lower stays the same as the lower shrouds.

As a "rule of thumb" it is common practice to make the upper shrouds of wire one size smaller than required for the lower; if there are three shrouds the uppermost is two sizes smaller than the lower.

Upper shrouds are generally ½ the strength of the intermediate and intermediate are ½ the strength of the lower; i.e., it is common practice on larger vessels to use the same wire on lower and intermediate shrouds, but fewer shrouds at intermediate portions—say 2 lower shrouds and one intermediate.

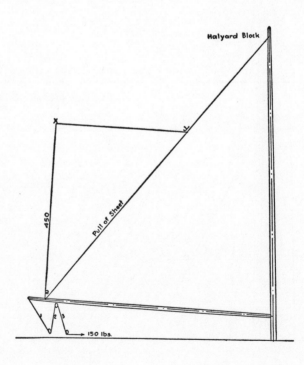

In lieu of the approximation of the sheet strain, the following may be used. Draw, to some convenient scale, the outline of the sail and spars involved, showing centerlines of the mast and booms or stays and sails, also the location and number of parts in the sheets.

The maximum pull a man exerts on a sheet is about 150 lbs. when "swaying up." Therefore, he can put a strain on the sail equal to this times the number of parts in the sheet; in this case there are 3 parts, so the strain is $3 \times 150 = 450$ lbs. In the sketch this pull is exerted on the boom between the after two parts of the sheet, so here (a), a perpendicular is erected to the boom having a height equal to the calculated pull, in some convenient units. At the extreme height (x) a line is drawn parallel to the boom or foot of sail. Next another line is drawn from a to the halyard-block on the mast—this represents the direction of the pull of the sheet. This last line intersects the line drawn parallel to the boom at y. Now measure the line ay, using the same unit of measurement used to lay off ax, and this is the pull of the sheet in pounds. If the boom of a sail is heavy, as in a large cruising schooner, it would be well to add the weight of the outer half of the boom to the pull of the sheet.

Calculation for Maximum Sectional Areas of "Split Sprits"

FOR CRUISERS ONLY

Spread, at from ⅓ to ⅖ the sprit length from the jaw end, is from 18% of the depth of the sail in way of the sprit, when round sections are used, to 16% for oval sections with their flat sides to the sail. The inside clear length of the sprit should allow for sail stretch, the outhaul and a small amount of shortening in the sprit due to "spring."

Clew strain, in pounds, may be given as follows:—

Main Trysails up to 200 sq. ft. = Sail area × .50 ⎫ This is also sprit-
    "   "   " " 400 " " = "   " ×.625 ⎬compression on its
    "   "   " " 500 " " = "   " ×.75 ⎭   long axis.

Moment around the maximum sectional area, in inch-pounds,

$$M_1 = S.A. \times \begin{pmatrix} .50 \\ .625 \\ .75 \end{pmatrix} \times \tfrac{1}{2} \text{ Spread, in inches (centerline of sprit to vertical axis of maximum section)}$$

For an indication of the section to be used, when made up in airplane spruce,

$M_2 = 1250 \times I/y$. In which I is the moment of inertia of the section around its vertical axis, and y is the distance, in inches, from this axis to the inner side of the figure.

Select a section for I/y to give M_2 slightly in excess of M_1. For staysails, M_2 may be somewhat *less* than M_1.

The above is for the lashed clew. For a single, three-part or four-part outhaul, the calculated M_1 should be doubled, increased by 50%, or 33%, respectively.

Where the sprit is applied to the mizzen of a ketch or yawl, due allowance must be made for additional sheet strain.

The amateur designer should not attempt a main trysail of over 250 sq. ft. in area, which corresponds to a total rig area of about 840 sq. ft. And he should bear in mind that the depth of the sail, clew to luff, should not be over 30% of the hoist.

Moments of Inertia

Solid Round Section $I = \pi D^4 \div 64$

Hollow Round Section $I = \pi \div 64 \ (D^4 - d^4)$. In which d is the inside diameter in inches.

Solid Oval Section—around long or vertical axis,

$$I = .785 \ B^3 A.$$ In which B is ½ the long axis, and A is ½ the short axis, in inches.

Hollow Oval Section—around vertical axis,

$$I = .785 \ (B^3 A - b^3 a).$$ In which b is ½ the long axis of the inner oval, and a is ½ the short axis, in inches.

The maximum spread should lie in a fair parabolic curve, between one-third and two-fifths the total length of the sprit from the jaw-end. The airplane spruce should show from between 12 to 15 annual rings to the inch, in section, and both arms should come from the same timber. When a hollow round section is used, the sprit should be in quarters. If in halves, the edge grain should be horizontal (or perpendicular) to the vertical axis. In the oval section the sprit arms are halved vertically or are even made up of four boards quartered vertically and with edge grain horizontal, or perpendicular to the long vertical axis.

Calculation of Mast Diameters

FOR CRUISERS ONLY

For unsupported masts (having no shrouds).

$$\text{diam.} = \sqrt[3]{\frac{16 \, PLf}{\pi e}}$$

where P = wind pressure in sails $\begin{cases} \text{sq. ft.} \times 1.15 \text{ small craft} \\ \text{sq. ft.} \times 1.5 \text{ large craft} \end{cases}$

L = length of mast in inches

e = maximum fibre stress $\begin{cases} 5000 \text{ lbs. for spruce or Ore. fir} \\ 5200 \text{ lbs. for hard pine} \end{cases}$

$$\mathbf{f} = \text{factor of safety} \quad \left\{ \begin{array}{l} \text{1.5 to 2 for small unballasted hulls} \\ \text{2 for small ballasted hulls} \\ \text{3 for large hulls with leg-of-} \\ \quad \text{mutton} \\ \text{3.5 for cats and gaff rigs} \end{array} \right.$$

With leg-of-mutton load may be taken as decreasing toward mast-head. The apparent strain at the headboards indicates that the line of strain is parallel to the leach and that the longer the line of leach the greater the strain.

(This formula is of doubtful value as an accurate guide in all design.)

For stayed masts (having shrouds)

The loads obtained (in panels) for the rigging may be used for calculating mast diameter. To the panels of load already obtained add the tension of the halyards as a uniformly distributed load, as well. This load may be represented as

$$(\text{sail area} \times .75) \times \left\{ \begin{array}{l} \text{2. for single-part halyard} \\ \text{1.5 for three-part halyard} \\ \text{1.3 for four-part halyard} \end{array} \right\} = \text{load}$$

As before, let half of each panel represent, graphically, the distance from chain-plate to centerline of mast. Divide this distance into the length of the mast and then multiply by the load in pounds. The procedure is exactly the same as in calculating tension of rigging, since the tension is converted to compression in a stayed mast. The thrust or compression of the upper and lower mast added together is the figure that must guide the maximum diameter of the mast. Theoretically, the diameter of the mast, above the spreaders, should only be sufficient to carry the load above that point, but in practice this is exceeded. It is usually best to design masts to a full taper which starts about ⅙ or ⅛ the total length of the mast above deck, the after side of the mast being straight and all the taper being on the fore side in profile. Athwartships the taper should be evenly divided between port and starboard. This is for round masts, of course.

The process of designing a mast to carry a given load is, first, to multiply the calculated load by the factor of safety, say 2.5 to 3, and then, by trial and error, to design a section having the requisite strength.

Without entering into an explanation of the theory, the following will serve as a guide in the drawing and calculation of mast sections to meet a given load.

Referring to the curve of strength of a 1″ spruce strut, formulae for the calculation of area and radius of gyration will be found. Assuming the designer has a given section in mind and that he has an idea of the approximate diameter required, he draws the section.

From this, and the formula given, he can calculate the radius of gyration. Next he converts the length of the mast to inches. Then he divides the length by the radius of gyration and the quotient is the ratio of length to radius of gyration. The ratio for a 1″ diameter spruce strut is shown at the bottom of the curve of strength figure. Choosing the ratio on the curve figure corresponding to the calculated one, the strength per square inch is obtained. Now, the area of the designed section is calculated and the strength of the designed section =

$$\text{strength per square inch} \times \frac{\text{area of designed section}}{\text{area of 1″ diameter spruce strut}}.$$

(The area of the 1″ diameter strut is constant, of course, .785, as noted on the curve figure.) Divide this strength by the chosen factor of safety and the quotient is the load the designed section will safely carry. By comparing this with the calculated load a conclusion, as to whether it is necessary to increase or reduce the designed section, will be reached.

Judgment must be used, in employing these formulae, as the condition of the spar-timber, type of rig, distribution of sail-area, and hull-form all influence the application of these calculations. In most cases, comparison is a better guide than calculation alone; a combination of both is ideal.

Drawing Lines to Inside of Plank

In waterlines drawn to the inside of the planking, the waterlines and diagonals are faired into the half-breadth of the "middle-line" (*i. e.*, the inside of the rabbet) at stem and sternpost. The sections likewise meet the "middle-line" at the keel. The half-breadth of the keel can be obtained by squaring out the thickness of the planking from the midsection at the point where it intersects the "middle-line" in the body-plan.

In drawing lines to the inside of the plank the half-breadth of the middle-line is fixed rather than the half-breadth of the whole keel. In the process of drawing the body-plan it is usual to check the half-breadth of the keel by the above-mentioned projection in order to be certain that the siding is not too great or too slight.

The outer edge of the rabbet may be obtained by squaring off the thickness of the plank on each waterline and section, where each intersects the middle-line on the half-breadth and body-plans; these points are projected to the corresponding positions on the sheer elevation and the outer rabbet is then swept in, passing through each point.

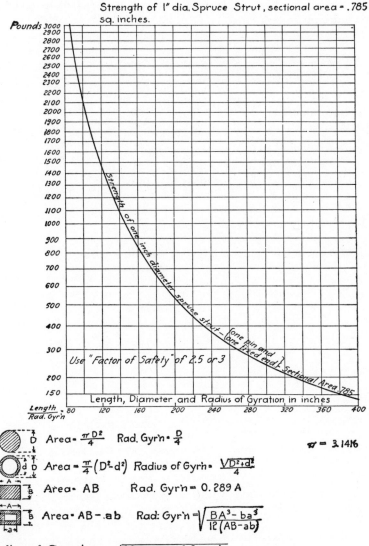

Strength of 1" dia. Spruce Strut, sectional area = .785 sq. inches.

$$\mathbf{\varpi} = 3.1416$$

Circle: D — Area $= \dfrac{\pi D^2}{4}$ Rad. Gyr'n $= \dfrac{D}{4}$

Hollow circle: d, D — Area $= \dfrac{\pi}{4}(D^2 - d^2)$ Radius of Gyr'n $= \dfrac{\sqrt{D^2 + d^2}}{4}$

Rectangle: A, B — Area $= AB$ Rad. Gyr'n $= 0.289\,A$

Hollow rectangle: A, B, a, b — Area $= AB - ab$ Rad. Gyr'n $= \sqrt{\dfrac{BA^3 - ba^3}{12(AB - ab)}}$

$$Radius\ of\ Gyration = \sqrt{\frac{Moment\ of\ Inertia}{Area\ of\ Figure}}$$

The Moment of Inertia should be taken about the vertical or horizontal axis of a figure as required by the direction of its loading.

The bearding line is the point where the inside of the planking intersects the side of stem, sternpost and keel. It may be projected to the profile from intersections obtained on the body and half-breadth plans.

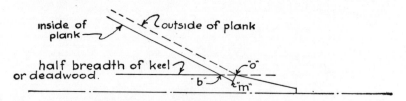

       "m" "middle" or "margin" line
       "o" outer edge of rabbet or "rabbet line"
       "b" "bearding" or inner edge of rabbet.
       "b" to "m" is the "backrabbet," utilized for fastenings.

See plate of schooner yacht *Dream* (page 151).

Sternpost should be sided larger at transom than at heel.

INSTRUCTIONS FOR TAKING OFF LINES OF HALF
MODELS AND DRAWING LINES

1. *Preliminary*

The half model, known also as the block model or builder's model, represents one-half of the ship divided longitudinally. It is usually made up of a series of "lifts" or pieces, either pegged, nailed, or held together by dowels. Sometimes these models are painted in the same manner as the original ships built from them. It is customary to mount these half models on a piece of plank known as the backboard, and on this backboard strips of wood to represent the profile of the rudder, the keel, cutwater, and the sternpost are fastened. Occasionally half-dowels are attached to represent masts and bowsprit. Very rarely does the half model show the ship's deck arrangement, and in this case the bulwarks are attached to the original model which only reaches to deck level. Such models, however, were built for decorations rather than for actual construction and are to be looked upon with suspicion so far as accuracy of lines is concerned. In most cases, the half model is made "to inside of plank" or "moulded," *i. e.,* actual shape of the frames.

In most examples of builders' half models it will be found impractical to separate the lifts or pieces for they are either screwed together or even glued in such a manner that an attempt to separate the lifts would damage the half model.

2. *Equipment needed*

In order to take off the lines of half models that may not be taken apart, or those that may be taken apart, the following equipment is required: *Wrapping, tracing, or drawing paper* of a sufficient size to draw the profile of the model completely. *Lead pencils*—4H will be found most suitable. *Straightedge*—should be equal in length to the overall length of the model or greater. (In very large models where straightedges cannot be obtained of sufficient length a chalk line may be employed to lay out the necessary long straight lines.) A *try-square* of the usual carpenter's type, with a graduated blade 6″ or more in length, is required. *Two triangles,* of the usual draftsman's type are necessary; one should be at least 12″ long, 30°–60°. *Large outside calipers* are necessary. They should be at least 12″ and should operate in such a manner that accurate measurements may be taken. *Lead bars* will be necessary to lift the sections from the model. It has been found that these bars must be of pure lead about ⅛″ or ³⁄₁₆″ by ³⁄₁₆″ square and from 12″ to 24″ in length. These bars should be formed by forcing the lead through dies of the proper sectional dimensions. If these are not obtainable, drawn bars may be obtained and split by use of a saw. Care should be taken that the lead bars be reasonably straight. This may be insured by tapping the bar against the straightedge. A *pair of dividers* of the ordinary draftsman's type, size 5″ or 6″ will be found useful. A *triangular scale* 12″ long, open divided, architect's scale, will be found necessary. *Marking pencils* for marking the model are necessary. (These may be of ordinary blackboard chalk, but it has been found that the "china marking pencil" is most satisfactory.) It is expressly directed that no models are to be marked with lead pencils which cannot be easily erased from the model or which will leave permanent indentations in the model itself. *Erasers, pliers, a pair of shears, screw driver, a hammer, a nail set, a few small wood dowels,* and *a piece of clock-spring or a flexible steel rule,* about 12″ long, should be at hand.

3. Procedure

When model may not be taken apart, the backboard (which is usually fastened to the model with screws) should be removed. A suitable space should be obtained, a table or drawing-board, on which to work. A piece of wrapping paper is first laid on the work bench and the half model is placed upon it so that its back, representing the center line of the ship, rests flat upon the paper. The next step is to run a pencil around the outline of the half model, thus obtaining the profile of the sheer, stem, stern and keel. The waterlines are represented by the visible lines between the pieces of wood or "lifts," making up the half model. These lines should be ticked on the profile where they intersect the stem and stern, great care being taken to locate them accurately. When the profile of the stem, cutwater, rudder, sternpost and keel have been mounted on the backboard, these may be transferred to the drawing by use of a separate piece of paper, rubbing with a soft pencil and then obtaining a template by use of the shears. When such information is at hand it should be transferred to the drawing as accurately as possible, and any other decoration which may be shown on the half model should be carefully reproduced by means of measurements obtained either by rubbing, or by actual lineal dimensions obtained by ruler or divider. The location of the bowsprit and the mast, if shown on the model, should be transferred to the drawing and carefully marked for identification.

The model is then removed from the drawing. The back of the model and its top should be carefully inspected for markings of any kind, such as location of masts, location of the centerboard, location of deck structures, dimensions, names of vessels built from the model, or any other information of any kind whatsoever, which may appertain to the ship—its builder, its owner, or its construction.

With a straightedge or chalk line, connect the horizontal waterline points (the line between the "lifts," or pieces of wood forming the model). Draw with a straightedge a baseline parallel to the waterlines, about 2" or so below the lowest point of the keel, and erect perpendiculars from this, to the extreme ends of the profile of the half model. Beginning at the stern lay off on this baseline equally-spaced station lines or sections. These are to be not exceeding 3" apart on large models. (On very small models 1" spacing is best, and on models from 2' to 3' long 2" spacing should be employed.) In laying off these stations care should be taken that a sufficient number be employed to obtain accuracy in fairing the lines on the drafting board. If a model shows a very full-ended hull, for example, it may be best to space the stations 1" apart at bow and stern until the "dead-flat" is reached, where the stations should be 2" or 3" apart, as seems most desirable. If the vessel is sharp, as in a yacht, and if the model be under 40" in length, 2" spacing will be found satisfactory. On the baseline erect perpendiculars by use of the triangles and straightedge, extending the lines from the baseline to well above the sheer line of the drawing (sheer line represents top of model or underside of rail cap).

Replace the model on the drawing, taking extreme care that its outline coincides exactly with the lines originally drawn and that the waterlines on the model agree with the ticks originally placed on the plan when the outline was drawn. Now with a "china marking pencil" tick the model at each station, on the top (sheer) and on the bottom of the hull (rabbet), or if stations intersect the stem and sternpost at the bottom of the model, this also should be ticked. Very often it is possible to transfer these station lines across the deck to the outboard sheer of the model while it remains up on the drawing, by use of the triangle, squaring against the table or drawing (so that one side is square to the drawing and the triangle is flat against the top of the model). Thus the section or station lines are brought outboard square to the back of the model (or centerline of the hull). It will be observed that by this means the stations are projected across to the outboard face of the model, and it is usually possible to draw the stations across the curved surface of the model, by use of a clock-spring or flexible steel rule, with the marking pencil.

When all stations are marked thus, remove the model from the drawing and with the try-square check the top of the model against its back to see whether or not there is any crown in the top (that is, whether or not top and back are at right angles). If there is any crown it will be necessary to reproduce this on the drawing by means of the try-square and a pair of dividers. The crown may be measured by holding the try-square against the back of the half model at each station, the blade extending over the top of the model and measuring the difference between the sheer at the back and at the outboard side with the dividers. (This crown may be due to warping of the model; it is rarely shown intentionally.) It is usually desirable to connect the station lines across the back of the model before proceeding further.

Next, make a template or rubbing of the transom. This is done by placing a piece of paper upon the transom of the model and rubbing the outline with a soft pencil. Removing the paper from the model a template is cut out with the shears. In making a template one straight side of the paper should coincide with the back of the half model (or centerline of the ship). In most ships the transom is set at a rake to the keel and in the profile this is represented by a straight line showing the rake at the centerline of the ship. The straight side of the template should be laid against this line so that the template lays at right angles of that portion of the profile of the vessel, and its outline should then be drawn. The curvature of the transom athwartship is obtained by use of the triangle or try-square and dividers; laying the model on a flat surface and placing a triangle against the transom so that one side of the triangle rests squarely upon the work bench, measure with the dividers the difference between the centerline of the transom and the outboard face of the transom at the extreme breadth. Transfer this measurement to the drawing and roughly sketch in the profile of the transom as seen when the model is viewed broadside on.

In many models both the sheer height of the rail-cap (top of model) and that of the planksheer, or deck, are given. In the case of the latter, the line of the underside of the deck at side is indicated by a scribed line running around the outside of the model, more or less parallel to the sheer. In rare cases, this may be formed by a lift or paint line. The height of the bulwarks thus indicated should be picked off the model at some convenient station (where the side of the vessel is nearly perpendicular) and this height transferred to each of the stations on the plan. Care should be taken, particularly forward, to check upon the actual height of the bulwarks indicated on the model, for in some vessels the height of bulwarks is greater forward than amidships.

With the dividers, prick on the drawing at the bottom of the model's outline, the half widths of the keel at each station; these may be transferred directly from the model, where the keel half-breadth at the rabbet is indicated by a scribed line or, in a sharp model, by a distinct angle in the surface of the model. With the two triangles square out, from the station line on the drawing, the height of the sheer or the top of the model. Measure the width of the model at each station, from the back or straight side to the outside or outboard side, at sheer height, by means of the calipers, and lay these points off on the drawing; marking the station number close by for identification. Taking some convenient waterline, say approximately at the load-waterline or line of flotation of the ship in service, pick off by means of the calipers the breadth of the model at each station, measuring from the intersections of the station and waterline on back and front and transfer these measurements to their corresponding stations on the drawing, squaring out from the station line. Bend the lead bar to the form of the foremost station, marking the point where the bar intersects the keel line, waterline and the sheer; then transfer the bar to the drawing and place it so that the marks on the bar coincide with the sheer, waterline, and rabbet (or bottom of the model) and draw in the curve line which should pass through the calipered and measured points on the drawing, if the bar is handled carefully. By means of the same procedure obtain the sections at the rest of the stations, transferring each in turn to the drawing. The greatest care should be used in marking the bar and in bending it, to see that a correct section is obtained and transferred to the drawing. If there is a projection on the model, such as a moulding representing the plank-sheer at deck or the rail-cap, it is usually best to make a notch in the bar with a knife so that the bar may fit snugly against the model above and below this planksheer, which in turn can be transferred to the drawing by means of the dividers or calipers, as previously directed for locating the deck-line. In handling the lead bar reasonable care should be taken so that the model is not marked.

When all the sections have been transferred and all the measurements checked, markings on the model should be cleaned off with a damp rag and the model should be remounted on the backboard. It is important that care should be taken that no permanent marks be left on the model and the greatest care should be used in reassembling the model on the backboard to avoid marring either the model or the pieces of wood representing the keel, cutwater, rudder, etc. When the model is reassembled it should be replaced on the wall or in the position from where it was obtained.

3a. If it is possible to take the "lifts" or sections of the model apart, the following instructions are to be observed: The model is to be removed from the backboard as before directed and its outline traced in the usual manner; position of the mast and all markings, decorations, etc., are to be transferred to the drawing. The shape of the keel, rudder, stem, and sternpost, cutwater and the location of masts, etc. are to be recorded in the same manner as previously directed. The waterlines are to be located in the same manner and the station lines are to be placed on the drawing as previously directed. The station lines are to be transferred to the model as previously explained only in the case of the midsection; other sections are to be merely extended across the top of the sheer (or top of the model).

In inspecting the model it may be observed that there is a line scribed on the back and top of the model, square to waterlines and centerline of hull; this is the midsection or "master section" used by the builder in taking off the lines. If possible, this line should be duplicated on the drawing. At a convenient distance below the profile just drawn, run a line parallel to the waterlines, which will be the model's centerline viewed from above or below. Square down lines from each end of the model's profile and the intersections of the waterlines with stem and stern. Likewise, extend down the line of the "master-section" or midsection.

Now the model should be taken apart. If the model is screwed together it is directed that the screws be removed with great care in order that they may not be broken or damaged, or the model marred. In old models that are held together with round or flat dowels, carefully observe how the dowels appear to be tapered before attempting to knock them out. It is observed that square dowels, which extend above the top of the model when in position, are usually tapered so that they must be forced downward to remove. Round dowels, however, may occasionally require to be forced upward rather than downward. This can only be decided by testing, and the small wooden dowels and light hammer should be used in removing dowels in order that they may not be marred. It is usually found that some of the lifts are nailed together or pegged together, and great care should be taken in removing these nails or pegs in order that damage to the model may be minimized. Lay each successive lift or section with its back edge to the centerline so that the "midsection" vertical line on the back of the model coincides with the "master-section" on the plan; then it will be found that the ends of the "lift" or section will correspond with the lines squared down from the corresponding waterline in the profile. Trace each lift outline in succession. When the sheer is reached it will be found that the curvature of the sheer or top of model will prevent it from lying flat upon the paper. It will be necessary to take off the half-breadth at each station with the calipers, and run the line in from these measurements when transferred to the drawing. Reassemble the model, and take off with the lead bar the shape of the midsection in the same manner as directed for models that cannot be taken apart. Likewise, take off the shape of the transom by use of the template as herein directed. As in the case of the models that cannot be taken apart, the position of the height of deck-line on the profile shall be obtained. Directions for the reassembling of the model, previously given, apply to these models as well.

4. *Notes on decorations, paint, and other details*

Many models are painted in the same manner as the ships built from them. The draftsman should record the position of all gilded lines and painted waterlines; record all colors of paint used on the model; if the spars are indicated by dowels the color of these should be recorded in painted models.

5. *Notes on rough drawings*

All information, historical and technical, that is obtained by the draftsman, is to be written on the drawings. Since, in most cases, the half models are made to represent the shape of the hull to the inside of the planking, it follows that the sheer or top of the model is usu- ally the *underside* of the rail-cap and the height of the deck in profile is to the *underside* of the deck at the side of the hull. Lines on the drawing, representing these, should be identified accordingly. If the model shows the length and height of a raised quarterdeck, the loca- tion of the "great-beam," or break in the deck, should be clearly marked and identified.

6. *Drawing Lines*

a. Draw profile or sheer elevation, reproducing same location of sta- tions and waterlines shown in rough drawing. Show sheer, waist, or deck, and all decoration shown on model. Show location of masts and other details as indicated on model and in the rough plan. Procedure for locating half-breadth and body-plan center- lines is the same as outlined in the chapter on Lines (Chapter III). If model was taken off by taking the outlines of the lifts, establish stations on the rough plan and transfer their locations to the lines. (See note below.)
b. Lay off sheer half-breadth in the half-breadth plan. (Fairing in the station half-breadths measured on top of the model, as re- corded in the rough plan.) Establish half-breadth of rabbet as recorded in the rough plan.
c. Lay off sections in the body-plan, reproducing those taken off by

use of the lead bar, or from half-breadths lifted from the water-lines at each station on the rough plan, when outline of lifts is shown. Half-breadths of rabbet and sheer, as well as heights, are measured from the views previously drawn. When midsection is drawn (outline of lifts being recorded in rough drawing) its form and deadrise may be checked from that shown in the rough plan, as taken off the model with the lead bar.

d. Fair in quarterbeam buttock, established as directed in Chapter on Lines (III).

e. Fair in one waterline forward, approximately the load-waterline position.

f. Fair in all waterlines as explained in Chapter on Lines (III).

g. Establish and fair in buttocks as explained in Chapter on Lines (III).

h. Establish diagonals and fair in, as explained in Chapter on Lines (III).

[NOTE: When outlines of lifts (waterlines) are taken off, the stations may be laid off on the rough plan with spacing same as directed when sections are to be lifted from the model by means of the lead bar. The stations should be drawn perpendicular to the centerline of the lifts and to the base line used in the profile, in the rough plan. These stations are reproduced in the lines.]

These instructions are similar to those employed by the U.S. National Museum in marine research.

INSTRUCTIONS FOR BUILDING CARDBOARD
HALF MODELS

The cardboard half model will be found useful in visualizing the form of the hull after the lines are drawn. The model will enable the draftsman to visualize the shape of the boat since the effects of perspective can be seen.

The first step is to lay out the profile of the boat as shown in the lines, on a piece of white cardboard of sufficient thickness to be fairly stiff. This profile should show the load-waterline, each of the stations, the rabbet, sheer and the keel, stem and stern. When these have been drawn from the lines (on the same scale as the lines, of course) the profile should be cut out and laid aside. Then each of the sections shown in the body-plan in the lines should be redrawn on pieces of cardboard. This may be done by using tracing paper as the transfer paper. After tracing a section the back of the tracing paper is rubbed with a soft pencil, then laid on a cardboard and traced. The rubbing on the back of the tracing paper will leave a mark on the cardboard.

On each section the centerline, the load-waterline and rabbet should be marked as well as the sheer. The shape of the transom may have to be projected from the lines if the transom is set on a radius. In the model it is not necessary to duplicate this radius, however; rather the transom may be projected as a flat surface set at the proper rake. When these sections have been drawn on cardboard and cut out, they should be fastened to the profile at their equivalent stations. The fastenings may be made by use of desk pins. The load-waterline of each section must coincide with that of the profile, and the centerline of each section must be on the equivalent station line on the profile as well.

A light piece of cardboard is then laid on top of the model and pinned on the profile so that it follows the shape of the sheer. This piece of cardboard should be longer than the model and somewhat wider than the half-breadth of the hull. The location of the half-breadth of the sheer at each section is marked on this cardboard as well as their locations fore and aft. This marking, of course, is put on the underside. The cardboard piece is then removed from the sheer and with a batten the expanded half-breadth plan of the sheer is struck off. This is cut out, and the cardboard is refastened with pins to the profile, and to the sections, so that they are square to the profile.

It is now possible to bend a few strips of narrow cardboard, fore and aft, around the model in the form of battens. These may be pinned to the sections. It is not necessary to finish these models by planking them up. A few cardboard battens bent around will enable the draftsman to visualize the shape of the boat well enough. The use of the model may lead the designer to make alterations in the lines to correct optical illusions caused by perspective.

Index